UNDER THE IRON HEEL

UNDER THE IRON HEEL

By
LARS MOËN

WITH 18 ILLUSTRATIONS

J. B. LIPPINCOTT COMPANY
PHILADELPHIA   NEW YORK

Foreword

ON OCTOBER 22, 1940, I LEFT BELGIUM, AFTER I HAD practically abandoned hope that the German military authorities would permit my departure before the end of the war. When I was suddenly offered the alternative, on October 8, "leave now or remain until the end of the war," I left. I had chosen to stay in the face of the German invasion, but I had no wish to go on living under the German occupation. The invasion was quickly over—but the occupation bid fair to stretch out interminably, with life becoming more difficult each day as food grew less.

It was only when the Germans realized the impossibility of finishing the war before winter that they consented to the departure of any foreigners. I am still astonished that permission was given, even then. We had seen too much, and it was presumably to prevent our talking about what we had seen that every obstacle was placed in the way of our return to our native countries—an attitude which persisted after official permission to leave had been granted.

Fortunately, I believe, my passport gave no indication that I was a former newspaper man, and my treatment by the Germans was influenced by no desire to make a good impression. When the lightning invasion was followed by the gray, dreary days of the occupation, there were no reporters to tell the story of War and the Little People. This book is that story.

You will find in it no startling exposé of Belgian state secrets, but a great deal of what the Belgian people think of King Leopold, of their former government and of the capitulation; no sensational interview with Hitler or Goering, but a great deal of what the common soldier who does their fighting thinks of them and of the war; no exclusive economic statistics about conditions in the occupied countries, but a great deal about what that situation means in terms of the daily life of the Little People.

For this is their war. They did not want it, and had little to do with starting it, but they may have a great deal to do with finishing it; the outcome is largely dependent on their morale and staying power. Twice within a quarter of a century their little world has been turned upside down, and they are ready for any effort, any concession, any experiment that may offer even a slight hope of putting an end to a situation grown intolerable.

The Little Man, be he soldier or civilian, no longer believes in the old illusions, and this "droll war," as the French once called it, is only understandable if that is borne in mind. I have no wish to assume the role of a prophet, but it is already abundantly clear that this war will bring widespread social and economic change, whatever its outcome; the old geographic boundaries are no longer the primary issue.

Since such changes must, in their very nature, affect great masses of people, I have tried as far as humanly possible to keep my own opinions out of this and simply to report in a straightforward way what I have seen.

When the war came to Europe, on September 3, 1939, I was doing a job of scientific research in Belgium. I was anxious to complete that job, and despite warnings from the American consulate I stayed on, hoping to finish at the beginning of June, 1940, and to return to America; I hoped that Belgium's neutrality would be respected, or that if she were attacked there would be ample time to leave.

When the war came to Belgium, I was living in Antwerp in a small hotel called "In the Shadow of the Cathedral." As the name implies, it was directly across from the great edifice which housed, until the war, Rubens' "Descent from the Cross." From the outbreak of the war I had been the sole permanent resident, and the beginning of hostilities found me there with only the elderly widow who was the proprietress, her daughter, and the chambermaid, a young cousin from the country. I had originally chosen the hotel for its central location, and that fact made it an ideal observation post for the events which followed. Just behind the building was the old City Hall, a masterpiece of Flemish architecture; the other side of that, the waterfront. A stone's-throw away was the entrance to the tunnel under the river, through which the Allied armies in Flanders passed on their way to the front—and again passed in the other direction a week later; through which, also, streamed the endless, sorry throng of refugees from Holland and eastern Belgium.

My research work was being done in a factory in the suburbs of Antwerp, in the town of Oude-God, or Old God. The plant normally employed four thousand workmen, of whom considerably more than a thousand were in the Belgian army.

When the Germans came, from fifteen to twenty a day were billeted at my hotel. Each German arriving in Antwerp, from the humblest private to the general, visited the cathedral, and many of them remained to eat in the restaurant of my hotel.

Six weeks before my departure, because of the increasing scarcity of food, I moved into a working class neighborhood, near the factory, where I boarded with a baker's family.

Thus the war and the occupation as I saw them were very much the war and the occupation as they were being experienced by civilians and soldiers of both sides. During the four-day journey to Lisbon with fifty-one other American refugees, the ten days in Lisbon, and the ten days on the boat to New York, I had the opportunity to compare notes with refugees from nearly every country in Europe; everywhere the pictures they drew were much the same.

This book is the story of the occupation as it appeared to one living under it, and the views in it are largely those expressed by the men and women with whom I came into contact. I have not always indicated the precise source of each scrap of information—in some cases, to do so would have unwarrantably prolonged the tale, and in others, serious complications might have followed for persons still living in occupied territory. Aside from that, nothing has been suppressed which seemed relevant to the story, whether favorable to one side or to the other.

CONTENTS

9

III

CONSOLIDATING THE OCCUPATION

IV

DEATH IN THE MORNING

V

The Great Exodus Begins

VI

The Swastika over the Cathedral

VII

THE WAY BACK

VIII

LIFE MUST GO ON

IX

WHAT A GERMAN SOLDIER THINKS ABOUT

X

BOMBS IN THE NIGHT

XI

HITLER MISSES THE BOAT

XII

CONDUCTED TOUR: BRUSSELS-LISBON

XIII

WHERE WILL IT END?

ILLUSTRATIONS

UNDER THE IRON HEEL

I

Daily Life Under German Occupation

THOUGH ONLY A FEW WEEKS HAVE PASSED SINCE I WAS IN Belgium, I already turn on the light in the evening without wondering whether the shade be tightly drawn or not. I order a second cup of coffee without wondering whether I would not rather save the stamp for the morrow. I find the clean tablecloth, with its implication of the availability of soap, perfectly natural and normal. When a plane flies over at night, it is only for an instant that I think of those other planes, circling far overhead, sometimes for hours, before letting loose their cargo of destruction on our heads, or, worse still, the low-flying black planes lurching just above the rooftops, staggering under their load of sudden death for the folk across the channel.

There is nothing more astonishing about war than the ease with which the abnormal becomes the normal, and looking back now I find it difficult to believe that only a little while ago I was living and working in a world which had grown perfectly natural, and which now seems to me quite mad.

The dangerous things in war are not difficult. Few persons, I find, are badly frightened in an air raid, unless the bombs fall very close indeed. What is much harder is to put up with the little annoyances and petty dislocations of everyday life—the unheroic things, too small to awaken an answering stimulus of courage, but great enough to determine the ultimate morale of a people. More German soldiers have complained to me about the annoyance of living with only what one can carry in one's pockets than about the danger of having to advance through machine-gun and artillery fire.

In the routine of daily life, habit is the great simplifying force—waking up at a certain hour, a time-tested breakfast menu, reading a newspaper with which we are familiar, taking a particular train or streetcar to work, making our purchases in shops where we waste no time in searching for the departments that we want—these familiar actions, requiring a minimum of effort, leave our time and attention free to deal with new problems that arise. When this tissue of daily habits is shattered, as it has been by the war, life suddenly becomes fatiguing and much more difficult. A sudden danger, or something equally critical, calls up hidden resources of courage and self-sacrifice in any normal person; the disruption of routine produces only irritation.

The importance of these things is especially great in the occupied countries, for the people are not even at war. They are innocent bystanders in a conflict which concerns them vitally but about which they can do little or nothing, save to submit to the hardships and privations—and often the danger—endured by the combatant populations. Even the German soldiers in the occupied countries are merely "occupation troops" with nothing to do and less than half the pay they would receive on active service.

To give a fair picture, then, of daily life in the occupied areas, it will be necessary to speak of many things which may seem almost trivial, for we are concerned here not with people at war, but with people living in a mockery of peace.

I was, I believe, unusually well placed to observe this important side of life in a subjugated country. My familiarity with French, Flemish and German permitted me to pass frequently for a Belgian—a fact which led many persons to speak to me much more frankly than they would have, had they known I was an American; this was particularly true of the German soldiers. Then, too, I was living in a small hotel where I had been installed for nearly a year, so that I was more like one of the family than a lodger. During the German attack, I was the only man in the hotel, and when the Germans arrived in Antwerp, I passed as the proprietor of the hotel until we were reassured as to the behavior of the Nazi troops toward women. These things brought me into close touch with the daily problems of running the hotel, and the private lives of those persons with whom circumstances had thrown me in such close contact.

So long as the war goes on, life will continue much as it was when I left, save that it will grow progressively worse. Should the war end the "wrong way," this gradual deterioration will not necessarily stop with the termination of hostilities.

I shall usually be speaking of Belgium, but my remarks will, in nearly all cases, apply with equal force to Norway, Denmark, Holland and occupied France. Life in these countries, totally dislocated during the period when the Nazi legions were smashing their way across Europe, has now been stabilized at a level not likely to alter much while the war remains a fortress war, save for a gradual worsening.

In that daily life, the outstanding feature is the pre-occupation of every man, woman and child with the question of food.

In 1937, while I was living in Soviet Russia, carrying on research work for the motion picture industry, there was a retrospective exhibition of paintings by many artists, under the title: "Twenty Years of Soviet Art." What seemed to me most significant was the fact that of the paintings shown for the years from 1918 to 1922—the years of famine and stark misery—more than half were pictures of food. Succulent steaks, shimmering fish and great baskets of fruit were portrayed almost tenderly and left no possible doubt as to what a Russian thought about at that time.

If Belgian artists were to paint at the present time, I have little doubt that they would seek similar subjects—but I question seriously whether any of them are doing much painting. The Russians, during the blackest years, were buoyed up by hope. The peoples of the occupied countries face a future so vague that they wish, but scarcely dare hope, for deliverance from their misery.

Every conversation came around sooner or later (and usually sooner) to the question of the food supply; over and over, one heard phrases, such as:

"I know a farmer in St. Nicholas who will sell you a hundred pounds of potatoes, if you can haul them yourself."

"I found a half pound of coffee this morning. If you hurry, the shop may have some left."

"The meat ration is going to be cut down again next month, I hear."

"A friend of mine in a sausage factory let me have a

pound of salami without stamps, but don't say anything about it!"

"Last month I managed to buy thirty-two loaves of bread over and above the ration, but it won't be possible any longer. I don't know what I'm going to do. You can't explain to five children that there's nothing more to eat because there aren't any more stamps."

Thus it goes, with a thousand variations; the verb "to eat" is conjugated in every possible way whenever two people meet. The ability to get a bit of extra food is the real mark of affluence. Greater friendship has no man than the shopkeeper who sells you a bit of something without stamps, at the risk of having his shop closed if he is caught.

To be quite clear, no one was actually starving at the time I left. Perhaps no one will actually die of starvation during the winter of 1940-'41, but everyone is a little hungry and everyone knows that as the months go by the supply of food will become smaller and smaller.

That certainty is based on something more than pessimism. They know that the Nazis have hauled off to Germany all the stocks in the country and destroyed a large part of the means of production. They know that dairy cows are being slaughtered and hens killed for lack of feed, so that milk and eggs will become steadily scarcer. They know that there will be no chemical fertilizer for the farms next spring. Worst of all, they are sure that what food they do succeed in producing will again be carted away to Germany or used to feed the occupation troops living in Belgium (officially half a million, actually nearly twice that).

This is not, of course, the German version. In September, 1940, an analysis of the economic situation in the occupied areas published in the official German press stated that at the time Germany invaded Belgium, the latter had a food supply sufficient for one month only— and was, therefore, only being kept alive by the compassionate humanitarianism of the Germans. That statement had two obvious purposes: to continue the pretense of German "protection" of the peoples she had subjugated, and to cast further discredit on the former Belgian government by implying that it had failed to provide the most elementary essentials of life for the people.

The truth is—and no one knows it better than the Germans—that when the attack came Belgium had on hand stocks of every essential commodity and foodstuff sufficient for from two to four years.

As an industrial nation with a high population density, Belgium had to depend on imports for a large portion of her food and raw materials. When the blockade made such imports difficult, the government built up stocks, far above the peacetime level, of essential foodstuffs and the raw materials necessary to carry on normal manufacture. As trans-shipment of commodities and materials was also an important activity, a great amount of warehouse space existed for this purpose, chiefly in Antwerp.

To make matters doubly sure, plans for rationing were worked out as soon as the European war started, since it was obvious that shipping would be heavily curtailed and the war a long one. Within less than two weeks a census of all foreigners was taken, so that the state might know exactly how many persons required to be fed. Ration cards were printed and a complete organization set up, though actual rationing did not commence until a short time before the German invasion. It was strongly rumored at the time that the chief reason for instituting the cards was not so much a real or potential shortage as the desire to convince Germany that there was no surplus. Germany was at that time bringing considerable pressure to bear on Belgium to export foodstuffs and materials to her, and important quantities were being so delivered, though not so much as from Holland. (At that time, also, it was no secret that French iron ore was coming into Belgium for transshipment to Germany, which repaid it in coal for transshipment for France. This, coupled with the fact that freight trains steamed through the Maginot and Siegfried lines every afternoon, carrying goods from France to Germany and from Germany to France, as was common knowledge, made the Belgians rather bitter about the blockade, for it seemed that the only countries affected were the little neutrals.)

Up to the actual week of the invasion, however, a fair number of ships continued to put in at Antwerp, and if there were a few minor restrictions, life continued to be perhaps the most comfortable in Europe at that moment. Belgium is not, comparatively, rich in resources, but by hard work her people have managed to reach an average standard of living which is relatively high in normal times.

When rationing was put into effect, shortly before the invasion, the quantities allowed were such that no one suffered seriously. Almost the first act of the Germans after occupying the country—certainly the first act of which we heard—was to reduce the rations drastically, in many cases by half and more, so that what had been ample became a bare sufficiency.

Ration cards had been issued to every man, woman and child in Belgium, including foreigners, upon presentation of an identity card or other suitable document. It was necessary to present this card at the beginning of each month to receive the stamps for the period beginning on the tenth. The stamps merely bore numbers, and each month the newspapers announced the commodity, and quantity of it, for which each number would be valid.

The routine of obtaining the cards was agreeably simple, compared with the red tape which usually surrounds official matters on the Continent. However, I was spared even the few formalities which it involved; an elderly municipal official, who lunched regularly at the hotel, took my identity card and brought it back next day with my ration card.

After the occupation by the Germans, the same cards and stamps continued to be used and the same Belgian officials nominally administered the organization. At the end of September, 1940, it became necessary to register with the authorities the name of the shop from which one intended to make these purchases during the month, and certain principal commodities could then only be bought in the store for which the card was registered.

Precise figures concerning the rations would be meaningless, since they changed every month; furthermore, the problem was not so much to exist on the quantities of food for which you had stamps as it was to find even a reasonable portion of the actual merchandise to which your stamps theoretically entitled you. When a given commodity began to be scarce, it was rationed; when it had totally disappeared from the shops, its number was transferred to some other foodstuff.

The situation was considerably complicated in Belgium by the fact that so many of the people, having been through

1914-'18, knew what to expect and bought up the greatest possible quantity of everything not yet rationed. This hoarding made the general situation even worse than it would otherwise have been. In Holland, where the people had no experience of war, this did not happen to any serious extent. The remedy would be a house-to-house search, but up to the time I left nothing of the sort had been attempted, though the Gestapo had raided and closed a few shops. In any event, the effect is a temporary one, since these private stocks will soon be exhausted and there will be no chance to replenish them.

Police control of the stores and restaurants was, however, extremely severe. Shortly before my departure, a meat market near my hotel was fined about three hundred dollars and closed up for selling a pound of meat without receiving the proper stamps. A large hotel in Brussels was closed for serving a meal without stamps.

The situation was further complicated by the fact that all of the German soldiers must be fed by the country in which they are quartered. Those in barracks are fed by the army kitchens, which requisition the necessary foodstuffs through the intermediary of the Belgian municipal authorities. Those billeted in private homes and hotels, and those merely passing through, receive special ration stamps entitling them to a far higher allowance than a civilian receives.

The number of German soldiers in Belgium at any one time is about one-tenth of the total civilian population, but this tenth undoubtedly receives one-third as much foodstuffs as the whole of the Belgian people.

However, the major factor was not hoarding, nor was it the necessity of feeding the army of occupation. If the

Germans had left in the country the stocks of foodstuffs on hand at the time of the invasion, there would have been no serious shortage before the winter of 1941-'42.

The German army completed the occupation of Antwerp at about eight A.M. on May 18, 1940, and by three P.M. on the same day huge army trucks had been backed up at the warehouses and were emptying them of all merchandise. There was not even a check made of the contents of cases and bales; everything went into trucks and took the road to Germany.

Not, of course, that these things were stolen. The German army permits no looting, and the individual soldier caught stealing anything whatever, save food of which he is in need, is shot without trial.

Therefore, quite logically, everything taken from the warehouses was duly paid for. The owner of the goods (if he were still in Belgium) needed only to put in a bill for the confiscated merchandise. He then received, in a very short time, a bond for the entire value of the goods—to be redeemed by the Belgian taxpayer!

In the same way, the Germans have purchased large quantities of foodstuffs directly from the farmers, paying with so-called "occupation money."

This money deserves a special word in passing, since the German army uses it extensively in all of the occupied countries, and it has an important bearing on the manner in which merchandise has been drained off from them. Although the soldiers refer to it as "occupation money," the official name is "Reichs Credit Bank Voucher" and it is only by courtesy that it could be called "money" at all, since it is backed by nothing whatever. It is printed on the spot as needed, in printing plants installed in great motor

STAMPS FOR SOLDIERS

At the right are shown the ration stamps issued to German soldiers not eating in barracks. Those shown are for coffee, each stamp entitling the holder to one-sixth of an ounce of coffee—if he can find it! Two stamps equal one cup of coffee, and another stamp is necessary for sugar, should that be desired. The allowances for soldiers are far higher than those given the civilian populations of the occupied areas, and materially greater than those for civilians in Germany. The stamps for soldiers are undated, so that those not used during one month may be employed the following month, if desired.

STAMPS FOR CIVILIANS

Each month, on presentation of their ration cards, civilians receive stamps such as those shown at the left, and the newspapers announce the items and amounts of each for which the stamps will be valid in that particular month. All stamps are good only during the month for which they are issued, and some must be used during a particular five-day or ten-day period; if the corresponding merchandise is not found during that time, the stamp expires.

trucks, and there is no evidence that there is any control whatever over the amount printed or any hypothetical backing which it may have.

The unit of currency is the "Reichsmark," as distinguished from the "Rentenmark," which is the present unit in Germany proper. In each country an arbitrary exchange rate has been established—twenty francs to the mark in France, twelve and a half to the mark in Belgium, one and one-half marks to the gulden in Holland—which in each case is about double the nominal value of a real German mark. This simple economic practice has, naturally, doubled the purchasing power of the German soldier, who is paid exclusively in occupation money, and has doubled the rate at which the soldiers have managed to empty the stores of merchandise—of which the soldiers receive the right to send eleven pounds per month home without charge.

The Reichsmark has no value in Germany, and though the same bills are used in all of the occupied countries, it is categorically forbidden to take them from one occupied country to another.

When I returned from Belgium to America, it was necessary for me to pay certain excess baggage charges in Paris. The simple way to do this would have been to take a small sum in Reichsmarks, but this was "verboten." It was necessary, therefore, to obtain from the Currency Section of the German High Command a license to buy a suitable number of French francs, then go to a certain bank and buy them.

However, we are getting rather far from the question of rationing and the food shortage.

Certainly the most serious matter of all, when I left,

was that of fats. The situation might be summed up as in St. Patrick's description of the serpent population of Erin: "There are no fats in Belgium."

It is unfortunate that fats should be precisely that commodity which Germany lacks the most and needs desperately; unfortunate, too, that the same fats which are so essential a part of human diet should also be the source of glycerine, itself the source of high explosives.

The ration permitted was far too small for normal needs, but it was impossible to find even this negligible amount. Meat as purchased has already been trimmed free of fat before delivery to the shop. Margarine was available when I left, for the first time in months, the allowance being about two-thirds of a pound per month, but butter was only a memory.

The same shortage of fats made soap virtually impossible to find. Bars of Palmolive soap were being sold illicitly in October for thirteen times their original price. The allowance was a bar of soap per month for all purposes, toilet and domestic, and the odds were against finding even this one bar. No provision was made for hotels and restaurants, so clean sheets and tablecloths were becoming increasingly rare. Bleaching powders had made their appearance on the market as substitutes for soap, but their effect on fabrics was disastrous.

The next serious shortage was that of potatoes, though the question appeared to be chiefly one of distribution. The importance of potatoes in the Belgian diet is something difficult to convey to an American reader, accustomed to a much more varied diet and a greater choice of vegetables. Belgium is a considerable producer of potatoes, and consumes an enormous quantity of them; as the bread ration grew progressively smaller, potatoes became more and more the most important item of food.

Fortunately, Germany is herself a considerable producer of potatoes and there was no indication that she had taken any serious portion of the Belgian crop. It is largely that fact which will keep the Belgians alive until the 1941 harvest. Potatoes make up a large part of any meal, even in peacetime, and in the case of the poorer families they form the main item of diet.

Despite the fact that there seemed to be plenty of potatoes in the country, they were extremely difficult to obtain when I left, and shops were allowed to sell only about four pounds to a customer at a time.

The reason appeared to be that the peasants were refusing to sell at the low price fixed by the Germans. When the Nazis occupied Belgium, they decreed that all prices must remain at the May 10 level. They have not done so, but the rise in prices is far less than would have normally occurred during a period of rapid currency inflation.

As the potato harvest approached, stories were current in Belgium, assiduously spread by the peasants, that an infrequent disease had attacked and largely destroyed the crop. There has been no evidence that this was true, and there is reason to believe that the rumors were circulated to prevent possible confiscation of the crop by the military authorities.

That did not occur, but the price was fixed by decree at about three cents a pound, not much above the pre-invasion level. During the summer, potatoes were not rationed, but as soon as they were sufficiently mature to be stored, they were placed on the stamp system. Buyers for the stores then attempted to obtain deliveries from the peasants and were curtly told that they had none, which was merely another way of saying that they would not sell at such a low price.

It was obvious when I left that if the Nazis were going to continue this regime of forced economy, they would have to carry it to its logical conclusion, seizing the potatoes and placing them on sale at the decreed price or else recognizing the normal play of the laws of supply and demand and permitting a moderate increase in price. The result would, of course, be only temporary, but the immediate situation would be relieved.

Meanwhile many of the poorer families, who could afford little else than potatoes, were going very hungry. Only a fortnight before my departure, the police closed a grocery shop near the City Hall because of a free-for-all fight which occurred among women shoppers over a small quantity of potatoes remaining, which was obviously not enough for all of them.

The importance of this dearth of potatoes would perhaps not have been so great, had not the quantity of bread been limited. The bread ration had been reduced twice by the German authorities before I left, and while it could scarcely be reduced further and be called a ration, there were serious indications that there was not enough flour in the country to assure each person of that small amount. The quantity worked out at about four slices a day, and the quality was becoming progressively poorer. There has been no white bread since the beginning of Nazi rule, and only one kind of flour was being milled, which appeared to be a mixture of wheat, rye and corn meal, with perhaps dried peas or other substances as a "filler."

The baker received flour only in return for the stamps

which he had received from customers for the previous period—so if he let anyone have bread without stamps, he not only risked police action but automatically diminished his supply of flour by just that much for the following month.

I came in close contact with this problem by virtue of the fact that during my last six weeks in Belgium I boarded in a small *pension* run by a baker (on the theory that when food is scarce, a food shop will have a little more than is likely to be found elsewhere). The day of my departure, the baker had flour on hand sufficient for the next twenty-four hours, and had not been able to obtain assurances of any immediate delivery. Only the week before the town of Lier, near Antwerp, had been entirely without bread for four days, since none of the bakers in the community had any flour whatever.

In the absence of any figures which might be trusted, it is impossible to say with certainty whether such occurrences were due to a breakdown in distribution—or whether, as appeared far more likely and as most Belgians believed, Belgium was reaching the bottom of her flour barrel.

In the opinion of those of my acquaintances best qualified to know, the continuance of any bread ration at all would depend, by the spring of '41, upon whether or not Hitler chose to send back to Belgium some of the wheat which he had taken away—and no Belgian whom I knew considered that a serious possibility.

The Belgians did not hesitate to speak their minds, with more frankness than prudence, on this subject to the German soldiers in their midst, and the reply was so standardized and unvarying that it was obviously what they had been taught to say:

"Our leader lets no one starve—but you can't expect to be allowed to gorge yourselves while *we* starve. National-Socialism means a fair division of everything. If your food supplies have been taken away to Germany, it is only in order to store them safely and divide them fairly. You'll be all right."

However, every Belgian knows that there is no lack of storage and refrigeration facilities in his own country. He knows, too, that the population of the German Reich is ten times that of Belgium, so when a Nazi speaks of "a fair division" of Belgian stocks he is not impressed by the degree of dietary security thus offered him.

Within the narrow limits of the rationed allowance, the situation was still somewhat better regarding meat, at the time I left, than for potatoes and bread. Owing to the great amount of livestock being slaughtered for lack of fodder, there was little difficulty in obtaining the five pounds of meat allowed per person per month, though it was limited almost entirely to beef of indifferent quality. Despite the pretended price control, meat prices had advanced sharply, in some cases nearly a hundred per cent.

Belgium produces a considerable amount of vegetables and fruit, and in a normal year this is an important export item. Since the only remaining export market was Germany, there was, in the autumn of 1940, a fairly ample supply of fruits and vegetables. The great majority being of a perishable nature, the beginning of October saw supplies already dwindling.

So much for the staple necessities. As to the rest, there is not much to say. Sugar was more plentiful in Belgium than in the other occupied areas, since the country is a considerable producer of beet sugar. The ration was two pounds a month, which works out at about four and one-half lumps a day for all purposes. Salt was obtainable only in small quantities, and growing scarcer.

Beverages offered something of a problem. Each person is entitled to a ration sufficient for thirty cups of coffee a month, but at the time I left there were already more persons with stamps than with coffee. Every German arriving in Belgium rushed to buy a few pounds of coffee and send it home, which in itself made a huge drain on available stocks. By October, an increasing number of cafés were serving *ersatz* coffee with little resemblance, except in color, to the real article, and it was evident that there would soon be nothing else. Tea disappeared in the early months of the war, since the Belgians are no great consumers of this beverage and stocks were limited. I myself solved the problem by using linden tea, made of the leaves and blossoms of the linden tree and gathered locally. This tea, ordinarily used for medicinal purposes, was drinkable but somewhat flat; I was assured, however, that it was "very good for me" and doubtless it was.

More serious for those with children was the milk situation. Nominally, the ration was about a pint a day, which on paper appears reasonably adequate. The joker in this was that only skimmed milk might be sold, and it was frequently impossible to find one's pint even of this blue and watery fluid. Other milk products, such as cheese, for which this part of the Low Countries has always been famous, were virtually non-existent. All butter-fat took the road to Germany, and the German soldier received each day an allowance of butter considerably larger than he could eat—which explanation no doubt contented Belgian children obliged to drink skimmed milk.

The foregoing will, I hope, give a fair idea of the food situation as it was when I left Belgium, with the average person receiving a quantity of food adequate for one smallish meal a day, though he might spread it out over three. A quantity of food, in short, sufficient to maintain life. If that level could be maintained throughout the war, there would be little starvation; everyone would be a bit hungry, but there would not be much serious privation.

My own weight, when I left Belgium for America, had fallen from a normal 170 pounds to 145 pounds; my height being five feet eleven inches, that obviously indicated a definite degree of undernourishment.

However, the months I saw were the best months, and it was abundantly clear that each succeeding one would see a worsening of the food situation. Next summer's crop will relieve the pressure for a time, but so much of the means of production has been and is being destroyed that a vicious circle has been created—a circle which will grow progressively smaller.

So much for the general food situation in Belgium. What I have said, however, is based on ability to purchase all of the foodstuffs which their new masters graciously allow them—and not all of Belgium's families are in that happy position.

Families of the unemployed, receiving the equivalent of about twenty-five cents a day—families of the men who are still prisoners in Germany, receiving a similar allowance; even families of the great mass of workers employed only half-time—could barely afford the staple necessities rationed to them, let alone the little luxuries, such as fruits and vegetables, not governed by stamps.

I did not come into much direct contact with such families, but shopkeepers and others who did spoke with unconcealed bitterness of the misery which already left many families sitting at home with literally nothing to eat. That, however, is an economic question only indirectly related to the question of the food supply itself.

In Holland and Denmark, themselves great producers of foodstuffs, the situation was somewhat better; in parts of France it was materially worse. It would be fair to say, then, that conditions in Belgium represent a fair mean of conditions in the occupied countries.

In Denmark, for example, there were 25,000,000 hens at the time of the invasion. By late autumn of 1940, only six months later, a prominent Danish business man told me, there were 7,000,000, since there had been nothing to feed the others. The same reduction of the poultry population has been going on in Holland and Belgium, so it was clear that eggs, already extremely scarce when I left, would be virtually unobtainable by the summer of 1941. The means of production of many other staples were being similarly whittled down, and about the only factor tending to increase the food supply to any extent at all was that a great many people were preparing vegetable gardens for 1941.

Any such discussion of the food situation as the foregoing inevitably raises a question which cannot, in all fairness, be evaded—a question which, as I write this, is occasioning a great deal of discussion in the American press and elsewhere: Should we feed the inhabitants of the occupied areas?

Perhaps by the time this appears the question will have been cut short by the fact that we shall be feeding them, or have definitely decided not to, but so much ill-informed discussion has appeared that I should like to present a point of view on the matter as it appeared from Belgium.

It is dangerous to pretend to speak for a whole nation, especially when millions of lives may be the issue at stake, and I shall not claim to do so. I did, however, discuss the matter with a very great number of Belgians in all walks of life, especially after it appeared reasonably likely that I should be permitted to return to America, and what I shall have to say represents the fairest cross-section of Belgian opinion that I can write.

The average Belgian, I believe, does hope that America will send food. Hungry people would always rather be fed than not. But if any of that food is to reach German soldiers or civilians, then the Belgians would, in the last analysis, rather go hungry.

I have never talked with a Belgian who believed, seriously, that the occupied areas could be fed without a great deal, and perhaps the lion's share, going to their new masters.

That presents, I realize, a slightly confused picture, but the issue is a confused one to the Belgian as well.

The pro-German and anti-British Belgians, to be sure (and there are a very great many more than is realized here, though their number was diminishing daily when I left), have no doubts whatever about the matter. They would like to see American food pour into the country, with the Germans receiving the major portion. I assume, however, that what is being discussed is not the plight of the Fifth Columnists who sought eagerly for the absorption of their country into the Greater Reich, but of what I like to consider the great mass of the Belgian people, who, if not always strongly pro-British, are at any rate staunchly pro-Belgian. It is of them that I am speaking here.

There are really two quite separate questions involved, and it will perhaps clarify the issue if we define them:

1. Should the Belgians and other oppressed peoples be fed?

2. If so, could this food be prevented from reaching Germany?

On purely humanitarian grounds, of course, nearly everyone would rather feed the Belgians than not; even the German soldiers often give them what they can spare from their own rations. However, only one phase of the question is really important, even for the Belgians themselves—or, more accurately, especially for the Belgians. That is: what will be the result, in terms of the conduct and outcome of the war, if we do or do not feed the hungry millions?

Some opponents of relief—ill-advised, it seems to me—have asserted that we should not feed the occupied areas for the reason that when those peoples become sufficiently hungry they will revolt and overthrow German rule.

That is not a very realistic view of the matter. A very large share of the population of the oppressed areas would already like to revolt; a fair share would risk their lives willingly if there were any hope of success.

There is no such hope, and any failure to recognize that simple fact is wishful thinking of the most harmful sort. The people of Spain tried to meet machine-guns, tanks and airplanes without adequate arms. They made a magnificent fight of it, with such aid as they were permitted to receive, but in the end they failed. Any attempt by Belgians, Frenchmen, Danes to revolt against the Germans who are everywhere in their very midst, would be far more hopeless.

Those who have not seen the German military machine in action will not appreciate the full force of that statement. The oppressed populations, who have had that machine roll over them once, have no illusions on the subject. Today that machine has had added to it all the equipment captured in Holland, in Belgium, in France and elsewhere, and so long as the mass of the German soldiers remains loyal, there is no slightest hope of successful revolt.

Furthermore, observation has convinced me that it is a fallacy (though an oft-repeated one) to say that starving people revolt. Hungry people, perhaps, given competent leadership, but starving people never. A starving man becomes listless, apathetic, indifferent.

I saw that look recently on the faces of people in Spain when I passed through en route to America—hungry and weary and no longer capable of caring—as I saw it on the faces of starving peasants along the lower Volga and in the Ukraine in 1932 during what was, I hope, the last great famine which the Russian people will have to endure.

There is an old adage: "To tame a wild beast, starve it." Whether that be true of animals or not, I have no experience, but it would seem to be abundantly true of human beings.

The increasing pressure of starvation in the occupied countries is, however, certain to have one important effect: it will breed an ever-growing hatred of Nazi Germany, and the importance of that must not be underestimated, even though there is little hope that it will mean open revolt.

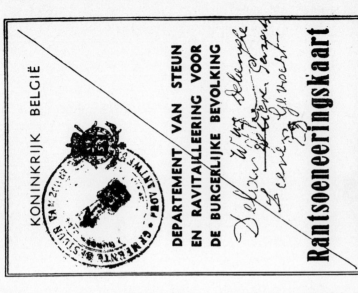

KONINKRIJK BELGIË

DEPARTEMENT VAN STEUN
EN RAVITAILLEERING VOOR
DE BURGERLIJKE BEVOLKING

Rantsoeneeringskaart

ONDERRICHTINGEN

De rantsoeneeringskaart is strikt individueel en persoonlijk. Zij is alléén geldig als zij samen gaat met de eenzelvigheidskaart en, voor de personen van min. dan 16 jaar, als zij samengaat met de eenzelvigheidskaart van de persoon die me det de hoede van het kind belast is.

Het verlies van de kaart moet onmiddellijk aangegeven worden aan de Gemeentelijke of Intercommunale Steun- en Ravitailleeringsdienst. Zij wordt vervangen tegen betaling. Ieder misbruik, vervalsching of namaak der kaarten wordt bestraft.

De rantsoeneeringszegels worden afgeleverd door de Gemeentelijke of Intercommunale Steun- en Ravitailleeringsdienst van het gebied waar de titularis gevestigd is of zijn gewoon verblijf heeft, op overleggen :

1° van de rantsoeneeringskaart ;

2° van de eenzelvigheidskaart.

Iedere wijziging van domicilie of van gewoon verblijf dient aan de Gemeentelijke of Intercommunale Steun- en Ravitailleeringsdienst aangegeven.

Bij de aankoop van een rantsoen der aan rantsoeneering onderworpen produkten moet de overeenstemmende rantsoeneeringszegel aan den verkooper afgegeven.

Verloren rantsoeneeringszegels worden niet vervangen. De namaak of vervalsching van rantsoeneeringszegels wordt bestraft.

BELGIAN RATION CARD

The cover of the author's ration card in Antwerp, printed in Flemish and issued by the Belgian authorities operating under Nazi supervision. On the cover is written in the name of the shop for which it was registered, and at which the principal items must be purchased—if available.

For one thing, at the time of the occupation, a considerable share of the population of the Low Countries greeted the new masters with cordiality, and even enthusiasm. When I left, hunger was already convincing many of these potential Nazis that the Germans were not as admirable as they had thought. The more this feeling is intensified, the less they will fraternize with the German soldiers, and, in consequence, the greater will be the consciousness of isolation on the part of the occupation troops—an element which might well further influence their morale.

Furthermore, although organized revolt may be impossible, this hatred will lead to an ever-increasing amount of sabotage and non-co-operation.

The Germans, of course, lose no opportunity to spread counter-propaganda to the effect that the food shortage is due solely to the British blockade—but the Belgians have seen too many thousands of the gigantic German Railway trucks speeding along the highways to the Greater Reich, laden with confiscated materials, to take that statement seriously.

The deepening hatred of the Nazis as hunger grows might have one other military advantage. Should the time come when an expeditionary corps again lands on the European continent, hostility to the German army of occupation on the part of the civilian population will obviously have a considerable military importance.

If this were all that needed to be taken into consideration, however, it is doubtful whether the total military gain would justify a decision not to send food to the occupied areas.

Unfortunately, there is still the second question to be considered: Could food sent to the occupied countries be prevented from reaching German soldiers and civilians and thus prolonging the war?

Frankly, I don't think it could, unless precautions were taken far more elaborate than anything now being considered—and far more elaborate than the Nazi government would be likely to accept.

The favorite proposal at the moment seems to be to send food in small shipments and to cease sending further supplies immediately if a single shipment fails to reach the starving civilian population.

This point of view seems to me totally unrealistic. It is based on a complete failure to appreciate that it is not nations in the abstract that must be fed, but concrete individuals and families whose lives are controlled and regulated down to the minutest detail by the gray-uniformed soldiers who are everywhere in their midst.

To put it more directly, these well-intentioned persons overlook the fact that we would not *know* whether the food reached the civilian populations or not, unless a far more elaborate organization were set up than was the case during the First World War.

One of my main reasons for that skepticism is one that I hesitate to bring up, since it is certain to provoke indignant denials, but which I cannot in all fairness evade.

On at least a score of occasions, Belgians who lived under the occupation from 1914 to 1918—responsible business men, industrialists, municipal employees and private citizens whose honesty I had no reason to doubt—have assured me that a large share, and perhaps the major share, of all the food sent by America during the last war was diverted to feed the German army.

The details of how that allegedly occurred, through the

complicity of corrupt Belgian officials, is not important here. Perhaps it is completely untrue, or grossly exaggerated; in any case it is not susceptible of proof. However, on every occasion that I have met a Belgian who had lived through the last occupation, I questioned him about American relief—and I have never, on even a single occasion, found one who had received anything save some practically inedible salt fish and rancid lard. I do not pretend that there were no Belgian civilians who received anything else; it merely happens that I have never been able to find one.

That rancid lard, incidentally, has become practically a legend; if I happened to mention lard to a Belgian housewife, she raised her hands in horror, so whatever it was that reached the Belgians must have been pretty bad.

They all realized and appreciated that America had sent a great deal of more desirable food as well, but were unanimous in asserting that it had been eaten by the occupation troops.

Whether that be true or not, it focuses attention on a point which should be fairly obvious but appears to be somewhat overlooked: Unless the food is actually distributed by reliable American representatives directly to individuals, or at least individual families, on the spot, there will not be the slightest assurance that it does reach the civilian population, nor shall we even know of it if the chief beneficiary is the German soldiery.

This means that enough American relief workers must be stationed in every little town and village to supervise personally the distribution of supplies in small quantities directly to individuals upon presentation of identity and food cards.

The existing food-rationing organizations could be of great assistance, since they have accurate data on the population to be fed, but it would be out of the question to entrust them with any slightest part in the distribution, since they are entirely Nazi-controlled and could scarcely resist any effort to divert food to the army; in fact, with a Gestapo man always just around the corner, it is doubtful whether they would even dare to report infractions of the agreement.

An American relief organization on the scale I mention could no doubt be assembled, but the personnel would have to have something more than a desire to help and a willingness to face the risk of bombardments. Unless all those in charge of distribution were fluently conversant with the language of the country in which they were stationed, and were well informed on the general situation there, their control would still not be a valid one.

Assuming, however, that such an organization is possible, a more difficult question arises: Would the Nazi government permit such an organization to operate in the occupied areas?

I believe not.

Any plan for relief must be based on the obvious fact that a Nazi promise is worth rather less than nothing. The Nazis know that the rest of the world feels this, and they not unnaturally resent it, since it deprives them of one of their best weapons. Any suggestion, therefore, that we could not trust them and must ourselves control the distribution of food right down to the individual home would infuriate them.

If, however, the Germans were willing to concede this

point, there is still a greater military issue involved: Would the German High Command permit an organization of several thousand persons, citizens of a country which they consider unfriendly, to circulate freely throughout the entire occupied area?

It must be remembered that, by virtue of the very nature of this war, every square mile of the occupied countries is a potential theater of war. These thousands of Americans would inevitably bring to the now isolated peoples news of the outside world which the Germans try to keep from them, and a great deal of what the Nazis would consider "propaganda for the democracies."

More serious, the Nazis would never believe that such an organization was not carrying on, directly or indirectly, espionage for Great Britain.

Finally, German statements on the subject have made it probable that that country would demand, as one of the conditions, feeding of the German civilian population as well. We, of course, consider the population of Germany a belligerent one and that of the occupied areas non-belligerent. The Nazis, considering all of these peoples citizens of the Greater Reich, whether they like it or not, make no such distinction.

It is not easy for me to suggest that it would be unwise to feed the hungry and oppressed peoples of the Continent. A very large number of my greatest friends are at this moment wondering what they will have to eat tomorrow, and my natural instinct is to say: "Let's feed them by all means, and as quickly as possible!"

But this new war-against-civilians leaves no room for sentiment, and I know that those same friends would not, do not want, relief at the price of strengthening Hitler's hand.

If the Germans want those civilian populations fed, they would doubtless accept terms under which we could be sure of the destination of the food we sent. If not—and I strongly suspect that Germany prefers them hungry and submissive—then she would reject measures of control such as I have indicated, and in that case there is not the slightest doubt in my mind, at least, as to who would be the ultimate recipient of our well-meant aid.

II

Life Without Light

THE MATTER OF FOOD IS VITALLY IMPORTANT, BUT IT IS
by no means the whole of the picture. Life has been profoundly altered under the occupation in nearly every respect; so many things have been changed that it is difficult
to pick the most typical features and deal with them within
reasonable compass.

Shortage of food is not the only deficiency. It would
be difficult to name a line of merchandise which is not
deficient. Things manufactured in Belgium go chiefly to
Germany and the great number of items for which Belgium
was dependent on import are gradually disappearing from
the shops. Even imports from Germany were, when I left,
practically non-existent, and the same condition was true
throughout the whole of the occupied area. The shipping
lanes to Germany are today one-way roads.

It would be unfair to say that at the time of my departure the shelves in the stores were completely bare. There
was still merchandise, and a visitor to Belgium at that
time would have probably thought that the shops were putting up a very brave show of business-as-usual. Belgium
was still living on her reserves, and not all stocks were
exhausted after only a half year of occupation. What it
will be after one year, or two years, is another matter. At
the one end, further supplies have been cut off; at the
other, there has been the rapid depletion of stocks due to

47

hoarding by war-wise Belgians and reckless buying by merchandise-hungry German soldiers.

Woolen goods are virtually unobtainable. The German soldiers are miserably dressed and, according to their own stories, suffered greatly from the cold during the winter of 1939-'40. Hence they rushed to buy warm woolen under-clothing, and when a sharp cold wave in September forced me to look for something of the sort myself, the only thing I could obtain in the largest department store in Antwerp was a suit designed for a man of roughly twice my di-ameter.

Women's stockings are equally scarce; every German soldier bought a few pairs of silk stockings for his wife, sister or girl friend, not to mention silk underclothing of every description. When I left, two Belgian women out of three were going bare-legged, though the weather was no longer Californian.

In brief, the German soldiers bought anything and everything, and then purchased expensive leather luggage to carry what they did not send home via the army postal service. It was years since most of them had seen shops stocked with so much merchandise—some never had—and they made the most of the opportunity. Those who ar-rived only shortly before I left, and found the best of everything gone, complained bitterly of the greediness of the earlier purchasers.

Not only are the German soldiers well paid in occupa-tion money, but the exchange rate has been pegged at a level which makes everything half-price for them. As a re-sult, many of them not only spent their entire accumulation of army pay in the shops, but wrote home for every bit of money the family could scrape together, to be likewise converted into goods. I strongly suspect that many of the older Germans remember what happened to money at the end of the last war, and are wisely accumulating merchandise rather than paper currency of dubious worth.

Except for the increasing scarcity of staple lines of goods, business in the shops was going on much as usual. The Germans had instituted a twelve to two o'clock closing period in the middle of the day, which made matters inconvenient for working people who could shop only during their own lunch hour; some critics suggested that this was perhaps a Nazi device for the reduction of shopping by the civilian population.

Clothing had not, however, been rationed in Belgium when I left, though Holland was already on the same card system as Germany.

One thing noticeable in department stores was that the food department was closed off from the rest of the premises, and might only be entered through a single door from the street. To prevent possible food riots, the police allow only a small number of customers to be in the food department at one time, with the result that long lines wait outside in the street, sometimes for hours.

Another feature of shopping in wartime is that in the event of an air raid, everyone in the store, both customers and personnel, must take refuge in the nearest shelter. Since a raid may well last an hour, this lends a touch of uncertainty as to just how long your shopping will take you; fortunately, there are not many daylight raids in the occupied areas.

Important in the Belgian scheme of things, as elsewhere on the Continent, is café life. No feature of the American scene really corresponds to it; the Belgian café is neither a saloon, nor a restaurant nor a clubhouse, yet it combines some of the features of all of them. In an average Belgian street, one commercial establishment in three will be a café. Here the whole family goes in the evening—to play cards, to meet friends, to listen to music—and while there are cafés of all sorts, the majority are pretty orderly. For one thing, public establishments in Belgium may not serve strong drinks, and it is difficult to become drunk and disorderly on beer and wine.

Surprisingly enough, beer was one of the items which were still plentiful and of unchanged quality when I left. There had been frequent reports that the alcoholic content was to be reduced, but nothing had yet been done about it. Perhaps the grain being used for this purpose is considered unsuitable for food, or, I think more likely, the Germans feel that depriving the population of its beer would be too unpopular.

After beer, the most important item in the cafés has always been coffee, but it was becoming less and less so. For one thing, the ration stamps only allowed for one cup a day for each person; for another, it was necessary to have a separate stamp for the sugar; and finally, an increasing amount of not very good imitation coffee was being served, and the Belgian is accustomed to the very best.

Except for this limitation, most Belgian cafés were doing lively business, a large share of the customers being German soldiers, chauffeurs, railroad men and the like.

Entering a café in the daytime, everything seemed to be going on much as usual, save that a great number of those sitting about were wearing the field gray uniform of the German army, or had the yellow armband of its civilian employees.

The Belgians present did not allow this to disturb them seriously. Some ignored the Germans, some fraternized with them, but never did I see any effort to boycott them. There have been stories to the effect that in Norway and Holland, for example, patrons in a café get up and go out when German soldiers come in. That may be true in scattered cases, but I saw or heard nothing to confirm it.

It must be remembered, of course, that I was living in Flanders, where the inhabitants speak a language, Flemish, which is similar to Low German. My observation in France was more limited, but it was evident that the language barrier alone was enough to limit fraternizing between the occupation troops and the civilian population.

If café life in the daytime was almost normal, evening brought a different picture. The blackout has profoundly affected life between sundown and sunup, and nothing more deeply than café life.

Bright lights are an intrinsic part of café atmosphere, and the blackout has made bright lighting a problem, since not the faintest glimmer must be visible outside. Most Belgian cafés have windows taking up the entire front wall, which open out onto the terrace in the summer, and these make "occultation" difficult. A few of the largest cafés have hung heavy drapes and thick curtains, which permit of normal illumination on the inside, but this is the exception, and most establishments content themselves with a bit of moderately bright lighting at the back of the room and dim, blue-shaded lamps, or dulled red neon tubes, nearer the street. The result, in the latter case, is desperately depressing, and there is little inclination to linger.

The larger cafés still have their orchestras, but the regulations when I left Antwerp did not officially allow music after nine-thirty P.M. Dancing was limited to two nights a week. Thus there is little inclination to make a late evening of it, and in any case there remains the problem of getting home in the blackout. Public transport continues to operate until a fairly late hour, but ceases in the event of an air raid warning—and since such a warning may come suddenly any time after sundown, few late revelers risk the chance of being forced to stumble their way homeward through blacked-out streets.

For, under German rule, the blackout is a serious matter. Illumination was normal in Belgium from the beginning of the war to the invasion, and there was only one half-hearted rehearsal of blacking out the telltale lights. When the German attack began, occultation was ordered, but lack of preparation made it almost totally ineffective, and few took it seriously.

As soon as the Germans entered, matters altered sharply. If a German sentry saw a gleam of light he shouted a warning; if the light did not disappear, he shot it out. The measure was a drastic one, and the first result was a considerable number of smashed windowpanes and lamps—the second result being that people stopped joking about the blackout and rushed to buy blue paint, black lampshades, blue lamps and all the other necessary paraphernalia.

In France, of course, the total extinction of all outside light began with the crisis at the end of August, 1939, and I had the greatest difficulty at that time in buying a pocket flashlamp in Paris. In the end, I found a case at one shop, a lamp at another, and, after several hours of searching, a battery at a third store. When I revisited Paris in November, 1939, the blackout had become serious indeed, and heavy fines were being imposed on those who failed to observe the regulations. Nevertheless, French fliers assured me that Paris remained clearly and easily visible throughout the night.

An interesting sidelight on the curious economic effects of modern warfare was that at that time, before the invasion of the Low Countries, the largest electric lamp factory in Europe was in a serious financial position due to the fact that the Continent was no longer using electric lighting on any scale worth mentioning; the recession of civilization had begun.

I can never forget an incident which impressed upon me for the first time just what light means as a part of civilized life. Returning from wartime Paris to a Belgium still at peace, I had traveled all evening in a train practically without lights. I could not read; I could not even see the faces of my fellow travelers. At Quévy we were in Belgium; a railway employee came into the compartment, screwed a lamp into the overhead fixture, and suddenly there was LIGHT!

Any statement of that fact must seem somewhat banal, but the simple reality brought a surge of joyous feeling of what it meant to be in a country at peace that cannot be described. I was not to feel that sudden contrast again until nearly a year later when my train crossed the international bridge to Irun and I watched my last German sentry fade into the distance.

Living in a country at war, light becomes the very symbol of decent, civilized life—and the eternal, unending darkness, broken only by parachute flares, "flaming onion" tracer bullets and exploding bombs, comes to stand for all the forces of destruction and misery.

Imagine a world in which your pocket flashlamp has be-

come as indispensable as your front-door key. Wending
your way home after dusk through the murky streets, the
only pedestrians you can distinguish are those who carry a
lighted cigarette or cigar. Many of them you bump into.
Every lamp-post, every telephone booth, every letter-box
means a potential collision. You stumble over each curb-
stone. You hear automobiles approaching, but barely see
the faint slits in their headlamps. You may not use your
electric torch in the street, unless you have made its light
nearly invisible by means of blue paint. Worst of all are
the bicycles, so common in the Low Countries, for you
scarcely hear them coming, and while not fatal, a collision
with one may be most unpleasant. The only helpful measure I ever discovered was to pick out, if possible, another
pedestrian going my way and to follow closely behind
him, detouring each time he bumped into something. The
method was not infallible, but it did simplify matters.

However, this was only one aspect of the problem, and
often the smallest, since one simply avoids as far as possible being out in the streets after dark.

Arrived at home, you have not necessarily finished with
the blackout. You stumble into the hallway, and perhaps
fall over someone's bicycle, placed there for security.
Eventually you fumble your way to your own apartment,
and turn on the "light."

I suppose one could call it that. The most frequent lighting unit is a 15-watt bulb, dipped in blue paint, with a
spot smaller than a dime left clear. Since not even this
must shine on the window, it will more likely than not be
enclosed within a deep shade, black on the outside, blue
within.

As a result, when you "turn on the light" the resulting

illumination would not dazzle even a person with the weakest of eyes. Directly under the lamp is a modest circle of light, perhaps a foot across, and bright enough to read by if you are directly in the beam. The rest of the room is in almost total obscurity, relieved only by faint gleams of diffusely reflected light.

There is, of course, a way around this interior gloom. Thick, heavy curtains over all windows, fastened along the edges with thumbtacks if necessary, will permit of normal lighting. However, few homes have window drapes so opaque that no light whatever is visible through them, and such materials are already difficult to obtain in the occupied countries, not to mention the expense of such curtains for large Continental windows.

Another solution is to cover all your windowpanes with blue paint—but the result is a blackout in the daytime which is even more depressing.

So in the end you learn to live without light, going to bed early and rising with the dawn, reading little (which you don't much mind because there are only the German propaganda newspapers and magazines) and doing by day such jobs as demand clear illumination.

If one reads little, however, one tends to smoke a great deal. I say "tends," because at the time I left it was becoming more and more difficult to obtain the means to gratify that inclination.

Before the invasion, Belgium was a smoker's paradise. Perhaps no country in the world offered so great a range of tobaccos, and prices were far lower than in the rest of Europe. A typical shop in Antwerp carried three hundred and fifty brands of cigarettes—Belgian, American, French, English, Italian, Egyptian, Bulgarian, Russian, Macedonian—and some two hundred brands of pipe tobacco, not to mention almost innumerable sorts of cigars at exceptionally low prices. Hence the Belgian smoker was exceedingly difficult to please, and if he could not have his favorite brand would go elsewhere.

Not today.

When I left, one no longer entered a tobacconist's shop and asked for a particular sort.

One simply entered and said: "Have you anything at all to smoke?" If there were no cigarettes, one took tobacco and cigarette papers, or pipe tobacco, or cigars, if one were lucky enough to find a shop which had any of these.

Practically all shops, however, had a sign on the door: "No cigarettes, no tobacco." In the beginning, that sign was taken down when supplies came in, but by the time I left most of them didn't bother. A small stock was received about once a week, and since the shopkeepers tried to keep this for their regular customers they avoided letting the general public know that there was anything on hand. Taking down the "No tobacco" sign resulted in the immediate formation of a long line of customers in the street, and within half an hour the shop had finished its sales until the following week.

Not that there is any lack of tobacco in the country. Stocks on hand at the time of the invasion were sufficient for four years. When the Germans arrived, all supplies of cigarettes were seized. When the factories resumed production, huge orders were placed with them for the German army, and obligatory fulfillment of these orders leaves little over for the civilian population. To make matters worse, one of the largest and most modern factories, belonging to Vander Elst, was destroyed during the Ger-

FRANCE

CARTE POSTALE

EXPÉDITEUR DESTINATAIRE

_____ _____

_____ _____

_____ _____

_____ _____

Après avoir complété cette carte strictement réservée à la correspondance d'ordre familial, biffer les indications inutiles. — Ne rien écrire en dehors des lignes.
ATTENTION. — Toute carte dont le libellé ne sera pas **uniquement** d'ordre familial ne sera pas acheminée et sera probablement détruite.

....................................., le........................... 194...

.... en bonne santé .... fatigué.

.... légèrement, gravement malade, blessé.

.... tué .... prisonnier.

.... décédé .... sans nouvelles.

de.................................. - La famille .... va bien.

.... besoin de provisions .... d'argent.

nouvelles, bagages. .... est de retour à ....

.... travaille à .... va entrer

à l'école de .... • .... a été reçu

.... • .... aller à .... le ....

....

....

Affectueuses pensées. Balsers.   *Signature.*

NEWS FROM THE FAMILY

This card, the only form of communication permitted between occupied and unoccupied France, bears the following: "After completing this card, strictly reserved for family correspondence, cross out the unnecessary indications. Attention—Any card on which the message is not purely of a family nature will not be sent and will probably be destroyed. (Place and date.) . . . in good health . . . tired . . . slightly, gravely ill, wounded; . . . killed . . . prisoner . . . died . . . without news of . . . The family . . . is well . . . need of provisions . . . of money, news, baggage; . . . has returned to . . . is working at . . . will enter the school of . . . ; . . . has been received . . . Go to . . . on . . . Affectionate thoughts. Kisses."

(Photo from P. Guillumette)

man advance, further reducing possible production.

Smoking, however, is not the only one of the pleasures of life that has been badly curtailed. Few of them have not. Entertainment, so essential to keeping up morale, limps badly.

The motion picture theaters, grouped into cartels by the German authorities and placed under the direction of Belgians sympathetic to the Nazi cause, are practically all open for business.

Two things, however, keep patronage at a low level—the films shown and the blackout. Not all the pictures presented are made in Germany, though the great majority are of Nazi origin, but only films which have been passed by the censor in Germany may be shown in the occupied countries. As the number of foreign films shown in Germany is limited, this makes a fare not likely to greatly tempt the fan. The blackout makes it necessary to go very early if you want to get home in comfort, and this also limits patronage.

Theatrical fare, when I left, was limited to a few revues acceptable to the Nazi censor and a "Strength Through Joy" theater presenting entertainment in German for the occupation troops.

It goes without saying that the radio had ceased to become a means of entertainment. Stations in the occupied countries were all under German control, and broadcast frequent news bulletins in that language for the soldiers. There were also interminable propaganda announcements in the language of the country, and heavy-handed musical entertainment in which brass bands took up the greater share of the time.

For some time after the occupation, Hilversum in Holland continued to broadcast good music, but on several occasions soldiers in the restaurant of my hotel, when this was being played, asked with some annoyance if it were not possible to get a good military band. The Germans were once a people with a considerable musical culture, but there was no evidence among the soldiers whom I saw in Belgium that any traces of it remain.

Loudspeakers in public places emitted German news bulletins at all hours of the day, since the soldiers demanded them, but few of the Belgians whom I knew listened much to the German-controlled stations, except from curiosity, and fewer still took the broadcast "news" at all seriously. The Germans knew this, thanks to Belgian frankness on the subject, and were as furious as they were impotent to do anything about it.

Soon after the occupation began, a decree was published imposing a penalty of two years in a concentration camp for listening to any other than German-controlled stations. This prohibition included specifically even the Italian stations, a tabu which cast some little doubt on Germany's confidence in her Axis partner.

The only result of this decree was that what had been done openly was done in secret. Few Belgians whom I knew failed to listen regularly to London, and I learned that the same was true in Holland and in France. Those who listen talk about it with discretion, for the Germans are especially severe with those who repeat news heard from non-Nazi stations, but they did listen, and, within the circle of their immediate family and friends, they did talk about it.

In the face of the total impossibility of checking up on what was coming over millions of loudspeakers, the Germans were, before I left, making constantly increased efforts to "jam" the broadcasts from London. They tried, on successive nights, every possible raucous noise, emitted on the same wavelength as London, but up to my departure they had not found any form of interference which made speech unintelligible, though music was completely ruined.

The only other source of information is, of course, the German-controlled press.

Before the invasion, the Belgian press was divided, some of the papers being frankly pro-Ally while others were pro-German, though not usually so frankly. All were obliged to keep up a reasonable pretense of neutrality, but none of them really was. Under the occupation, the previously pro-German papers appear with little change save complete abandonment of the pretense of neutrality. A few of the others, completely changed, also appear; some have simply disappeared. In addition, there are new dailies in German for the troops.

The content of these papers can easily be imagined by anyone familiar with the controlled German press—dispatches glorifying German feats of arms, and everything possible to vilify the British government and the former Belgian government. Items concerning American isolationists receive great prominence; ex-Ambassador Cudahy's famous interview in London gave them front-page copy for days. No occasion is overlooked to prove that American aid to Britain is negligible and will grow smaller and smaller; no slightest doubt is left that America will never take up arms against an all-powerful Germany. Also, parenthetically, when I left the papers were leaving no slightest doubt that Mr. Wendell Willkie was going to be elected President of the United States by an overwhelming majority.

It is worthy of note that all of these newspapers print a certain amount of the news broadcast from London— branding it as "British hate-lies," of course—which shows that the authorities realize the extent to which civilians in the occupied areas listen to London, and seek to discredit the information thus obtained.

The German authorities, pursuing their policy of "making friends" in the occupied countries, operate the press censorship in such a way that a minimum of inconvenience is caused to the publishers. At "De Dag," for example, the Flemish-language Antwerp daily which is one of the most important in Belgium, a German captain arrives each day about an hour before press time. He then goes through the proofs, aided occasionally by a translator, and makes the smallest possible number of deletions. One of the publishers remarked that he had less trouble with the German censorship than he had had before the invasion with the Belgian censorship. That remark was a bit naive, since the pro-German trend of the paper's sympathies made it inevitable that the editors should have trouble with a Belgian censorship trying to preserve an air of neutrality, and relatively little trouble with a German control. Even making allowance for this, however, the attitude shown is an instance of the success which the Germans have undoubtedly had in many quarters with their policy of "friendship."

Despite this fact, it seemed evident that the Belgian reading public had not been won over so completely. No reliable circulation figures are available, but a great many of the people I knew had given up reading any newspaper

whatever and there was every indication that sales were
heavily hit.

Finally, it is perhaps worth mentioning that the only
product I ever saw unloaded in any quantity in the harbor
where the river barges come in from Germany was news-
print paper. The Belgians may have to go without food,
but they shall not lack propaganda!

As for magazines, only a few are published in Belgium,
even under normal conditions, but there was no lack of
German periodicals. Particularly in evidence was "Signal," the propaganda organ published in several editions
in various languages, well printed and richly illustrated.
This sold rather well.

There is considerable doubt in my mind, however,
whether all this propaganda effort, and the policy of a
state-controlled press, really achieves the result which its
sponsors fondly imagine.

After all, news traveled around before newspapers existed, and since people cannot be prevented from talking
the chief result of officially one-sided newspapers is to attach an importance and credibility to rumors which they
would never have in a country with a nominally free press,
or at any rate one in which various shades of opinion have
their organs of expression.

I have had the opportunity to observe at close hand, over
a period of many years, the operation and effects of a state-
controlled press in two countries, Germany (including occupied areas) and Soviet Russia.

Since I think this matter is an important one, I should
like to lay aside for a moment questions of bias and prejudice, ignoring the political systems involved, and, as an ex-

newspaperman, discuss the results as I witnessed them from day to day.

Although I have grouped them together, there seems to me to be a certain fundamental difference between the Russian press and the German.

Over a period of years in Moscow I regularly saw the German papers, and, of course, the local dailies, and had the opportunity to compare their treatment of events with which I was familiar.

The difference which then seemed to me most striking was that whereas news in the German press was frequently pure invention, the Soviet press sometimes suppressed or colored news but never, so far as I was able to observe, made it up out of whole cloth. What appeared in the Soviet papers was usually accurate; the only exception to this was a tendency, common to all Soviet agencies, toward over-optimistic statistics concerning future production, and, perhaps, occasional understatement concerning casualties and damage in wrecks and similar catastrophes. I mention this point because it has a bearing on the attitude toward the press in the two countries; few Russians doubt seriously news which appears in their daily newspapers, but they are prone to attach undue importance to rumors concerning that which does not appear; an intelligent German doubts anything he sees in the press.

That last statement may seem questionable in view of the apparent success of the German propaganda within Germany. Nevertheless, when I was last in that country, shortly before the outbreak of war, I encountered a surprising number of Germans who said to me, in effect: "Now, thank Heaven, we can find out something about what is happening in the world!"

The fallacy, I think, in the idea of the muzzled press is a simple one: it is the assumption that you can keep news from circulating if you don't print it.

As a matter of fact, you seldom can. Few things happen which are not known to a number of persons; with rare exceptions, each of these persons has at least two or three close friends or relatives to whom he tells even things supposed to be kept secret; each of these in turn has two or three more, and within an astonishingly short time the "secret" is known to nearly everyone.

This statement may seem as elementary as something out of a third grade reader—but failure to recognize this simple fact seems to me to be at the root of the whole matter.

An entire book, and an interesting one, could be written about the network of rumors, gossip and supposition that makes up the background of life in Moscow, Berlin or Rome.

I recall that whenever a new law was being drafted, a commissar had been arrested or a new long distance airplane flight was being planned in Moscow, we knew about it days and sometimes weeks before a word appeared in the press—"we" being just about everybody in Moscow. All sorts of rumors circulated, and the surprising thing was that most of them sooner or later proved to be true.

When the great "Maxim Gorki," then the largest land plane in the world, crashed during my stay in Russia, I knew about it in my own apartment in town within half an hour. This, of course, appeared immediately after in the newspapers, but it was an instance of the rapidity with which news circulates in a country where the press prints only part of it. News acquires a tremendously increased importance by virtue of its suppression; in the absence of free news, people spread rumors far more industriously than would otherwise be the case and, what means more, they pay greater attention to them and take them more seriously.

In a country with no open censorship of news, readers pay little attention, for the most part, to rumors of which they find no confirmation in the press. In a censored press, on the contrary, they learn to read between the lines, and often attach the greater importance to that which does *not* appear in the papers.

I again saw this abundantly demonstrated in the occupied little countries. In these areas, readers were accustomed to relatively uncensored news; there was, to be sure, a mild censorship from the outbreak of the war to the invasion, but this was concerned only with avoiding sentiments too partial to one or other of the belligerents and disclosure of secrets prejudicial to the national defense.

Suddenly confronted with a press not remarkable for its impartiality, the reaction was exactly what might have been expected. The pro-Nazi elements in the population naturally gloried in the new-found "freedom of the press." The rest of the population turned to rumors for consolation.

The variety and frequency of those rumors defies description. Every acquaintance you met throughout the day had a few new ones and several old ones. As is nearly always the case, most of the stories purported to originate in what a high German officer had said, or what an eyewitness had seen, or, perhaps oftenest of all, what the London radio had announced. Many, doubtless most, were fantastically untrue, and merely represented an example of mass wishful thinking—but a surprising number eventually proved to be correct, demonstrating the difficulty, if not impossibility, of totally bottling up the truth.

To take a simple instance: One day, toward noon, a British scouting plane flew over, doubtless taking photographs. The moment it emerged from the clouds, a terrific barrage of anti-aircraft fire began crackling on all sides, and two German fighters went up to engage the enemy ship. There was evidently a slight lack of co-ordination between the two services, for one of the Messerschmitts was hit by Nazi anti-aircraft shells and came down in flames.

The next day, a full account appeared in the Belgian press—perfectly accurate save for the fact that the destroyed plane had become a British craft. There was nothing surprising about this, but more significant was the fact that just about everyone in Antwerp already *knew* that the plane brought down was a German fighter. No one was fooled, and confidence in the German-controlled press, already weak, was further torn down.

The reason I speak so categorically of this particular incident, though I did not actually see the plane at close enough range to identify it, is that I had three confirmations of the facts: a friend of mine living near the airport saw the ship crash; a newspaper editor told me that he had had a photograph of the wreckage ready for publication when the censorship stepped in; and, most conclusive of all, one of the German pilots who ate frequently at my hotel told me, before the false version was published, that the dead pilot was one of his mates.

A surprising number of the completely false rumors masqueraded as something broadcast from London. I was able to listen to the B.B.C. news bulletins pretty regularly, if cautiously; for one thing, as an American, I was perhaps less worried about facing a German tribunal, and for another, I lived alone, and had no need to worry as to whether any of my immediate friends or relatives might inform the police.

Thus I usually knew pretty well what London had said during the day, but the rumors circulating on that score were often far more colorful than anything the conservative British radio had given out. Almost invariably, these were stories of remarkable British victories and staggering German defeats, showing the "wishful thinking" principle at work; the fact that they were attributed to the London radio was an instance of the manner in which rumor-mongers try to make their tales credible. This citing of the British Broadcasting Corporation as authority for otherwise questionable statements was, it seems to me, a significant mass recognition of the fact that most people (even if they did not admit it) placed more credence in the London broadcasts than in those originating in Dr. Goebbels' office.

Rumors were particularly rife after a night's bombardment by the R.A.F. These were a weird mixture of the true and the untrue concerning the objectives hit, but they served a useful purpose, surprisingly enough. After such raids, the German-controlled press gave great prominence to stories of bombs which had fallen (as they all too frequently did) on homes, schools, hospitals and the like, but there was never a word concerning military objectives attained.

The intention was obvious, and had it not been for the "word-of-mouth" news service, most Belgians would have been convinced that the R.A.F. never bombed anything save civilians, and merited the name "Air Pirates" which the German press and radio gave it a thousand times a day.

However, before leaving this question of censored news, it must be made clear that the question has two sides; long-continued propaganda is not entirely without effect. Even those who do not believe what is printed may have their judgment warped by their ignorance of things which are withheld. Although, as I have said, there are thinking Germans who are not deceived, they are all too few, and the peculiar docility of the German people has undoubtedly made it possible to mislead them with false news to a greater degree than any other people.

But on the whole, I am more than ever convinced, since living under the occupation, that censored news and the suppression of truth in the press is what the English aptly call "a mug's game"—a largely wasted effort.

Letters were, of course, also being censored throughout the whole of the occupied regions.

During the first months after the invasion, there was no postal communication whatever for civilians. The destruction of railway lines and bridges during the retreat of the Allied armies meant that for some time no trains ran, and postal facilities became non-existent. The German army ran a special mail trucking service for the soldiers, but even they complained for some time of long delays and irregular receipt of news from home.

Then a few private postal services sprang up. Certain bookshops in Antwerp accepted letters for transmission to Brussels, and vice versa, the charge being about fifteen cents. Not long after, the German field post began carrying a small quantity of mail between important cities at the normal postal rate, the only restriction being that the letters must be unsealed.

Then, as trains began to run here and there, postal service within the country took on the semblance of normality, though communication with the outside world remained uncertain and slow; a letter to or from America took three to four weeks. Officially, the censorship allowed only correspondence in Flemish, French or German, but in practice an occasional letter in English got through. The reason for this ban was simply that the censor's office was not yet equipped to deal with English language letters, and it was promised that this deficiency would soon be made good.

In Holland, for example, it was already possible to post letters in any language, and there were airmail connections, via Germany and Italy, with the Clipper from Lisbon, which did not exist in Belgium.

This was not because the Dutch people were especially favored, but largely because in Holland there was far less fighting and less destruction. Furthermore, as the Dutch queen and her government had fled, a new Nazi government under Seyss-Inquart was rapidly set up, which busied itself with the reorganization of such civilian services. In Belgium, although the government had likewise fled, the refusal of King Leopold to co-operate with the Germans, and the latter's fear of setting up a government without him, had prevented the appointment of a civil governor and new administration, so that the country was still under military rule when I left—infinitely to be preferred in many respects to Nazi civil administration, though perhaps not as active in organizing certain aspects of civilian life.

Train service everywhere in the occupied countries was far below normal. One of the chief efforts of the Allied armies in retreating was to make the railroads unusable, and the damage done prevented their operation for a considerable period. The most urgent repairs to blown-up lines were made by Nazi Labor Service battalions, who followed closely on the heels of the army of occupation. Working under the supervision of German railway engineers, these Nazi youths built temporary wooden bridges and cleared up enough of the wreckage to permit of the passage of troop trains and military supplies. After these emergency repairs were completed, systematic reconstruction began with Belgian civilian labor working under German direction. When I left, most of the main lines were in operating shape, with schedules greatly reduced, but many smaller lines were still out of commission. Local trains might be used freely, but the through trains were purely military and might be boarded only by civilians who had obtained the necessary permission from the military authorities. To obtain such permission, it was usually necessary to have urgent business (of interest to the German army), a relative seriously ill, or the like, but much depended on the good nature of the particular official with whom one came in contact. Every train carried at least one German railway employee, and several of these men were to be seen at each station.

Typical of present-day railway service was the usually excellent electric line between Antwerp and Brussels. Normally, these trains covered the thirty-mile stretch in as many minutes. When the Allied armies withdrew, they blew up all the bridges, wrecked the station and lines at Mechelen (or Malines), the midway point, and took with them all the blueprints showing the wiring of the power supply and signalization, which proved the greatest obstacle of all to a rapid resumption of traffic. For some time after the occupation private bus services offered the only means of getting from the one city to the other. Finally, the Germans managed to get the line running from Brussels to near Mechelen and from a point a few miles away to Antwerp. This service was then opened to the public, with a bus line connecting the two ends of the gap. Gradually, the line was repaired so that the two ends came within walking distance. At that time it took about an hour and a half to cover the thirty miles. The week before my departure, the schedule was speeded up so that it was possible, with luck, to make the journey in 45 minutes.

One feature of these trains is worth mentioning as an instance of the German tactlessness which tears down much of their indefatigable effort to make friends of the subjugated peoples.

Every train has at least one entire coach, and often more, exclusively reserved for members and employees of the German army, and every window in this space is conspicuously marked with stickers to that effect. When these seats are occupied, no one pays any special attention to the matter; after all, the Germans are operating the railways, and it is not altogether unnatural if they choose to give priority to their soldiers.

Unfortunately, it frequently happens that many or all of these seats are unoccupied, and on such occasions a few of the more daring souls among the Belgian standees invariably take some of these empty seats—to be promptly evicted by the conductor. As the latter is a Belgian, he is apologetic about the matter; he has no choice, and is merely carrying out orders, but he usually adds a few remarks under his breath about Germans in general which might rather shake the complacency of his new masters if his observations came to their ears. As for the crowd of standees, they profit by the fact that French and colloquial Flemish are unintelligible to the majority of Germans, and stage a noisy protest meeting.

If the Germans were as wise in carrying out their policy of conciliation as they imagine, they would avoid stupid and irritating practices of this sort. If the Belgians might only occupy these seats when there were no soldiers in them, the matter would pass almost unnoticed, but when fifty or sixty Belgians must stand throughout an entire journey, within view of an empty coach, even though it be a non-stop run and no more soldiers can possibly come aboard, the feelings of the standees may be imagined without difficulty.

In many of the big things, the pretense of friendliness is well carried out; it is in the little things that the arrogant belief in the superiority of the German race—and, naturally, the profound inferiority of all conquered peoples —comes to the surface. These little things will, in the long run, determine the attitude of the people of the occupied nations toward their new masters.

III

Consolidating the Occupation

EVEN THOUGH IT BE TRUE THAT THE GERMANS HAVE SOME-
times erred badly in the little things, with irritating and
even infuriating effect on the population of the occupied
countries, it would be self-deception to suppose that they
have made an entirely bad job of the occupation.

On the contrary, they have done an amazing piece of reconstruction, overshadowed only by the impressiveness of
their military feats, and it would be a grave mistake to re-
fuse to face that fact.

Almost before the shock troops had given way to the occupation forces, the German economic specialists and ad-
ministrators appeared, with their ever-present briefcases
stuffed with complete plans for "business as usual" in the
conquered area.

Admittedly, the ultimate beneficiary of most of this activity was to be Germany, but it was equally true that for
the oppressed populations this "business as usual" meant
the closest semblance of "life as usual" which it was possible to create under the circumstances.

The force of the expression, "Life must go on," is not
always appreciated; in wartime it becomes more than ever
a basic verity. People who have had their homes destroyed,
their relatives and friends killed, their nation brought low,
turn with grim desperation to their work and the humble
routine of daily life—the only thing they have left.

German efforts to rebuild as much as possible of normal, daily life for the civilian populations are therefore of the utmost importance for keeping up the morale of the conquered peoples, quite aside from the purely economic aspect.

The first business premises to be entered by the invaders, I believe, were the banks. At noon on the day of their arrival in Antwerp, a short walk through the business district showed me that they had already forced the doors of the principal banks.

Resumption of payment by the banks was of course vital to any resumption of business and industrial life, and as soon as possible after an inventory of the assets (and the confiscation of those useful to Germany) the banks reopened. At the time I left, those with bank accounts were permitted to draw a thousand francs a month (normally about thirty-three dollars), some persons being allowed to have more if they could demonstrate that they had no other source of income, so that the money was needed for living expenses. Special arrangements were made for large commercial firms, but factories were still having difficulty in obtaining funds for payroll purposes.

Payments by the banks were made indiscriminately in German occupation money or Belgian currency, the latter being still in circulation. In fact, much of the Belgian money, at the time of my departure, was obviously newly printed; after all, it costs the Germans no more to print from the Belgian plates than from their own, and since neither is backed by anything, the results are the same.

Those with safe deposit boxes were permitted to visit them in the company of an officer of the German financial service. All foreign securities and valuables negotiable abroad were then confiscated; September 27, 1940, was fixed as the deadline after which it was illegal to possess any foreign money, stocks, bonds or other negotiable values. Even my American Express checks, purchased before the war, had to be declared, and I had to obtain permission from the German command to bring them out with me.

Credit must be given to the German authorities, however, for far-reaching efforts to return as many Belgians to work as possible. However selfish the motive may be, Belgian employees and workers have inevitably benefited by the application of this policy.

All business establishments were obliged to reopen and to take back their employees. This undoubtedly worked some hardship on employers in many cases, but it kept a considerable number of workers earning and spending money and to that extent greatly retarded the economic collapse which will come when there are no longer enough raw materials and merchandise to keep the wheels of business turning.

The position of Belgian factories was somewhat more complicated. A German officer was placed in each establishment, nominally in charge. Actually, while nothing may be done contrary to his orders, the Germans have profited by the lessons of the last war and made this control a purely nominal and almost amiable affair. There is little interference with the administration of industrial plants, so long as the directors are not openly antagonistic.

The real problem, however, is that of markets. Belgian industry lived largely by export, and the local market is not enough to keep most factories working at normal capacity. Before I left, there was beginning to be a small amount of export business to the Scandinavian countries,

Holland, Finland, Switzerland and France. Transport was limited and uncertain, and the total amount of business which could be done under these circumstances was not large.

Many factories, therefore, were working on a half-time policy, in order to give some work at least to the greatest possible number of their employees.

The factories most favored, naturally, were those which were willing and able to manufacture a product needed by the Germans. Such plants received banking facilities, raw materials, transport and a large market, and, needless to say, were working full-time. On the other side of the ledger, these plants were being paid for the merchandise delivered in paper money of dubious worth, and, most serious of all, ran a greatly increased chance of bombardment by the R.A.F.

Some three hundred and fifty Belgian factories were destroyed during the invasion, and employment conditions could not be expected to be normal. It is not improbable that Germany's slowness in returning Belgian prisoners to their homes, despite repeated promises, has been due to the fear that too many of them would remain unemployed and thus constitute an eventual danger of discontent and possible trouble.

Strenuous efforts have been made, since the beginning of the occupation, to persuade Belgians to work in Germany. Posters everywhere stress the need in Germany for skilled workers of every sort, and offer the most tempting conditions. Thousands have accepted this offer; special trains have taken them to the Reich, and the Belgian newspapers have been filled with photographs of their departure, their journey and their arrival in Germany. Their families must be left behind, but a portion of the workers' wages may be sent to those at home.

The great mass of Belgian workers, however, has not shown any wild enthusiasm at the prospect of working in the Reich. Those who have gone have been either enthusiasts for the Hitlerian regime or those in such desperate circumstances that there seemed to be no alternative.

A special agent came to Antwerp from Germany, for example, to recruit longshoremen to work in Hamburg and Bremen. The men, who had had little to do since the occupation, gathered at their headquarters in the harbor to listen to the German representative. At the close of his speech, which painted a glowing picture of the ideal life of a worker under Nazism, the men shook their heads and began to turn away, as one of them later told me.

"You see," their spokesman volunteered, "we're not interested in working for quarter-pay."

The German agent was bewildered, and protested that he had offered them excellent wages.

"Yes," admitted the longshoreman, "that's true, but two hours on the pier and six in an air raid shelter means eight hours on the job for two hours' pay, and we're not interested. And anyway, there's too much rain in Hamburg for our taste."

The German was nettled, and insisted that while the climate of Hamburg was perhaps not ideal, it was certainly no worse than that of Antwerp.

"That may be," conceded the spokesman, "but we're thinking about a special kind of rain—English rain!"

The longshoremen remained in Antwerp.

This unwillingness to go to Germany to work on the part of most of the jobless led, shortly before I left, to the ap-

COMMENCEMENT OF RECONSTRUCTION

Civilians are here shown at work on repairs to a bridge near Sartrouville, on the important line between Paris and Le Havre.

(Photo from P. Guillumette)

EMERGENCY FERRY SERVICE

While bridges are being rebuilt, a small ferryboat transports pedestrians, an automobile and a horse across a small French stream.

(Photo from P. Guillumette)

plication of a new technique.

Unemployed men reporting to receive their small relief were told that a job had been found for them. Their card was held, and they were told to report at another office the next day, where they would receive the new job and the return of their card.

At the time specified, these men went to the office in question. Here they were told that there was a job for them —in Germany. If the man refused, his card was held and he was ineligible for further relief; if he accepted in the face of this threat, his only hope was the possibility that the examining physician might declare him incapable of making the journey. How many men have been thus "recruited" is not known, but many have refused.

Letters arriving in Belgium showed that a great number of workers had been obtained by Germany among the Belgian prisoners still in that country. Men who had a useful trade or professional skill were given the chance to leave the concentration camp to accept work; those who agreed were "farmed out" singly or in small groups on the responsibility of the employer, who fed and housed them and answered for their detention. Since, according to letters, almost anything was preferable to the monotonous idleness and near-starvation of a concentration camp, many had accepted work, and these undoubtedly made up a large portion of the 25,000 Belgians said to working in Germany.

In spite of all these measures, the number of unemployed in Belgium was large, and will grow larger. The question naturally arises: To what extent will the discontent engendered by this and the general situation lead to sabotage directed against the army of occupation?

The answer to that, of course, depends a great deal upon

the duration of the war. Taking the situation by and large, the amount of sabotage during the first half year of the occupation was great enough to give the German gendarmerie a few headaches, to be sure, but not enough to be considered a serious indication of incipient revolt.

In Belgium, there has been more sabotage in the Walloon part of the country than in Flanders. The Walloons speak a language closely related to old French, and their hatred of the Germans has persisted undiminished since the last war, when they were the greatest sufferers from Prussian oppression.

The principal form of sabotage, throughout all of the occupied countries, has been the persistent cutting of German military telephone wires.

When the troops first arrived, army electricians immediately installed a field telephone system. The wires—rubber covered cables about the thickness of a lead pencil—were at first simply laid in the streets. Within a few days, all these wires were off the ground and had been strung on hooks fastened to the front of buildings along the street, to telephone poles, lamp posts and other convenient supports.

The wires were still easily accessible, however, and it was not surprising that they should provide a constant temptation to those who wished to hamper the Germans in any way possible.

No figures are available, but indirect evidence showed that during the first half year these field telephone wires were cut pretty regularly. There were frequent posters threatening the most dire punishment for those caught tampering with the telephone wires, and imposing an enormous fine on the municipality in which the offense occurred.

This evidently proved inadequate, for shortly before I left a new measure was adopted. In a Walloon village where the wires had again been cut, all of the returned soldiers were rounded up and sent back to prison camp in Germany—to be returned only if and when the guilty person was turned over to the authorities. This measure, it was announced, was to be generally applied throughout Belgium.

Frequent radio broadcasts from the German-controlled Dutch stations made it evident that the same tampering with telephone wires was happening there, too.

Further than this, there was little evidence that acts of sabotage on any important scale were taking place, and while cutting field telephone wires doubtless irritated the German officials and caused them occasional inconvenience, the results were not usually of great moment. It was a difficult thing to prevent, since the blackout made it impossible to keep the wires under surveillance throughout the night: this impotence no doubt contributed to the fury which the Germans displayed when the wires were cut.

However, if acts of sabotage were of minor importance, there were a great many arrests of civilians for public criticism of Hitler, of the Nazis and of the German army. The mayor of a village near Brussels received a long prison sentence for asserting that bombs which had fallen in the center of the Belgian capital had been dropped by the Germans themselves to discredit the R.A.F. in the eyes of the Belgians. A salesgirl in an Antwerp department store disappeared because when a German officer asked to see bathing suits she asked him if it was for swimming the Channel. A Belgian woman made a remark derogatory to Hitler in a café near my hotel; she was arrested on the spot and not seen again.

It would be both unfair and untrue, nonetheless, to exaggerate this matter. The Belgians continued to speak their minds pretty freely, and the majority of the Germans respected them for their honesty. It was only the occasional Nazi fanatic who "saw red" when a Belgian implied that Hitler was something less than a deity or that Belgium had been better off before the arrival of the German legions. The higher officers and the simple soldiers were, for the most part, human and tolerant; worst of all were the under-officers, or sergeants, who seemed to be selected for their brutal arrogance, stupidity and violent pro-Nazi convictions. Such difficulties as I got into through my incautious habit of saying pretty much what I thought were invariably with sergeants. One of these, in particular, came to my hotel a score of times, usually drunk and always offensive. He was trying to win the affections of the chambermaid, with a total lack of success, and vented his displeasure by addressing noisy remarks to me about politics and the superiority of German culture as exemplified in the Nazi army. One evening, he became particularly annoying, and I permitted myself the satisfaction, for once, of telling him exactly what I thought of Nazi hoodlums of his stamp, with a few remarks about his Leader and government thrown in for good measure.

He became purple with rage, and it was probably just as well that his superior officer had not given him permission to carry his automatic that day. Choking with fury, he bent over and shouted at me the affirmation that he was an educated, cultured person (spitting in my face at each sibilant), and that the German army would know how to deal with low swine like me. He then stiffly demanded my name, which I gave him, and strode out unsteadily.

There was no sequel to the affair. He did not know that the man to whom he went to make the complaint had known me for many years before the war, and I understood later that he had received a harsh reprimand for drunkenness and conduct not calculated to create a good impression of the German army. However, I learned to confine my freedom of speech, from then on, to officers and privates, far more disposed to be human.

There was, for example, Lieutenant Perlt. This man, only a lieutenant in army rank, was nevertheless the police official who dealt with all questions of sabotage and censorship in the Antwerp area. He had been a police official all his life in Dresden, and was, I believe, one of the organizers of the Gestapo, not as a Nazi fanatic but as a capable and efficient police administrator.

I came to know Lieutenant Perlt rather well, and saw him on several occasions. He should, I suppose, have been a fire-breathing dragon, instead of which he was a courteous and conscientious police official who knew how to temper justice with mercy. That impression is not based on his reception of me, for I was, after all, the citizen of a neutral country, and, in addition, was sent to him by a superior officer—but is the result of a quite different case which came to my direct notice.

A Belgian was arrested by the German police for remarks of a violently pro-Belgian nature, and derogatory to the Nazis. Brought before Lieutenant Perlt, the man stuck to his guns.

"I am still a Belgian," he said. "If you win the war, I suppose I'll have to get accustomed to thinking of myself as a German—but you haven't won the war yet, and if you are chased out of here, as I believe you will be, I'll still be a Belgian."

Lieutenant Perlt was silent for a moment. Then he straightened up and banged his fist on the desk.

"By God, the man is right! Let him go!"

I shall not pretend that such a case is typical; unhappily, there are all too many sorry instances of the direct opposite—but I feel it is important to remember at this time that not all Germans have forgotten how to be human beings.

Much of the criticism which circulated among the Belgians took the form of anecdotes and humorous stories. This phenomenon is common to all dictatorships: I have encountered many of the same stories, in a practically identical form, in Italy, in Germany and in Russia.

One of the best of these yarns which was circulating when I left was equally popular in Denmark and Holland.

According to this tale, a decree went out that after a certain date no grain might be fed to chickens; they must receive only *ersatz* stuffs.

A Gestapo inspector was sent round to check up on how the farmers were observing the decree. At the first farm he visited, he inquired what the farmer was feeding his chickens. "Oats," was the reply, and the hapless farmer received a long sentence in a concentration camp.

At the next farm, the same question brought the reply that nothing whatever was given the poultry.

"But," objected the inspector, "that seems impossible. Your chickens look so fat and well fed!"

"It's very simple," replied the farmer. "I have two thousand hens and one rooster. I call the rooster 'Adolf' and he takes the hens out to eat up all the neighbors' feed!"

Many of these barbed criticisms took the simpler form of wisecracks. For example, a Belgian would say to you: "Did you know that the Gestapo raided the Jewish quarter yesterday?" Upon your expressing ignorance of that fact and curiosity as to the reason, he would reply: "Yes, they were looking for the staff of Moses, which he employed to take the Jews across the Red Sea!" Or: "Do you know that there is a merchant in Deurne who has a sign in his window reading: 'We would rather do business with Germans than with Belgians'?" Upon your expressing suitable indignation, he would add: "He's a coffin maker."

At the time I left, the German impotence to invade England, at least for the moment, was the favorite subject of jest. One of the most frequent German marching songs is "We Are Going to England"; Dutch children run along behind columns of soldiers singing this, making motions with their arms like a man swimming, and chanting in unison, "Blub-blub! Blub-blub!"

The Germans didn't like this very much. A Dutch chauffeur, working for the German army, told me on one occasion that in his village in Holland, which he named, a group of children had been sent off to a concentration camp in Germany for this; whether that be true or not I cannot say.

Most infuriating of all to the Germans, no doubt, was the very general and freely expressed conviction of the Belgian population that they, the Germans, could not win the war.

When the Germans arrived, they announced that the war would be over in fifteen days. At the end of the first fortnight, the war was still due to be finished in the next fifteen days.

Every statement of this sort was greeted by the majority of Belgians with a skeptical smile, a derisive laugh or even open scorn. At first the Germans could not comprehend the stupidity of people unable to see the simple, obvious fact that they would terminate the war victoriously and decisively within a few weeks.

As time wore on, and the war did *not* terminate, victoriously or otherwise, within the period promised, the irritation of the Germans was increased by the fact that the skeptics had been right.

Belgian disbelief, in turn, has been fortified by these repeated German failures to end the war by a specified date, and it would probably be correct to say that today the majority of Belgians do not believe that Hitler can win. I received that impression living in Flanders, the stronghold of pro-German sympathies, and in other parts of Belgium the conviction that the Nazis would lose was far stronger.

During the late summer and autumn of 1940, mass opinion might have been summed up as follows: "Either Hitler will win the war quickly, before winter sets in—or he will lose it slowly, over a period of several years."

By the time I left, it was pretty obvious that Hitler would *not* win before the onset of winter, and the Belgians drew the (to them) obvious conclusion.

It is important to note, however, the second part of the above statement: "or he will lose it slowly, over a period of several years." They did not say: "Or England will win." There seemed to be no very general belief that England could win decisively; the feeling was rather that unless Hitler won quickly, his vast military machine would slowly disintegrate.

Belgian opinion of Germany is a mixed affair, impossible to discuss without considering separately the four million Flemings and the four million Walloons.

The Flemings are a close kin of the Dutch; their language is, with slight difference, the language of the Netherlands. A large share are peasants.

The Walloons are close to the French; the Walloon language is a form of old French, and most of them speak modern French as well. A large number of them are industrial workers.

Quite naturally, the Walloons feel a strong kinship with the French and the Flemings with the Germans. Actually, the latter resemblance has been much exaggerated; the Flemings have a fierce love of independence and a background of struggle for freedom throughout the centuries which is an element almost totally lacking in the German character.

Unfortunately for Belgian unity, differences between Flemings and Walloons have been major issues in Belgian politics since the last war. Practically speaking, one half of Belgium could not even talk to the other half, and self-seeking politicians have capitalized on the resulting situation.

So far as one can sort out the facts in a situation tangled up with bitterness and prejudice, it would seem that the cultural standard among the industrial Walloons has been higher than that among the peasant Flemings. As a result, the Walloons exerted a preponderant influence in the educational system, in the army, and elsewhere. The Flemings, being more prolific than the Walloons, have been increasing in numbers more rapidly than the latter, until they have become the majority of the total population, and in consequence have demanded more and more energetically the dominant voice in affairs.

It is particularly unfortunate for a country so small to be split into two strongly marked groups—but it seemed to me that if there had been mutual confidence and good will the question could have been smoothly settled on a basis of cultural autonomy. However, I strongly suspect that what the politicians of each group sought was not to obtain autonomy but to impose their will on the other half as well. This would have been bad enough in itself, but matters were aggravated by an intense propaganda carried on by Germany in Belgium in support of Flemish nationalism for several years before the war. Money was spent liberally in subsidizing newspapers and magazines, as well as clubs representing the most extreme phase of nationalism.

One of the extremist Flemish politicians, for example, gained his entire reputation by going about Antwerp with a paintbrush and defacing signs in French. It was almost inevitable that this violent Francophobia should lead to an open sympathy with Germany and the Nazis on the part of many of the Flemings.

I saw an example of this soon after the arrival of the army of occupation. I was walking along the street with an acquaintance, a high German military police official, whose task it was at the moment to confiscate Belgian automobiles for the army. A Fleming whose touring car he had already taken saw us from across the street, and came over to inquire when he would be paid for the car, and how much.

Assuming that I was a Nazi, he turned to me and said: "You know, it's a hard blow for me to have to do without my car—but if it will help to smash France, I'm glad to do it!"

The smile of hatred on his face showed that he thought very well of himself indeed for these sentiments; could he have heard the contemptuous remarks made about him by the German official afterward, his complacency would have been badly jarred; traitors are rarely respected by those whom they aid. The Flemish nationalists think of themselves as relatives of the Germans, and equals; the Germans think of the Flemings as distant and definitely inferior relatives. Bit by bit, the Flemings are finding that out.

It would be highly unfair, however, to imply here that all Flemings, or even Flemish nationalists, were pro-German. The noisy ones were, but I would hesitate to suggest that they were in the majority. Many of the Flemings remembered 1914-'18 too vividly to have any sympathy for German conquest; others had too great a love of personal freedom and democratic institutions to feel admiration for the Nazi regime. As an instance of this, Flemings were, on the whole, extremely kind to the Jewish refugees from Nazi Germany during the years preceding the war. One of the many cases which came to my direct attention was that of a Flemish business man, violently nationalistic and openly pro-German, who nonetheless willingly did a very great service for a Jewish refugee whose papers were not in order, though he did not know the man and had not even seen him.

Parenthetically, there was no anti-Semitism in Belgium up to the time of my departure, even under the occupation. Belgian extremists began pasting stickers on the windows of Jewish shops immediately after the German soldiers ar-

rived; within two days the military authorities had compelled their removal. German soldiers traded indifferently
in Aryan and non-Aryan shops, and were seen in company
with Jewish girls as often as not. I can offer no definite explanation of this fact; I merely record it.

When the German soldiers arrived in Belgium, the pro-
German elements among the population greeted them with
undisguised joy; their Germanic brothers had come to
"liberate" them from the Walloon yoke. Other Flemings,
prepared to be hostile to the invaders, were completely
baffled by Germany's new policy of "making friends" at
almost any price with the conquered peoples. They expected violence and brutality, instead of which the soldiers
were courteous and friendly. This, coupled with Germany's
military successes in the few weeks following the conquest
of Belgium, led to a considerable swing of Flemish sympathies toward Germany.

As time went on, and people began to recover from the
experience of having the Western Front roll over them,
they began to think more and feel less. They began to realize that Germany was draining Belgium of all her carefully accumulated supplies. Prisoners returned from German camps with tales not calculated to stir sympathy for
the Nazis. German severity began to show through the
kindliness. Most of all, people began to be a little hungry.

The result was what might be expected: enthusiasm for
the invaders waned. There were still pro-Germans, but
their number and influence had declined considerably.

As for the Walloons, they hated the Germans before
their arrival and have seen no reason to alter that feeling.
In consequence, the Germans have treated them with far
greater severity than they have the Flemings.

Taking the Belgians collectively, the greater number do not, today, very much like the Germans, and do not think they can win the war. Part of that is quite naturally wishful thinking, but it would be a mistake to suppose it is nothing more. They have seen the efficiency of the Hitler machine pass a certain peak and, as they believe, start to decline; they believe that the enthusiasm of the German soldiers will continue to diminish, and that it can never be brought again to the peak which it reached in May, June and July, 1940. Most of all, they believe that Hitler's autarchic economy will collapse when there are no more well-stocked countries in Europe to be raided.

As to England, Belgian opinions are strongly divided. Not all those who wish Germany to lose also wish England to win. Many hope that England will be as badly smashed as Germany.

This matter is an unpleasant one, but it would be a mistake not to face it. Great Britain has shown a remarkable ability for making enemies during the past ten years, and matters cannot be mended by pretending that these enemies do not exist. During all the years of appeasement, British liberals cried warnings that England, through her refusal to defend democracy, would find herself quite without friends in the world when the time came when she was forced to defend the very existence of the empire. Those predictions have, in a very large measure, come true.

I never found anyone on the Continent who believed, even now, that England was fighting for democracy, or for anything other than the continued existence of the British Empire. Opinions as to the outcome of the war are therefore colored very largely by the individual's opinion of the British Empire; many of those in Europe who are pro-

German are so only because they are violently anti-British.

Belgium and England enjoyed the best of relations until about 1930. Then England instituted Empire Free Trade, which was no doubt a thoroughly defensible measure from the British point of view, but had the effect of wrecking Belgian foreign trade to a degree from which it never recovered.

Perhaps the Belgian man-in-the-street was only vaguely conscious of this, but from 1932 onwards he saw one small nation after another being sacrificed on the altar of appeasement, for which he held Great Britain responsible—and being himself the citizen of a small country, he took the matter very much to heart. Britain's non-intervention policy in Spain was particularly damning to British prestige in Belgium.

Churchill's policies have revived a certain amount of hope that even a victorious British Empire would be a different power from that which went into the war—but however unpleasant the fact, it is wise to realize that there are a great many Belgians who would as soon see a victorious Nazi Germany as a victorious British Empire, if the latter were to play the same role in Europe that it did before 1939.

The early months of the invasion did not materially help the prestige of either France or Britain. When, on the first day, the Allied armies sped across Belgium to meet the invader, there was a wave of popular enthusiasm. When, only a week later, they fled behind the Maginot line, or tried to, enthusiasm fell to a very low level.

The chief reason was that after years of reassuring promises that they would "take care of Belgium," the French and British had shown themselves as impotent to aid her as to aid Poland. For a week, German planes had filled the skies of Belgium, and scarcely an Allied plane had appeared to challenge their mastery. Strong antagonisms already separated the British and French forces, with the result that in many sectors both put up an extremely poor show. Worst of all, British and French soldiers, lacking the discipline of the Germans, did more looting and destruction than the invaders.

I was not disposed to believe this, when I first heard it, and set it down to German propaganda. As time went on, however, I talked with so many persons who had actually suffered such depredations that I could no longer reasonably doubt it. Apparently the Allied soldiers considered that the refugees who had fled, leaving behind them their homes and business establishments, would never return anyway—so whatever they had abandoned was fair game.

British propaganda from the beginning of the war was often badly handled, and this, too, alienated a good bit of sympathy in the small countries. The presentation of the Norwegian campaign was especially unfortunate. For a certain period, the British bulletins made it appear that the Allies were driving the Germans out of Scandinavia; suddenly, from one day to the next, it was announced that the Allied forces were evacuating Norway. Whatever imperious necessity may have dictated this, the effect on British prestige in Belgium was damning. When I left, there was considerably more confidence in British news bulletins than previously, but a great many Belgians listened to Berlin and London and struck a mean between the two as coming closest to the truth; perhaps they were not altogether wrong.

Probably one of the most damaging things to British prestige was the inactivity of the British forces from the outbreak of the war to the invasion of the Low Countries, and from Dunkirk to the autumn of 1940. It is difficult to feel enthusiasm for a belligerent power which apparently does not try to fight.

The evacuation of Dunkirk, it is only fair to say, made a favorable impression in Belgium. The German radio did its utmost to make it appear that the British had slunk away in cowardly fashion—but the Belgians had heard the unending German broadcasts promising that the British army in Dunkirk should be annihilated down to the last Tommy, in the most horrible fashion which the mind of man had ever conceived, and when the British, despite these threats, got away, the Belgians gave them credit for their first real achievement of the war.

It is safe to assume that as time passes Belgian sympathies will swing farther toward the British cause as dislike of the Germans grows—and as British blows become harder and surer.

It is relatively simpler to sum up Belgian opinion of America. America shares with one other country all of Belgium's hopes of ultimate freedom and a new world order. The other country is Soviet Russia.

That bracketing of the United States and the U.S.S.R. together as the hope of the conquered countries may be puzzling to some, and even infuriating to others. I can only record the facts as I have seen them.

The Belgians, like the other peoples of the Continent, do not believe that Great Britain alone is strong enough to smash Germany. They believe that without American aid, England would already have been forced to yield to the superior force of Germany.

Knowing that this is a war of materials rather than men, they feel that American intervention would be decisive, and they cannot understand why America is so slow to realize the menace that is directed against those things for which she stands.

The average Belgian, I am sure, is confident that America will come into the war, and he hopes that it will not be too late.

Before the invasion, many of the Flemish nationalists aped the German opinion of America: that the United States would fight only if a great deal of money were to be made out of it. I did not hear any of that sort of talk after the occupation began.

The reason that Belgians—devoutly Catholic, strongly conservative—look with hope toward Soviet Russia is not so complicated as might be imagined.

There is a very general conviction in Europe that Russia, in making a pact with Germany, was only seeking to delay the day when she will have to come to grips with the Nazis herself; a conviction, too, that at the proper time, when Germany has been sufficiently weakened and her enemies sufficiently strong, Soviet Russia will jump in and help in giving the death blow.

I give this opinion, widely held, for what it is worth. I shall have more to say of its social and economic repercussions elsewhere.

The element in Belgian public opinion least understood abroad, I believe, is the attitude of the Belgians to King Leopold. Surprising as it may seem to outsiders, the Belgians do not consider Leopold a traitor, a coward or a deserter. On the contrary, he is, to all the Belgians, one of the greatest heroes in their national history.

Never have I heard it suggested—even by the most pro-French Walloon—that there was the slighest collusion with the Germans on the part of their king. I shall have more to say of this matter in another chapter, but I feel it is important to note here, in considering the state of public opinion in the occupied countries, that their king was and is a national idol. Every Belgian feels that the capitulation ended a hopeless situation, which could only have brought catastrophe and served no useful purpose; they believe that the first few days of fighting demonstrated clearly that all of Belgium's military preparations were utterly inadequate against the German war machine, and that no effective help could be looked for from France and Britain.

I have never heard a Belgian express the opinion that their king and government had erred in refusing a military alliance with its old comrades-in-arms; they feel that so long as Belgium had to deal with a France which put all her faith in intricate fortifications, and a Britain which thought that sea power was enough, there was little hope of fruitful aid.

My own observation, plus talks with many refugees, would indicate that what has been said of Belgium is, in the main, true of the other occupied countries.

Norway and Denmark, of course, have always tended to be pro-British. Sympathies in Holland, to a great extent, went to Germany, but that has been altering rapidly under the occupation, and there were indications that sabotage and other forms of resistance were more prevalent in Holland than in some of the other occupied areas.

The people of France are so bewildered and confused that it would be difficult to say what they think. Before the collapse, a very considerable portion of the French public was violently anti-British—a fact not without its bearing upon the collapse itself. Today, sentiment is divided, but there is little question that there has been a large swing of sentiment away from Germany, if not toward England.

The picture is a confused one; I wish it were otherwise, but to simplify it would make it untrue. Public sentiment in the occupied countries is confused by so many issues— national, racial, political and economic—that it cannot be summed up in simple and direct fashion. This chaos of public opinion is going to render very difficult the arrangement of a stable and satisfying peace, whatever the outcome of the war.

P.S.—As this book is going to press, an American friend of mine has arrived from Antwerp who left there in mid-December, 1940. His account of recent developments in Belgium confirms my belief that there would be a progressive deterioration of living conditions during the winter. Potatoes, he reports, have become practically unobtainable, not more than a pound being allowed to each customer on those rare occasions when there are any at all in the shops. The meat situation is worse, fats continue to be an unknown commodity, bread is of the poorest quality. The tobacco situation has grown materially worse, and the alcoholic content of the beer has been reduced. Some little damage has been done in the business district of Antwerp by further R.A.F. night raids, including serious destruction of buildings on the Place Verte, beside the cathedral; there is a strong presumption that night raids have caused important damage in the port, as the Germans have now closed this area to civilians. "Invasion rehearsals" continue to take place in the harbor, great numbers of tanks being taken aboard ships in the Schelde, then run off in formation by means of drawbridge arrangements on the barges and other craft.

IV

Death in the Morning

At four-thirty on the morning of friday, may 10, i
was partially awakened by a persistent droning noise. Still
half asleep, I looked at the clock, turned over, pulled the
covers above my head and was immediately lost in slumber.

At four-forty-five, the noise returned, accompanied this
time by other and more insistent sounds. Then I sat up; I
had recognized the noise. The last time I had heard that
surging crescendo of sound fill the air had been on the
Champs-Elysées in Paris, during the vast military review
on July 14, just before the war; before that, I had heard
it many times as formations of heavy bombers had passed
over the Red Square in Moscow during the annual cele-
brations. Now the powerful drone of many motors was
punctuated by an almost continuous crackle of anti-aircraft fire.

Probably, I thought, German planes were flying over on
their way to bomb England; for several days Luftwaffe
pilots had been violating the neutrality of Belgian skies
every few hours, coolly disregarding the fire of the ground
defenses. Annoyed at the disturbance, I got out of bed;
sleep was impossible.

Through my window the gray cathedral loomed against
the serene blue of a calm and lovely sky. As I watched,
gray bombers—fifty of them—passed overhead in impec-

cable formation, flying so low that I could easily see the crosses painted on their wings. Around them floated, with macabre loveliness, feathery, white wreaths of smoke as shrapnel burst at intervals of a few seconds. Every anti-aircraft battery in Antwerp seemed to have joined in the chorus of exploding shells, and still the great gray ships sailed on, precisely aligned and never deviating from their formation. As they disappeared in the direction of the river, the guns grew silent.

Here and there around the square, heads peered from windows, and men, heavy-eyed and bewildered, shouted to their neighbors questions which no one could answer. The consensus of opinion was that England was in for the worst bombing of the war.

As five o'clock approached, I kept one eye on my watch. If they came again exactly on the quarter-hour, I should begin to have my doubts as to whether the bombers' goal were really England.

The minute-hand marked the hour, and at that precise moment the gray squadron, or another identical with it, sailed into view, and the air was again filled with the pulsating rhythm of motors and the sharper beat of the anti-aircraft guns, firing their shots in groups of four. Then came a new note—a deep, earth-shaking blast in the distance, not followed by a shell-burst.

Still I could not believe that bombs were being loosed over Belgium. We were at peace—but were we? I tried all the Belgian radio stations, but there was nothing on the air. With the passage of the bombers, there was left only the silence of a radiant spring morning. Men, hastily dressed and not yet fully awake, descended to the street; a few stood on rooftops across the square, watching the sky anxiously. It had occurred to no one that there might be any danger. I decided to go below, to see whether I could find out anything about what was happening.

In the restaurant I found Marie, the maid of all work, busy putting the dining room in order for the day. Her face was pale and anxious, but she knew no more than I of what was going on. I went out into the square.

The barber next door, usually jovial, was standing before his shop, looking glumly at the sky.

"I suppose it's war," he said, bitterly. "Can't they leave us alone?"

Frans, from another hotel a few doors away, joined us, his beret pulled down tightly over his uncombed hair. He looked at us questioningly.

"Are they on their way to England—or are the *boches* going to attack us again?"

The proprietor of the café at the other side of the hotel paused a moment from his regular morning task of washing the sidewalk.

"They're not for England," he said, soberly, "they're for us. I could see them turn from my back window, then circle round to come over again."

In silence we watched the sky. At five-fifteen the bombers reappeared, and again at five-thirty. No bombs fell near us, but we thought we detected explosions in the distance. After five-thirty they did not come again, and I wandered back into the hotel. Marie was still busy putting the restaurant in order. She paused a moment in her sweeping and looked at me anxiously.

"Do you think it's war?"

There didn't seem to be much room for doubt on that score, but there would be time enough for the realization of that reality when certainty came.

"We'll hope not," I said, lightly. "It may be just another bit of heavy-handed Nazi diplomatic pressure. If it's war, there'll be something on the radio about it. I'm going upstairs to listen for a bit."

I went up to my room. There was still nothing on the air, so I tuned the set to Brussels and left it on, then sat down to think over the situation in which I now found myself. In another three weeks I should have been finished with my work at the laboratory—then off to Genoa and back to America. Genoa suddenly seemed very far off indeed. What would happen now to my work? I looked around the room at the technical gear and books about which all my waking hours had been centered since the outbreak of the war. Was I going to be obliged to leave all that behind, and the job unfinished? After all, if the Germans were coming in, it would be no walk-over. A million Belgians would be under arms before night; the French and British were, I knew, standing at the frontier, ready to come to our aid instantly. Surely I could finish out the three weeks somehow!

There was a faint sound as the carrier wave of Brussels came on the air.

"This is Brussels speaking! Brussels, Antwerp and Amsterdam were raided by the German air force this morning. Bombs were dropped, and it is feared that there were numerous casualties. The government has been sitting throughout the night and is still in session. Keep listening for further bulletins."

Then there was silence again.

Brussels—and Amsterdam! Holland was in for it, too. I tried two of the Dutch stations, without success. A bulletin from London merely repeated what I already knew. I turned back to the wavelength of Brussels, and began to put a few of my technical notes in order. The same bulletin as before was repeated from Brussels at intervals, but nothing new was added.

At seven-thirty, I tried the radio again. This time a powerful broadcast in German cut through. Dr. Goebbels was speaking in person. For nearly half an hour he read a violent denunciation of the governments of Holland and Belgium, and recited the list of their intolerable crimes against the sovereign majesty of the German Reich. Belgian and Dutch newspapers had dared to express sentiments friendly to France and Britain. Was that neutrality? Some papers had even dared to criticize the Nazi government. Was that neutrality? More Belgian troops were massed on the German frontier than on the French border—as though there were anything to fear from Germany! German planes lost over Belgium had been shot down. Was that neutrality?

His envenomed words went on and on, growing more hysterical and more ridiculous as his indignation mounted. The stupid Belgian and Dutch governments had thought they could deceive the German government, but they had failed. Germany knew that Allied military experts had been visiting Belgian airfields, planning to enlarge their facilities so as to use them against Germany. Allied troops were already in Belgium. Belgium and Dutch troops were to be the spearhead of a vast attack against the German Reich, who wanted only to be their friend. They had spurned German friendship—now they should taste German vengeance. There was one that was never deceived, and he had seen through their pretense of neutrality to their schemes for aggression against the Reich—so the Leader had given the order to occupy Holland and Belgium at four-thirty that morning, and the German legions were again on the march. If the Dutch and Belgian people were sensible, they would greet the German soldiers as friends and as deliverers from the oppression of the Allies, and would enjoy the boon of German protection—but if they were stupid enough to repulse Germany's friendly gesture, then Germany would annihilate them! Heil Hitler!

At eight o'clock, Brussels announced briefly that Belgium and Holland had been invaded by German troops, and that Germany had delivered an ultimatum to the two governments several hours later. The government was still sitting in Brussels.

Turning the radio off, I went downstairs. I told Marie what I had heard. She sped to the foot of the stairs and called up to the elderly proprietress:

"It's war!"

The old lady came to her door, and demanded to know the source of the information. She considered this for a moment, then said, "It's not possible. Germany won't be so foolish!" She went back to bed.

Marie began to cry, silently; of her six brothers, five were in the army, and all were stationed along the Albert Canal. My breakfast was on the table, and I sat down, without much appetite, to consider the position. The first thing would be to visit the factory; the bombs which had fallen that morning had seemed to be in the direction of the plant. There would be complications; I was expecting a batch of new samples in a few days; probably production would be held up. Three weeks to go—and if I couldn't complete them, everything I had done since September would be wasted.

While I was still at breakfast, the elder daughter of the proprietress arrived with her husband, a Swiss, and their three-and-a-half-year-old daughter, Andrée. She waved to me from the square, then ran on ahead of her parents.

"Did you hear the boom-booms this morning?" she called to me from the doorway. "Were you scared? I was! I hid under the covers. Where is Rambeau? Was he scared?"

Rambeau was the very large and very black cat who honored the restaurant with his haughty and majestic presence. I explained that he had not liked the shooting very much, and had disappeared into one of the basements around the square.

She considered this gravely.

"He wasn't afraid. Perhaps he wanted to sleep because he was out late last night. Can we play house, or do you have to go and work?"

I thought I should have to go and work, and Andrée sighed.

"Well—anyway, we can be papa and mamma having breakfast in a restaurant, can't we?"

Upon my agreeing that there seemed to be nothing to prevent that, she removed her hat and coat, seated herself beside me, and proceeded to devour what remained of the bread and jam. Her parents, who had come in meanwhile, were more grave than usual. Andrée's father wanted to take the family to Switzerland immediately; her mother was reluctant to be separated from the rest of her family for the duration of the war, probably several years.

Presently he left for the Swiss consulate and to talk to

a few compatriots. The morning passed without incident, but posters decreeing full mobilization were up, and re- servists on their way to join their regiments went by at fre- quent intervals, their uniforms bearing every indication of having been hung for years in an out-of-the-way closet.

There was no enthusiasm and no surge of patriotic feel- ing. This war had hung over everyone's head for years; mobilization had come to be almost a normal state of things; bungling European statesmen had muddled along from Manchuria to Munich, making war more inevitable with each false move. Since September, Belgians had gone to bed each night knowing that the morning might bring the war to their doorsteps.

Now it had come, and the capacity for feeling anything about it had been exhausted. The war was a dirty, messy job that had to be gotten over with, but there was no wave of delirious excitement such as had marked 1914. Grimly, men rejoined their regiments; others set about taking such measures as could be taken, now that it was too late, to protect their homes against air assault.

In that respect, the situation in Belgium was appalling. In all Antwerp, there was only one air raid shelter worth mentioning; this was in the basement of the City Hall, and had been fitted up for municipal employees. Otherwise, no steps whatever for passive defense had been taken. A few small efforts had been made at the beginning of the war, but Germany had protested on each occasion that such measures were an insult to her, and the matter had been dropped as an appeasement move; subsequent develop- ments made it not unlikely that Fifth Columnists had played no small part in sabotaging the work of air raid protection. Even in the crisis which had now materialized, the municipal authorities gave no guidance and no help.

During the Munich crisis I had been a director of a small factory in London, so I had some familiarity with what needed to be done. The proprietress of my hotel had lived through the German occupation in 1914, and together during the morning we did what was possible— clearing out the cellar and stocking it with essential provisions, putting sandbags at the front, pasting crisscross strips of gummed paper over the windows and arranging improvised blackout lights.

At noon, the Brussels radio announced that the Belgian government had declared war on Germany. This created no excitement, for it merely confirmed what was already a fact. Andrée's father returned presently and announced that arrangements were being made to evacuate all Swiss nationals by special train.

Immediately after lunch I walked to the American consulate, to see if any helpful suggestions were to be found there. I found the consulate in a state of utter confusion. Every room seemed to be crowded with elderly American nationals in a state of panic, demanding to be told what to do, and what the consulate was going to do. Each demand was met with the helpful reply: "You were warned last August to go back to America, and told that if you remained it would be at your own risk."

I heard that remark a good many times from then until my departure. I have no doubt that the attitude which it implied saved the State Department a great deal of trouble, but it gave the Americans caught in Belgium the proud distinction of being citizens of the only neutral country which did not make any move to protect or aid its nationals. Every country had warned its citizens to leave the war zone at the outbreak of hostilities, but every foreign office, with the exception of the American State Department, had recognized that persons who chose to stay on under such circumstances had serious reasons for doing so, and were not necessarily to be treated as miscreants. Even little Rumania was arranging for a special train to evacuate her nationals from Belgium; I had some difficulty in explaining to citizens of other countries why only America could not afford measures of this sort—but then, of course, we *had* been warned that there might be a war.

I was better off than most Americans, for the reason that several members of the consular staff were personal friends of mine, outside of office hours. I saw one of these, and found him feeling very much as I did about the whole sorry situation. There was nothing the consular staff could do. He suggested that it would be wise to leave, if possible, but had no notion as to the best way to go about it. The French frontier was closed, it appeared, to everything except troop movements, but it might be possible to get through in a day or two. Several Americans who had cars had already left, on the off chance of being able to pass the frontier.

Feeling little clearer about the situation, I left the consulate and eventually arrived at the factory. I went first to the business office, and found several hundred employees milling about in the main lobby, waiting to be paid off. The plant was to be closed, I learned, from Friday to Tuesday; on Tuesday a further decision would be taken in the light of developments. My own department chief had already left for France with his wife and five children, and it was almost impossible to learn anything about the chances of carrying on my own work. My contract contained a clause providing for cancellation in the case of invasion, at the option of either party, but I had no wish as yet to take advantage of this.

Eventually I found one of the commercial directors with whom I had been working. He was badly shaken by the whole business; five incendiary bombs had fallen in his garden that morning, missing his house by a few yards; explosive bombs had fallen not far away.

There were, he told me, thirty-five known dead in Oude-God. One bomb had partly demolished an insane asylum, killing several of the inmates and employees; in the confusion, some twenty of the inmates had escaped, and had run about the streets of the town in their nightclothes for several hours before being recaptured. A considerable number of houses had been badly damaged, but the factory was untouched.

Nothing would be decided about the future operation of the plant until Tuesday, and he suggested that if I wished to leave immediately, the firm would release me from my contract. I declined, and said I would wait until then, at any rate.

I left him to go around to the laboratory, to see for myself if everything was in order. It was located in Lieven Gevaert Street, which ran at right angles to the thoroughfare in front of the main office. As I entered the street, I saw that considerable damage had been done at the far end, beyond my working headquarters, and when I reached the laboratory I saw that every house from the corner right up to the house next door had received some damage, but that my own premises had escaped without a scratch.

Since this was the case, I walked down to the corner to survey the results of the raid before going inside. Fragments of brick and stone lay about the street and broken glass crunched beneath my feet along the sidewalk. Windows were shattered, and the fronts of houses bore deep scars from flying bomb fragments. This was trifling, however, in comparison with the scene which I found at the end of the street. The Lindenhof Hotel, on one side, had received a direct hit from a bomb, evidently of considerable size, and was completely wrecked. Most of the roof was missing, all the windows were smashed and wreckage was strewn all about. An iron street-lighting fixture in front of the hotel was twisted and broken. The sign marking the streetcar stop had a hole in the middle where a fragment of the bomb had flown through.

The greatest damage, however, had been done on the other side of the street. The fronts of several business premises were completely wrecked; the façade of the pastry shop on the corner had been caved in as completely as though a heavy tank had been driven into it. Stone, concrete and iron had been pulverized and hurled about the street. Here and there an effort had been made to commence clearing up the debris, but everyone was still too dazed by the events of the morning to show much interest in the matter.

I knew all of the shopkeepers affected; most of my buying had been done in these same stores for the past year. I talked with a few of them, and learned that, astonishingly enough, no one had been hurt in the Lindenhof, which had received the direct hit, but that casualties had been heavy on the opposite side of the street, both in the business premises and in the apartments over them.

Six persons had been killed in the building on the corner, in which the pastry shop was located, including the proprietor. He had been out on the sidewalk, winding up the shutters for the day, when the bomb had exploded across the street. His forearm and most of one hip and thigh had been carried away, and he had lain on the sidewalk for more than an hour without attention before anyone had dared venture outside. Despite heavy loss of blood, he had lived on for several hours.

This tragedy affected me doubly: the dead man had been, if not a friend, at least a very pleasant acquaintance, with whom I had often stopped to chat for a few minutes about the war after selecting some of his unusually excellent pastry. He had served throughout the First World War without a scratch, and now he was dead, killed in the first minute of the German attack on Belgium, while going about one of the humble tasks of his quiet daily life. More directly unnerving, however, was the fact that only three weeks before the invasion I had engaged a room from him; only at the last moment had I decided that I preferred to remain in Antwerp, and canceled the arrangement. Two of the six casualties in the building had occurred in the room in which I would have been sleeping that very morning, had I not chosen to remain at my hotel.

My lucky star had, I felt, rather worked overtime that day. My laboratory, filled with costly equipment and containing technical notes which would have been irreplaceable, had escaped destruction by a matter of fifty yards— and I had myself escaped a similarly disastrous fate by virtue of a decision to which I had attached no importance at the time.

I went back to the laboratory. Everything inside was in perfect order, though I found the elderly Flemish woman who acted as caretaker badly shaken by the bombing. She

announced that she was going to sleep at her sister's house
in another part of town that night; I could not blame her.

From time to time a lone German raider passed over
during the afternoon, but only a few bombs were dropped,
apparently in the direction of the flying field, which was
not far beyond the factory.

I filled a large box with notebooks and apparatus and
returned to my hotel. Leaving the box in my room, I went
out for a short walk in the port with a friend. The streets
wore an almost normal appearance; men in uniform had
become a common sight during the eight months that Belgium had been partially mobilized. Not many men of military age were on the street in civilian attire; the mobilization posters prominently displayed before the City Hall
made clear the reason for that. Many women were out
marketing. Those who remembered the last war were taking no chances, and were stocking up on as much food as
they could obtain. Food cards were already in force, but
the quantities allowed were liberal, and many items were
not rationed at all.

I was accompanied by André, a Belgian ship's officer
and the fiancé of the younger daughter of my hotel proprietress. His ship had returned from the Mediterranean
only a day or two before, and would soon be off again. As
a sailor, André was exempt from military service, but he
told me that several members of the crew had resigned
that day to join the army, preferring the dangers of the
front to the risk of being torpedoed.

We walked slowly along the Eugene Van Dyck quai on
the waterfront. On one side were the docks and the Steen,
the old Flemish castle which is now a museum; on the
other stood a row of nondescript shops and cafés such as

might be found along almost any waterfront. The sidewalk was crowded with women shoppers.

Suddenly everyone stopped and turned as the roar of a low-flying German plane filled the air. The crowd scattered and ran as the crack of a machine-gun cut through the throb of the motor. Near us, one woman fled for the nearest basement, leaving in the street her two children, aged about two and five, who stood paralyzed with fright. André and I gathered them up and pulled them into the shelter of a doorway, just as machine-gun bullets spattered along the street and the plane flashed overhead.

It did not return, and after a few minutes people began to reappear on the street. André and I returned to the hotel; we left the two children searching for bullets in the street. There were no casualties.

Now that it was over, I remembered what a Spanish soldier had told me during the civil war in that country: "The Germans can drop all the bombs they like—there's always a good chance that they'll miss you, and if they don't, you'll never know what happened. But when a plane flies just over your head and starts machine-gunning you, that, señor, is just pure hell."

Back at the hotel, our story created something of a stir. Machine-gunning of civilians was soon to become too commonplace to be worth mentioning, but this was the first time we had seen it for ourselves. Little Andrée was particularly indignant, and bloodthirstily hoped the soldiers would "kill that Heil Hitler."

Refugees had been arriving steadily throughout the afternoon, I learned, and a considerable number were quartered in an empty shop building across the square. These were peasants who had lived in the zone within twelve miles of the Albert Canal, which was now the front line. They had been awakened at dawn and given five minutes—sometimes less—to pack up such belongings as they wished to take with them, then, before they were out of sight of their homes, these were dynamited to clear the ground for defense operations.

A regular customer of the restaurant, who held an important municipal position, told us that all schools and similar buildings were being cleared to make room for tens of thousands of refugees who would be arriving during the night.

I sat down to dinner, and had just started on the soup, when we heard planes overhead and the sirens began to wail. The air was torn by the screaming, blasphemous sound of a dive-bomber hurtling to earth. It seemed to be falling directly toward us, and I stood up hastily. At that instant the house shook and dishes rattled as we were deafened by a powerful blast.

Almost before it had died away we heard the shriek of another bomber diving, but before it had released its cargo we were all in the basement—Andrée and her parents, the proprietress and her daughter, André, Marie and a few customers who had been in the restaurant. The second explosion was followed almost instantly by the rat-tat-tat of a rapid-firing anti-aircraft gun as the plane zoomed up again.

In the dim light we huddled under the vaulted arches of the old cellar, thankful that the men who had built it, three centuries before, had believed in solidity and massive stonework. Short of a direct hit on the hotel by a large bomb, there was little real danger, but the concussion of each near-by explosion, transmitted directly through the earth, was terrific. Andrée was crying on her mother's shoulder, and the rest of us wore rather strained expressions.

Six times the inhuman crescendo of a bomber screaming to earth was followed by a shattering blast, at exactly equal intervals, punctuated by a furious anti-aircraft fire. Then there was silence, and after a few minutes we trooped up the narrow stairs to the kitchen, and back to the restaurant. By this time people were rushing out into the street, and hundreds were running toward the scene of the explosions, in the direction of the waterfront.

André, Elvire, his fiancée, and I joined the crowd. We had not far to go. Just around the corner, we could see the crowd gathered near the Promenoir, on the waterfront, and it was evident that the Congo liner, the "Albertville," had been the target of the attack. André had once been an officer on her, and we hastened to see if the great ship had been damaged.

One crater, more than twenty feet across and perhaps ten feet deep, was barely twenty yards from the "Albertville," but the ship itself did not bear a single scratch. Paving stones six inches in diameter had been hurled as much as two hundred feet by the explosion, but none had done any material damage. There were many shattered windows in the buildings across the street, but the thick, circular porthole windows of the liner had resisted the concussion.

By this time several thousand persons had gathered on the scene, and the police were having difficulty keeping them under control, but we pushed through the crowd and searched for the evidence of the remaining bombs. We found the craters scattered along the shore of the Schelde, the widest miss being a good two hundred and fifty yards from the ship. One bomb had fallen near the Steen, a museum; one had damaged an old barge.

This was my first direct observation of the work of the "Stuka," or German military co-operation dive-bomber, and the results, in terms of material damage and accuracy, were not impressive. Six dive-bombers had attacked a large ship in broad daylight and with no interference from fighter planes: the nearest bomb had missed the target by fifty feet and the others by greater distances ranging up to seven hundred and fifty feet; perhaps the pilots had been sufficiently worried by the anti-aircraft fire to have released their bombs inexpertly, but the barrage had not been a heavy one. Six bombs of considerable weight had been expended, and the total result was a few craters, a few trees stripped of their top branches, several broken windows in a museum and slight damage to a dilapidated barge.

That is, with one exception. A round iron structure about eight feet in diameter and six feet high—a public convenience found throughout Europe but not in America —had been crumpled as effectively as though the legendary giant supposed to have once inhabited the Steen had stamped on it with one of his colossal feet.

Herr Goering had turned the flower of his air force loose on Belgium's proudest liner—and his aces had succeeded in flattening out a public comfort station.

We went back to the hotel, and I managed to finish my dinner without further interruption. Later, André, Elvire and I went around the corner to the Amical Café, where we usually foregathered when André was in port. The café was in almost total darkness, and as there were two air raid alarms in rapid succession, we did not remain as long as was our custom.

A City Hall employee, whom I knew slightly, was standing at the bar, and he informed us that one hundred and fifty thousand French and British soldiers would pass through the near-by tunnel under the Schelde during the night, on their way to the front. This information, which later proved to have been entirely correct, was given in a manner typical of the carelessness which reigned in Belgium at that time. The municipal employee knew me only very casually; I might just as easily have been a German agent—and a few sticks of dynamite that night while the troops were marching through the tunnel would have had disastrous consequences for those inside, and blocked the remainder on the far shore until daylight, at least.

Back at the hotel, we found everything downstairs in darkness, the large front windows making it impossible to arrange blackout curtains on such short notice. We were all tired, having been awakened by the bombardment at four-thirty that morning, and soon after nine o'clock everyone retired. I took from my trunk the civilian gas-mask which I had been issued in London during the Munich crisis, and the flashlight which I had purchased in Paris during the week before the outbreak of war, then lay down to try to sleep. I did not bother to undress fully, for I felt reasonably sure that there would not be much rest that night.

Tired though I was, I found difficulty in getting to sleep. The day had been more of a strain than I had realized, and I had time now to take stock of the manner in which my little world had been kicked into complete chaos by the German aggression.

I had gambled heavily on the chance of being able to

finish my work before Belgium was pushed into the war, and I had lost. If I left now, nearly three years of hard work under difficult circumstances would have gone for nothing; an uncompleted color process was no process at all, and it was not yet far enough along so that I could complete it in America, away from the factory; it might be done after the war, but that possibility was wreathed in complete obscurity. If I did not leave, and the factory closed, I might well find myself stranded in the war zone, or even, if the worst happened, in German-occupied territory.

The problem seemed one with no happy solution, whichever way I turned, and I presently fell into an uneasy sleep, to be awakened sharply by the sirens. It was not yet ten o'clock, and *they* were already there again! It did not promise well for the night.

Struggling into my dressing gown, I stumbled down the narrow and rather tricky stairway from the second floor to the basement. Again we were all assembled, this time in various stages of undress, and there was little conversation as we waited sleepily for the "all clear" signal. Then we disappeared in various directions into the darkness.

Half a dozen times, at close intervals, the same thing occurred, and each time the assembly in the basement grew smaller. Finally we ceased entirely to go below. There were several further alarms, as we learned next morning, but we were too tired to care about anything else that night.

V

The Great Exodus Begins

THE WEEK WHICH FOLLOWED THE BEGINNING OF THE German attack on Belgium was crowded with so many events that it would be difficult, and even misleading, to deal with it in day-to-day sequence. With nights spent in the cellar, and days spent in dodging from place to place between raids, time became a confused notion; when the world is falling into bits, the clock and the calendar cease to have any significance. The events of the first day of the invasion are clear and separate in my memory; everything after that, and up to the evacuation of Antwerp by the Allies, is a jumbled period with no precise chronology. Days stand out as separate entities only when there is a period of rest between one and another.

On the second morning we began more serious preparations for the new state of things. We decided that since there were only a few of us in the hotel, it would be more sensible to sleep in the cellar than to stumble up and down the stairs during the night. Mattresses and cots were taken below, and Marie spent a good portion of the day arranging things as comfortably as possible.

I listened to the radio much of the time, but there was little to be learned. Brussels and Antwerp broadcast guarded communiqués which indicated that heavy fighting was going on along the Albert Canal, but said very little about the way things were going. London gave glowing

116

accounts of the spectacular dash of the Allied forces across Belgium, but little news of what they were doing. Paris made it clear that there was heavy German pressure in the direction of the Belgian forts, but gave no clue as to whether it was succeeding.

From the Dutch stations came reports rather more specific. It was evident that murderous fighting was taking place along the Dutch border, and that the heaviest German attack was, for the moment, concentrated there. This was to be expected, since the von Epp plan, which the Germans were evidently using, called for a quick, crushing blow at Holland, then the crossing of the more weakly fortified Dutch-Belgian frontier, a dash across Belgium to the Maginot line, and on into northern France.

No one in Belgium had any great degree of confidence in the ability of the Dutch to resist the attack. Holland was weak, the military training of her men was inadequate, equipment was woefully insufficient, and, worst of all, the number of Nazi sympathizers in the army and out of it was very high.

Radio bulletins from Holland were, despite this, optimistic; in fact, it might be said that up to the very minute of capitulation, judging from the news reports, the country was winning on all fronts. Fantastic figures were given for the German aerial losses, which were repeated at frequent intervals by London, Paris and Brussels—suffering no diminution in the process.

The most significant feature of the Dutch broadcasts, however, was the description of the mass air attacks of the Nazis; in them, for the first time, the word "parachutist" took on for us something of the apprehensive, deadly meaning that it was soon to have for everyone in the area which was under attack.

The first seriously alarming news from the Belgian front was the announcement that the Albert Canal had been crossed at one point by the Germans. The canal was Belgium's first line of defense, expected to hold for at least a month, and it was a bad sign that it had been broken through so quickly. The radio report put no unfavorable construction on the event, however, stressing only the heroism of an officer who had sacrificed his life to blow up the bridge across which the Germans had advanced, and which was the only bridge across the canal which had not been blown up at the appointed time. The bulletin further indicated that the German forces which had crossed the canal had now been surrounded.

During the second day of this period of uncertainty, Charles, the son of the hotel proprietress, came home on a rapid visit from his artillery unit. His regiment was moving up to the front that night, and he had slipped away on a bicycle for a brief farewell. Such absences-without-leave were a typical feature of Charles' military life, and, indeed, of the whole Belgian army. Ever since the beginning of the mobilization, before the outbreak of the war, scarcely a week had passed without two or three visits from Charles, usually without leave. A rule provided that a man might miss two roll-calls, but not three, without punishment, so the soldiers left late in the day, after one check-up, and managed to return the next morning just within the period of grace. On a Sunday, Charles had often assured me, scarcely a third of his regiment was in barracks.

The effect of eight months of this had not benefited the morale of the Belgian army, but the officers had seemed unwilling or incapable of curbing it. The spirit of independence of a Belgian is not amenable to military discipline of the Prussian type, and it may well be that the high command felt that too much of a check-rein during the long, inactive period of mobilization would have done more harm than good. As it was, a delicate situation was created by the fact that a large majority of the officers were Walloons, so that many Flemish units were commanded by chiefs who could not even speak their language. Some of the Flemings spoke French, but the number was too small to make for easy communication between officers and men. There was also a feeling among the men that many of the officers owed their rank to family wealth and influence, rather than to ability and training; true or not, this belief did much to undermine the hold of the commanders over their men.

With the outbreak of hostilities in Belgium, King Leopold had taken over the supreme command, and Charles felt that this was the only possible action that might bring some sort of unity into the fighting forces. Many of the Flemings, it was true, suspected the king of pro-French sympathies, but since Germany was the aggressor, this no longer counted. Only a short while before the invasion, the king had created considerable popularity among both national groups by taking a firm stand and decisive action to end petty factional political disputes, and Charles was hopeful that the army would now stand united behind him.

Charles confirmed my impression that the Belgian government had known of the impending attack at least several hours in advance (a notion due to the statement in the very first radio bulletin that the Belgian government had been in session all night). They had been awakened in barracks, he said, soon after midnight, and told to be ready for the attack.

He returned presently to rejoin his regiment, and the war took on a more personal aspect for me at the thought that a staunch friend was on his way to the front, supremely confident that the Germans would not pass.

Meanwhile, for those of us supposedly "behind the lines," air raid alarms became too common to attract serious attention. We rarely went into the cellar during daylight raids, unless the planes were numerous or directly overhead, but we tried to be indoors at such times. This complicated life enormously; a simple trip to a near-by shop might mean a half hour spent in the first available shelter somewhere along the way.

Not a great many bombs were dropped. No doubt most of the planes which occasioned these alarms were on simple reconnaissance missions, but one could never be sure, and there was always the danger of being hit by falling shrapnel. Several buildings were damaged by "dud" anti-aircraft shells which exploded after falling back to earth.

Only on the rarest occasions did we see any French or British planes; the Belgian air force of one hundred and fifty ships was already practically out of action, and German mastery of the air was almost unchallenged. Belgian and Dutch airports had been destroyed on the first morning of the attack.

We did, however, see important concentrations of Allied troops, in addition to the number which had passed through on the first night. One French mechanized army took several hours to pass, and it seemed to us that its complement of tanks numbered several thousand, though this was certainly an exaggeration.

Refugees from eastern Belgium and Holland began to bring stories of the British and French in action; they spoke with unbounded admiration of the French anti-aircraft gunners, firing, with a contemptuous smile on their faces and a cigarette in their mouths, point-blank at dive-bombers, firing until their guns became overheated, or they themselves were killed or wounded. Enthusiasm for the Allies, and particularly the French, was high at that moment. If a French officer appeared in the streets of Antwerp, he was immediately surrounded by a cheering crowd. Few, if any, British uniforms were to be seen in Antwerp; it was not until I visited Brussels that I saw any important number of British officers and men.

On the whole, we received much more news about the fighting from passing refugees than we did from the radio and press, and most of it was bad news. In the light of subsequent developments, it is clear now that there were, among these refugees, a considerable number of German agents and parachutists, placed there for the express purpose of spreading rumors of disaster and defeat. These tales spread with fantastic speed, and played no small part in creating the panic which was to start one of the greatest migrations in history.

It was very soon after the beginning of hostilities that I saw my first parachutists. Police headquarters were located in the City Hall, just behind my hotel. Here I saw two young men brought in, who had been captured as they landed. Scarcely more than seventeen or eighteen years old, one was dressed in a gray business suit and the other in brown plus fours of typical Germanic cut and material. One of the police officers later told me that both had small

swastikas—a singularly unimaginative touch—sewn inside
their jackets, below the left armpit, to prove their identity
to the German agents they were to have contacted immediately after landing.

We began to have some idea of the scope and importance of the German parachutists' activities when the police
came around, about the third day, to remove from the
hotel all advertising signs for "Pacha" Chicory, a step being taken all over Belgium at that moment. As the police
officer explained, it had been discovered that the "Pacha"
signs bore on the back information for the use of German
parachutists; this was later confirmed by repeated radio
warnings.

Chicory is widely used on the Continent, as a coffee substitute, or as a mixture with it, and "Pacha" was the most
widely used brand of chicory in Belgium. In consequence,
every little food shop in the country had signs advertising
"Pacha." These signs had been printed in Belgium, but
complicity on someone's part had permitted the Germans
to put on the back of them indications useful to parachutists landing in the locality where that particular sign was
to be used. Thanks to this arrangement, a German parachutist needed to carry on his person no incriminating
maps and addresses; wherever he might land, he needed
only to find the nearest "Pacha" chicory sign, which might
be in a grocery shop or along a public highway, and on
its back he would find cryptic indications giving him the
location of the nearest German agent, and how to find him.

This incident had a considerable effect on public morale.
It was a disturbing indication of the ingenuity and thoroughness of the German preparations, and many persons
began to feel that Belgium would not be able to do much

against so powerful a foe.

Many Americans had already left Antwerp, but I had been keeping in touch with the consulate and knew that none of them had been permitted to enter France. There seemed to be little point in merely fleeing to the other end of Belgium, if I were unable to enter France, and I was determined to obtain a French visa, if that were possible.

The French consulate in Antwerp was already closed, and my only hope was the French embassy in Brussels. Trains were still running, and the Antwerp central station was crowded with refugees. I fought my way into a train, and arrived in Brussels without incident.

At our embassy, I found Miss Frances Willis, the competent and helpful secretary, as much without information as anyone else. Even governmental and diplomatic circles in Brussels had little idea as to what was happening on the front. There was a report that the French had destroyed the German mechanized column which had crossed the Albert Canal, and taken twenty thousand prisoners, but this was totally unconfirmed. As for the chances of getting away, she could not suggest anything definite; there were still a few trains running, but the French embassy had refused all applications for visas to enter France. If I wished to try, she would give me a letter to the secretary of the French embassy and I might go around there and talk to him.

There was nothing to lose by this, so I agreed. Armed with the letter, I went to the French embassy, eventually saw a minor official, and was told that if I would leave my passport I might receive a visa in forty-eight hours. Still skeptical, I left my documents and promised to return in two days.

I remained in Brussels until late afternoon, and about dusk I saw the finish of a fight between Belgian soldiers and German parachutists. The latter, this time in uniform, had dropped near the Ministry of War and other government buildings. Attacked by police and troops, several of them had taken refuge in a glass-enclosed shelter at a streetcar stop. Here they were shooting it out with automatic weapons in one of Brussels' busiest streets. The Belgian soldiers were greatly hampered at the outset by the fact that the street was crowded at that hour, but as the fight went on the number of pedestrians diminished swiftly, and the parachutists did not escape.

As soon as the street battle was over, streetcars began running again, and I returned to the North Station and took my train for Antwerp. In sharp contrast to the journey in the other direction, the train was almost empty; it was going toward the front, not away from it, and not many persons were traveling in that direction. Just beyond Mechelen, a German plane flew low over our train several times, and the few passengers lay on the floor as he loosed a few rounds of machine-gun bullets. The pilot evidently decided that we were not refugees, however, and hence not worth the bullets to terrorize us, for he soon flew away, and we arrived in Antwerp without further incident.

On the following day, about thirty German parachutists dropped near the Art Museum in Antwerp, and a heavy street battle took place. This time, the Belgian authorities were less fortunate, for in the gathering dusk nearly half of the parachutists escaped. The effect of knowing, that evening, that a dozen heavily armed German soldiers were at large in Antwerp did not materially calm the state of public nerves.

After a few days of this sort of thing, the fear of parachutists became a mass hysteria. Any stranger on the streets of a Belgian town was suspected, and if dressed as a priest, a nun, a Dutch soldier, or any similarly distinctive garb, was very likely to be arrested. Some were badly manhandled by the crowd before being taken into custody.

After the first few days, one stared at any strange passer-by on the street, who in any way attracted one's attention, wondering whether he were perhaps a parachutist— and as often as not, he stared just as hard in return, wondering the same thing. In the end, one suspected everyone except one's own circle of friends and acquaintances of being a parachutist—and no doubt it was just this sort of confusion which the Germans intended to create.

A German agent, no matter how clever, will always betray himself by his accent—a fact which was the undoing of many of them during the First World War—but this time the Germans had been more ingenious. Many of the parachutists were Dutch and Belgian citizens, with strong Nazi sympathies, who had been taken to Germany on one pretext or another a few weeks before the invasion. There they had received a brief course of instruction in parachute jumping. It was difficult, when not impossible, to identify them as parachutists, since they possessed genuine identity papers and a genuine Dutch or Belgian accent. Only when seen actually making their landing were such agents captured, and this happened all too seldom.

How much actual damage, in the way of sabotage and the like, was done by these agents dropped from the skies will probably never be known. What was more important, I am convinced, was their success in spreading panic, and thus starting the torrent of refugees which was to make a military defense of Belgium and France almost an impossibility.

The method was simplicity itself. A parachutist would enter a Belgian town, posing as a refugee from some village nearer the front. He would announce that the Germans were only a few miles away, and that they were slaughtering all civilians they captured. Within a matter of minutes, everyone in the town who could walk or ride had snatched up a few belongings and joined the exodus of refugees, spreading the tale of calamity as he went.

By the middle of the week, refugees went past my hotel in an almost unbroken stream of women, children and old men. The great majority were on foot. Those who had automobiles had long since departed; there was still an occasional delivery wagon or light truck, but these grew fewer and fewer. Old carts and wagons passed from morning till night, drawn by horses too poor for the army, or even by oxen. In the wagon might be piled at random chairs, a table, a bed, cooking utensils, and often the most useless objects, such as a potted palm, or an old phonograph, or a sewing machine, indicating the haste with which the contents of the load had obviously been chosen. Atop these objects would be perched the smallest children and the grandmother; beside the wagon, the mother and older children, and leading the animals, the old man.

Many had bicycles; on the vehicle were the youngest children and a bundle of belongings tied in a bedsheet or tablecloth; the rest of the family walked alongside.

Some had seen their homes destroyed before their eyes, none knew if he would ever see again the fireside he had so hastily abandoned. On and on they went, with grim, set faces, their eyes full of the horror they had already seen, their hearts heavy with the uncertainty that lay ahead. On and on they plodded, not caring where, so long as the enemy lay behind. More like soulless robots than like men, they trudged on, speaking not a word, scarcely looking at the towns through which they passed.

Many of the women wore trousers—not fashionably cut slacks, but a masculine garment snatched up at the moment of their hasty departure. Many wore felt carpet slippers; they had already walked many weary miles; no one knew how many more they would have to walk before they found rest. They were tired, too tired to care. They did not hurry, but they never stopped.

Saddest of all were the children, many of whom had already walked a distance that would have taxed the strength of an adult. Now and then a tired child, trying to keep up with the slowly moving procession, would cry a little, furtively; I never heard one whimper.

Misery behind them, and little hope ahead, they sought only peace. There was little hysteria in their panic; only a nameless, unreasoning dread moved their footsteps ever further from the oncoming terror. No one had told them to leave, no one had counseled them to stay. There was good reason why an able-bodied man of military age should flee; the experience of the last war, when such men were obliged to work in Germany, was ground enough. As for the others, most of them would have been spared a great deal of useless suffering if they had remained where they were.

I shall not pretend that I was not frequently tempted to pack a few things in a rucksack and join their ranks. During the whole of that week, I had a bag packed and ready, with those things that seemed most necessary, should leaving become unavoidable. If I did not go, it was mostly because I remembered an old adage from the time of the First World War: "In case of a gas attack, run against the wind or stand still; never run with the wind." Though no one realized as yet the speed of the German advance, there seemed little hope of outdistancing on foot an oncoming mechanized army. The sight, too, of the weary horde that went past my door from dawn to dusk, and even during the night, did not encourage me to join the ranks.

I shall always feel that a great deal of blame must be attached to the Belgian government for its total failure to attempt to meet this situation in any way. Never, so far as I am aware, did the national or municipal authorities make any effort to stop this senseless migration. A word from the authorities at the right moment might have materially altered the whole situation. At the instant of the invasion, every man and woman in Belgium turned to the radio for information that would be of assistance in that uncertain hour; never before in history, in any war, has a government had the means of reaching all its citizens so quickly and so effectively. Not only did the radio fail to give adequate news of the operations in progress, a fact which might be justified on the grounds of military expediency, but what was infinitely graver, the leaders to whom the people looked for guidance gave them no answer to the one question that most concerned them: What should they do? Perhaps the government itself did not know; perhaps the government was too busy with things which seemed more important. Looking back now, it is evident that the government might better have given more heed to the allaying of panic and less to some of those other matters, for in the end it was that panic-stricken throng of refugees which hampered the defense of Belgium so badly.

Indeed, after the first few days, there was no longer any impression that there was a government in Belgium. I do not criticize the former Belgian government for fleeing when the emergency came—no doubt its members believed sincerely that they were safeguarding Belgian interests in the best way they could—but I cannot refrain from criticizing them for permitting blind panic to seize a nation and failing even to make an effort to restore some measure of calm. True, many would have fled in any case, but the panic need never have reached the proportions which it did.

By the middle of the week, news began to reach us from the front of events during the start of the invasion. Many of these stories were false, some were true, but nearly all were unpleasant. The antagonism between Flemings and Walloons, which the Germans had nurtured so carefully, had served the latter's purpose well. We heard of whole companies of Flemish soldiers who had refused to open fire on the Germans, of others who had declined to obey the orders of their Walloon officers, or even shot them. Too much importance should not be attached to these stories, nor would I want to suggest that the blame lay chiefly with the Flemings. There is little doubt that many of the officers failed badly to measure up to the task created by the sudden German advance. Worst of all had been the conditions around Eupen and Malmédy, in the territory ceded to Belgium by Germany after the First World War. In these communities, Belgian citizens, still German at heart, had shot Belgian sentries in the back that morning of the attack to prevent giving the alarm and to make easier the crossing of the frontier.

As the week wore on, we continued to know little of what was happening but it was clear that things were going badly. When the radio announced the citation for special bravery of the Seventh Ardennes Chasseurs, the old lady in my hotel shook her head gravely and murmured: "That means that not many of them are left!"

Disastrous in its implications but unforgettably stirring was the wireless appeal of King Leopold to the defenders of the forts of Liége—a name which the last war had already made immortal. It was announced that the forts were isolated, and that the Germans were advancing beyond them. Communication was cut off, and the King, the announcer explained, would try to reach them by a broadcast message, in the hope that someone in the forts might be listening—might still be able to listen.

"Defenders of the forts of Liége! Defenders of the forts of Liége! This is your king speaking. The entire Belgian nation is watching with gratitude and admiration your heroic struggle. Your unparalleled resistance is delaying the German advance. Your sacrifice is not in vain. In the name of the Belgian people, I ask you to continue your resistance to the last man. Do not surrender!"

Meanwhile, we saw little sign of any military movements in Antwerp. The arrival of a British destroyer in the port, and the sight of an occasional French or British plane, gave us the feeling that the fight was still going on, but we knew pitifully little about the real turn of events.

I kept in close, daily touch with the American consulate, but they could not be of much help, and I gave them information as often as they were able to tell me anything

I did not already know. Early in the week, the consulate advised all Americans in Belgium to go, by any means available, to La Panne, the little Belgian border town which lies just across from Dunkirk. I was convinced that it would be useless to set out on foot. Fantastic fares were being demanded by taxi drivers for the journey to the frontier—five hundred and a thousand dollars were not uncommon. No one was being allowed, as yet, to cross into France, but I had the promise of a French visa.

At the American consulate I had made the acquaintance of an elderly compatriot, a former cigarmaker of Flemish origin, who was desirous of leaving and believed that he could arrange the matter of transport. On Wednesday, he came to my hotel and announced that an old acquaintance of his, a fish dealer, was prepared to take us to La Panne for the comparatively moderate sum of one hundred and fifty dollars. We decided to accept this, and I completed my preparations for an early departure on Thursday. Later, on Wednesday afternoon, I met a wealthy Belgian manufacturer, head of one of the largest plants in Antwerp, who had just returned from La Panne with his entire family. He told me that they had fled at the beginning of the German approach, and had been for several days in La Panne. "I decided," he told me, "that although I didn't know what was going to happen in Antwerp, it couldn't be any worse than conditions already were in La Panne, so I resolved to bring my family back here. At least, we are at home."

He told me that two hundred thousand refugees were sleeping in the open fields around the little frontier village. Bread, if you could obtain it, was selling at almost two dollars a loaf. No one, American or otherwise, was being permitted to cross into France. Later that afternoon, the American consulate confirmed this fact and I made a rapid decision: if I were fated to have the Western Front roll over me, it would be at home, in relative comfort, with at least a place to sleep and something to eat. We called off the trip to La Panne and I unpacked my bags.

Meanwhile, Andrée's parents had decided to leave for Switzerland on the special train which the Swiss government was running for the evacuation of its nationals. Her father felt that there was no guarantee that Switzerland would be able to stay out of the war, and if it were not, he had no wish to spend the remainder of the struggle in a German concentration camp. Hastily, they made their preparations for departure. As I had to go to Brussels in any case, to get back my American passport, with its now useless French visa, I proposed to accompany them as far as the capital.

Little Andrée bade a tearful farewell to her grandmother and her aunt—for the uncertain duration of the war, at the least—and to all of her favorite dolls save the one she was taking with her and we set out.

The central railway station was crowded beyond description. In the streets and along the open roads, the refugees had seemed merely apathetic; here, confined in a building from which the only exit which interested them was the gateway to the trains, human nature did not always show up at its best. Carrying far more bags and bundles than they could ever hope to transport to the end of their journey, men and women struggled brutally to reach the gateway that led to escape.

At the entrance to each train, a severe examination of personal documents was being made by the military authorities. At one side of the station, behind a guard of soldiers with fixed bayonets, stood six men of varying ages, suspected of being enemy agents. The crowd stared at them with sullen hostility, and it was probably just as well that they stood guarded by soldiers.

When the Brussels train arrived, the struggle to pass through the gate took on the proportions of a football scrimmage. There were many small children, and babies in arms, and for a few moments there was a serious danger that some of them might be trampled under foot or injured in the mêlée. Then, spontaneously, in several parts of the crowd at once, arose the suggestion that women and children should be allowed to go through first. The panic subsided, and men fell back, quietly and in order, as women and children passed through without further interference. The train was quickly filled to the bursting point, and the uncertain voyage to Brussels began.

The coaches were piled high with valises and bundles and no inch of space went to waste. I stood at one end of the coach, wedged in between the door and a baby carriage. Andrée and her mother were somewhere inside; her father stood near by. In the perambulator was a few months' old baby. I fell into conversation with the mother, a pleasant-faced young Flemish woman, still calm and smiling, though she had left behind her home and had given away to Belgian soldiers all the contents of her little drygoods store in a village some thirty miles beyond Antwerp. Possessions, she remarked, had little meaning at such a moment.

She told me, almost without emotion, the story of an incident the evening before in her village—an incident which seemed to me to illustrate particularly well the character which the fighting had assumed.

A French anti-aircraft battery had arrived in the town. As usual, someone in the village—probably the burgomaster, she thought—had promptly notified the Germans. Almost before the battery was fully set up and ready for action, the German dive-bombers appeared. As one of them roared to earth, straight at the battery, the young French artilleryman scored a direct hit with a three-inch shell. The plane burst into flames and began falling, crazily. Before he crashed, the German pilot managed, for a few seconds, to straighten out the blazing ship, and in his last few moments of life, loosed a final burst of machine-gun fire into the crowd of women and children gathered in the public square to watch the spectacle. Very often, later on, when the German radio, the German press and German soldiers protested that Nazi fighters never, under any circumstances, attacked civilians, I thought of that story, though it was only one of hundreds that came to my attention.

During the voyage to Brussels, German planes flew over several times, but there were no attacks, and we arrived in the capital safely. It was already late afternoon, and my friends did not yet have their tickets for the special Swiss train, so we left Andrée and her mother in a café near the South Station, from which the train would leave, and set out for the Swiss Railways office. So many conductors and motormen had been mobilized that day, that only a few streetcars were running, and it took us nearly two hours to get to the other side of town. Life in Brussels had come almost to a standstill. Arriving at the Swiss Railways office just as it was closing, we learned that the letter with the list of reservations, sent from the Swiss consulate in

Antwerp several days before, had not yet arrived in Brussels, thirty miles away, and my friends had no place in the train. There were supposed to be two more trains on the two following days, but the Swiss Railways agent frankly doubted that there would be any others after that night, and advised going to the station and simply attempting to board the train, which was scheduled to leave at nine P.M.

Armed with the tickets and a note to the Swiss official in charge of the train, we attempted to return to the South Station. Public transport was by then almost non-existent, and such few streetcars as there were, were packed with youngsters from sixteen to eighteen, who had just been ordered to get to France, somehow, by any means at their disposal, so as not to be captured by the Germans.

By the time we were able to reach the café where Andrée and her mother were waiting, it was nearly ten o'clock, and we had every reason to suppose that the train, most probably the last, had already left. With some little difficulty, we found the two of them in the total darkness of the café. Although it was already two hours past Andrée's usual bedtime, her mother told me that she had not once cried or complained. As Andrée privately explained to me, with the gravity of her three and one-half years, "Mamma already feels so bad about leaving grandma, that I don't want to make her feel any worse." She was still able to joke with me, repeating our favorite one, which consisted of shrieking "Lights out!", just like a Belgian policeman, when I lit a cigarette. She had thought the whole matter over, and informed me firmly that I would accompany them as far as Paris, from where, she explained, I could easily return to Brussels if I wanted to.

As rapidly as we could in the darkness, we gathered up

their heavy suitcases and packages, and set out across the square for the darkened railway station. All regular train service had stopped, but around the great station we felt, rather than saw, the crowd of thousands upon thousands of refugees, each with his little pile of bundles and baggage, waiting patiently through the night, for a rumor had flown about that another train would leave for Paris the next day.

All entrances to the station were locked and guarded, save one reserved for soldiers taking military trains. We could find out nothing about whether the train had left for Switzerland or not, none of the police even knew that there was to be such a train. Milling around in the darkness, we finally found a Belgian gendarme, who knew nothing about the matter but did think he could perhaps find out. He disappeared for five minutes and returned. The Swiss train was leaving in a few minutes, he told us, and if their documents were in order he would undertake to get my friends through the military cordon. Gathering up the load of suitcases and parcels, we followed him through the darkness to the doorway, where one small light permitted the officer in charge to examine the papers of those entering the station. A rapid explanation ensued, then an examination of passports and tickets, and a moment later they had disappeared into the deserted, unlighted emptiness of the station—the military cordon closed up again—and I was left standing alone in the crowd. From inside the station came the sound of Andrée crying, for the first time that night; she had discovered that I was not with them, and I had not even been able to say good-by.

After a restless night, with several alarms, I went to the French consulate. Most of the staff had already left, but

THE GREAT EXODUS BEGINS 137

I obtained my passport, and in it was the French visa which had been refused to so many, and for which I no longer had any use. Perhaps by coincidence, perhaps with a touch of ironic humor, it had been placed on a blank page directly opposite my last German visa.

I returned to Antwerp in a train practically empty. It was common knowledge by then that the Germans had broken through and were not far from the Belgian-Dutch border, and not many persons were traveling in that direction.

In Antwerp I found everyone in a state of complete hopelessness and despair. Holland had failed to maintain any useful degree of resistance, and the streets were filled with fleeing, demoralized Dutch soldiers whose one thought was to get as far from the front as possible.

All Belgian ships in the harbor had received orders to leave as quickly as they could for a French port. André's ship was sailing that night, and in the evening Elvire and I accompanied him to the far end of the harbor, where the "Gironde" was lying. On the way, we passed many sheds and docks which had been damaged by German bombs; once we saw the silhouette of a British destroyer riding at anchor.

Before we reached the ship, we were obliged by an air raid alarm to stop for some time. A few German raiders were passing over the harbor, perhaps looking for the destroyer. The experience was not an agreeable one. There was not the slightest shelter, and we were in the center of a vast expanse of paved street and harbor facilities. We had already seen once the manner in which cobblestones flew through the air when struck by bombs, and the thought was not a comforting one. Bombs fell on both sides of us, but none near enough to cause any concern, and soon after we were able to resume our interrupted journey. We saw André aboard ship, and returned to the hotel in silence; one more of my friends was leaving.

The next morning, a sixteen-year-old country boy, a relative of my hotel proprietress, arrived to see her. A shipload of youngsters was to leave during the forenoon, to be evacuated to England, and he was among those due to go on board. He remained for some little time, talking with his relatives, and failed to note the passage of time. Suddenly, he realized that he had perhaps missed the boat, and rushed away. In less than an hour, he was back, white-faced and unnerved. He had missed the boat by a matter of minutes, and as he had stood on the pier, watching the ship that should have taken him away, a German plane had flown over and machine-gunned the crowded decks. He did not know how many casualties there had been, but he knew that they were many.

That same morning, our milkman brought news that a children's home, almost next door to his house, had been struck by a bomb, and twenty of the children had been killed. There was, in this particular case, a mitigating circumstance: the children's home was near a large Belgian arsenal, and at such a time, it was certainly imprudent to leave the children where they were.

Several times during the day, attempts were made to bomb the British destroyer in the harbor. It changed its position frequently, but the Germans always seemed to know within a matter of minutes where it was to be found. However, the German marksmanship proved as inaccurate as before, and no hits were scored on the target.

On Thursday afternoon, the police came around to

notify us that for a period of forty-eight hours, no one might go out into the streets for any reason whatsoever. It was even forbidden to look out of a window. Newspapers had ceased publication, there was little news on the radio, and we had almost no idea of what was happening. It should be remembered that Antwerp was so near the border of Holland that some of the Antwerp streetcar lines actually went to the Dutch frontier, so it was clear to us that, now that Holland had fallen, we should not have long to wait for the arrival of the Germans in Antwerp. Rumors had been rife for several days that Antwerp would not be defended, but would be handed over to the Germans in order to spare the civilian population, if it became clear that the Allies must fall back.

Public morale was not improved when it became known that day that the burgomaster of Antwerp had departed in the night. This was in sharp contrast to the heroism of Belgian burgomasters in the First World War, many of whom, like the late Adolphe Max, burgomaster of Brussels, remained at their posts through the entire German occupation, stubbornly fighting for the rights of the citizens, whom they felt under an obligation to defend. It was common talk that the burgomaster of Antwerp had long been friendly with the Nazis, and had been banqueted by them in Germany on more than one occasion; whether there was any truth in these reports or not, I cannot say, but their effect on public confidence was disastrous. The Belgian people felt that they had been betrayed into the hands of the enemy and that there was little they could do about it.

When the police told us that no one might go out for forty-eight hours, I had an intuitive feeling that this meant that Antwerp was being handed over—that twenty-four hours were for the retreat of the Allied armies, and twenty-four hours for the Germans to take over. The prohibition even to look out of windows sounded much more like a condition dictated by the Germans than anything emanating from the Allied command, which had shown no such nervousness when advancing to the front through Antwerp.

During this entire week, all of my nights had been spent in the cellar. It had been uncomfortable at first, but it was much better than running up and downstairs each time there was an alarm, and I had learned to rest tolerably well there. There were four of us, the proprietress, her daughter, Marie, and myself, and at any other time the situation might have created a certain amount of embarrassment. As it was, the arrangement seemed the most natural thing possible, and bit by bit, we made the cellar almost cozy.

The chief drawback was the stuffiness. The first night we slept in the basement, the old lady got up irritably after about an hour, gathered up her bedclothes, and marched upstairs, muttering, "I'd rather be dead than sick!" There were many raids during the night, and on the following evening the old lady had already thought better of it. During the day we had cleaned out the cellar and done everything possible to remove the mustiness. Before the week was out, we were quite accustomed to it. Eventually I moved my portable radio below at night, and we were able to listen there to such scraps of news as were available, and even a bit of light music, which London never ceased to broadcast.

A great deal of inconvenience was created by the forty-eight-hour quarantine, which had come practically without any advance notice. There had been no chance to lay in any supplies, and many families went hungry during that period. I was far better off than most, for the hotel naturally had a certain stock of supplies on hand at all times.

Friday, the first day indoors, passed without incident. Forbidden though it was, we peered out of the windows from time to time, but the streets were practically deserted. No movements of troops were visible, but occasionally a motorcycle courier or an army truck sped through the town. Such movement as there was, was always away from the front, never toward it. The most disquieting sign was the departure of groups of firemen and police officers, still in uniform, some with bicycles and all with parcels and valises.

On the second night of our confinement, the bombardment became terrific, and to it was added a new note: for hours, we heard the sound of big guns firing, not far from Antwerp; the battle had reached our doorstep. If, as I believed, the Allied armies were going to pass through Antwerp that night, they would have to go through the tunnel under the river, which would take them past our door.

Presently I heard the whine of falling shells, followed by shattering explosions, very near, which shook the basement. With the monotonous regularity of metronome beats, one shell followed another, and the blasts became more violent as the shells fell closer and closer to the near-by tunnel. First I heard the sound of the distant gun, then the whine of the shell overhead, and finally, the crash as it burst; each time, the explosion seemed nearer, which may well have been the effect of my own imagination. As I lay there in the darkness, I knew that the others were awake as well, but no one spoke. There was little that could be said to comfort one another, and none of us, I suppose, wanted to say anything that would further depress the others. For that matter, I cannot remember that we ever spoke of that night in the months that followed; it was not something that we wanted to remember. For the first time since the beginning of the invasion, I felt deep, panic-stricken fear. The cellar seemed like a rat-trap. My imagination pictured what it would feel like if a shell came crashing and tearing through the floors above, to burst over our heads and bury us beneath the masonry which was our only bulwark against the battle going on above our heads. Worst of all was the feeling of total helplessness; I did not want to die, there—and if I went somewhere else, that might be the very place a shell was fated to fall.

By a determined effort of will, I forced myself to think of other things. I turned as much of my attention as I could muster to a vital technical problem in my work with color reproduction, which had been baffling me for nearly six years, and ironically enough, during that night, against a background of crashing shells and marching men, I found the answer to the problem, which had eluded me for so long. Strange as this may seem, the terrific effort to concentrate in the midst of this pandemonium had crystallized in my mind a solution which had, no doubt, been there all the time. Stranger still, subsequent experiment showed that the solution was the correct one. The satisfaction that went with this steadied my nerves somewhat, and my tense muscles relaxed.

Still the shells continued to fall near us, until finally, the earth seemed split asunder as a mighty explosion, which made the shell bursts insignificant and puny, rocked the hotel. The artillery fire ceased, and the rest was a dead silence.

Finally, unutterably weary from the hours of strain, I fell into an uneasy sleep.

VI

The Swastika over the Cathedral

TOWARD MORNING, AS A LITTLE DAYLIGHT BEGAN TO FILTER
down into the forward part of the cellar, which lay beneath the sidewalk, I was awakened by the sound of steel-
shod boots running along the street. Belgian or French
boots did not make that angry, metallic noise; I was not so
sure about British army footwear, but intuition told me
that it was the Germans who were there. Bursts of automatic rifle and machine-gun fire became more frequent,
and from time to time a heavier explosion suggested that
hand grenades were being thrown.

The three women were now also awake, and we discussed in a low voice what the significance of these noises
might be. Perhaps what we were hearing was the sound
of Allied patrols left behind to delay the German advance
—or had the Germans already arrived?

Shortly after eight o'clock, I decided to end the uncertainty, and despite the protests of the others, I went upstairs to try to see what was happening. I passed through
the kitchen and into the restaurant, half expecting to find
it already filled with German soldiers. I could see nothing
from there, for at the beginning of the forty-eight-hour
quarantine period we had hastily boarded up the street
windows and the front door. I went up to my room on the
third floor, and cautiously advanced toward the window.
There, below, just in front of the cathedral, was what I had

dreaded to see—a German soldier. The moment was a
bitter one, buts its grimness was relieved by a ludicrous
touch. The German soldier mounting guard over the great
cathedral was short, squat and bow-legged, and his mushroom-like helmet suggested a man who had been flattened
out by heavy pressure from above. As I peered down at
his ludicrous figure, an automobile drove up and a flag
officer in blue uniform with gold braid stepped smartly
out. The sentry saluted, and the officer entered the door
leading to the stairway which mounted to the top of the
cathedral tower.

I had seen all I wanted. I returned to the cellar, and
announced to the others: "The Germans are here!" Marie
was a bit hysterical for a few moments, but on the whole
everyone took the tragic news calmly. For that matter, they
had borne all the dangers of that eventful week almost as
though they had no nerves whatever; I can only imagine
what that week might have been, had I had three nervous,
panicky women on my hands.

They immediately announced that they were coming up
to have a look at the Germans, too, and I went to my room
to sort out a certain number of documents which I had no
wish to have the Germans find in my possession. By the
time I had gathered these together, and burned them in
the kitchen range, breakfast was ready.

The preparation of the morning meal had been considerably delayed and complicated by the fact that we
were now without gas, without electricity and without
water. It had been necessary to start a wood fire in the
kitchen range, and we used water that day very sparingly.
Luckily indeed, the old lady, wise with the accumulated
experience of the last war, had made us fill every avail-

able pail, tub and other receptacle in the place with water
on the day before, so with reasonable care we could hold
out for several days. All other public services had ceased
as well. The telephone was dead. There were no newspapers, and the radio stations were silent. No public transport was running, and only the older members of the police
and fire departments were on duty. More than half of the
population had fled, and we were living in a city of women,
children and old men, with no public services and few of
the actual necessities of life.

I have often seriously questioned, since, the utility of
this destruction of all municipal services by the retiring
Allied armies. Before the Allies left Antwerp, the gas
station was put out of operation, the waterworks wrecked,
electric power stations crippled, vital parts of the automatic telephone exchanges were dynamited, and the same
happened in Brussels and elsewhere. The intention was
plain, but there was never the slightest indication that the
Germans were actually hampered.

The dynamiting of bridges and railway lines was understandable, and doubtless defensible from a military point
of view, but the destruction of public utilities rather
showed, it seems to me, that the Allied command was still
thinking of the war in terms of 1914. Germany had, it was
true, made stupid blunders in the last war, but the Allied
staff counted overmuch on the supposition that Germany
had learned nothing from those mistakes. Certainly, the
British and French totally failed to realize the extent to
which the mechanization of the German armed forces had
changed the entire pattern of warfare. The Germans arrived in Antwerp fully expecting a complete dislocation of
public services, and they came prepared both to do with-

out them and to put them back into operation within a very
short time—at the expense of the Belgian tax-payer. Thus
the whole burden of the inconvenience and the cost fell on
Belgian civilians, and it will be very difficult ever to convince them that this wholesale destruction was necessary,
or even justifiable.

By the time we sat down to breakfast, it was nearly ten
o'clock. At barely one minute past the hour, there was a
sharp explosion on our doorstep and a vivid flash of light
between the boards covering the windows which sent us
scurrying toward the cellar. It was not repeated, and we
soon came up again. Later, we managed to piece together
what had happened: at exactly ten o'clock, the Nazi swas-
tika flag had been hoisted over the cathedral, which had
never flown any banner save, on special occasions, that of
the Pope. A moment later, a single shell from a French
battery across the river had struck the front of the cathedral near the tower, glanced off, and burst before our door.
It was fortunate that the windows were well boarded up,
for we later found the fuse-cap and several jagged pieces
of the shell within a few yards of the door.

Soon after, we were again startled by a knock at the
front door. Expecting to see a Gestapo agent, or at the
least a German soldier, we were reassured to find an
elderly Belgian policeman. He informed us that the quarantine had been extended for another twenty-four hours,
during which time no one might go outside, and anyone
seen looking through a window would be shot at.

By this time, heavy military motor vehicles were rumbling past constantly, and a number of them were parked
in the square directly in front of the hotel; some of the
latter appeared to contain munitions, other were filled with

drums of gasoline. Presently these went away, and their place was taken by a less disquieting field kitchen. As we watched this, German soldiers now began crowding around it to receive a hot meal. I had seen German soldiers before, many of them, but always in peacetime and on parade. Now, I was astonished at their shabby, dirty uniforms and unkempt appearance. There was nothing in this to justify surprise—after all, they had just come from the battle-field—but the result was something very different from the propaganda newsreel conception of the German army.

Theoretically, no civilians were to go on the street that day—but the framing of that regulation did not take into account the insatiable curiosity of a Belgian, which nothing can discourage. The Germans were there, the fighting was over, and the good citizens of Antwerp meant to have a good look at them. Furthermore, this was Saturday, and no one had been able to do any shopping since early on Thursday. Many homes were completely without food, bread had grown stale, and while no one was quite certain whether any shops would be open, nearly everyone decided to find out for himself. At first, a few Belgian women scuttled timidly through the streets, market baskets in hand. The German soldiers told them that, for all they cared, they might go out if they wished to risk the chance of snipers still being about; the Belgian police shrugged, and said that the Germans were now masters, so if they did not care, the police could do nothing about it.

Since nothing seemed to happen to these first adventurous souls, others soon followed. Crowds of children gathered around military trucks and groups of soldiers. To their astonishment, the Germans greeted them in friendly fashion, joked with them, offered them part of their food.

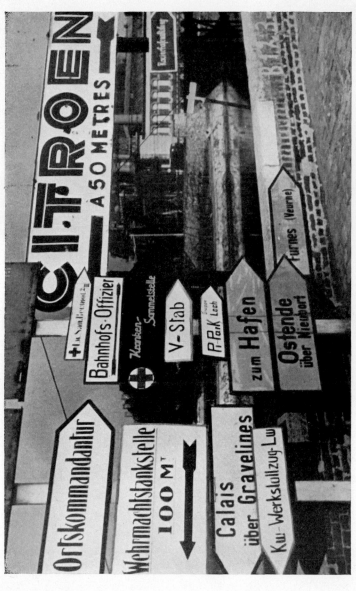

FRANCE—BELIEVE IT OR NOT!

Signposts were removed throughout France and Belgium when the war began, to make things more difficult for the Germans, but the latter arrived with complete sets of signposts in German, ready for use. The above is in Dunkirk, and only the Citroen auto sign remains to show that it is France.

(Photo from European)

Around in City Hall Square, a public distribution of bread took place. A tired and hungry policeman, who had been on service without relief for two days, leaped forward to catch one of the loaves of bread. At that moment, flashlamps lit up for a fraction of a second, camera shutters clicked—and photographs had been recorded to prove to the world that even the policemen in Belgium had been starving when the Germans came to rescue them. The distribution of bread was over.

Stories of the Germans' amiability rapidly spread, and by noon, most of the remaining population of Antwerp was in the streets. Men still went about a bit dubiously, and were careful not to talk French within earshot of the Nazis, but nothing occurred to cause the slightest alarm.

Early in the afternoon I decided to chance a visit to the American consulate, and I left the relative security of the hotel. Just across from us, directly in front of the cathedral, a rapid-firing anti-aircraft gun had been mounted. The location was one which afforded good visibility, but I could not help wondering if the choice had not been dictated primarily by the fact that a gun directly before the cathedral was unlikely to be bombed by the British. Several artillery horses were stabled within the deeply recessed main doorway of the cathedral, and the sidewalk all about was well strewn with straw and manure. I was almost tempted to ask the soldiers whether, at home in Germany, they also used cathedrals as stables. All along the side of the cathedral great motor trucks were ranged in long lines. A bit further on, I saw other motor trucks which had been driven onto the sidewalk and into the deep entrance of a large department store, with soldiers huddled about it anxiously. Everywhere there were soldiers, but chiefly in those places where they could best hide behind the civilian population. School yards, parks, and the broad, tree-studded avenues running through the central business and residential district of Antwerp—all were filled with tanks, trucks, and horse-drawn vehicles, all painted in the monotonous, if practical, field gray. Much of their equipment seemed very old, and Belgian veterans of the last war later told me that a great deal of it was the identical equipment used by the Germans in 1914, and scrupulously kept in readiness for the end of the long armistice.

The manner in which all of this equipment was brought into the center of Antwerp, and disposed in the midst of the civilian population, was in sharp contrast to the situation during the week that the Allies had been there. A large French army, with all its equipment, had been in barracks on the outskirts of the town, but except for an occasional officer about the streets, we would never have known that the French were there, and none of their equipment was ever brought into the town.

Traffic was badly tied up by the constant stream of German military vehicles, and to get away from them I took a short-cut through Rubens Street—where the house in which the great Flemish painter and diplomat had once lived was being restored to its original condition—and came out into the Avenue of France at a point directly opposite the consulate. Here, as elsewhere, I had to thread my way through a tangle of parked military vehicles to reach the other side of the street. It was pleasant, at that moment, to see the American flag still flying outside the consulate. I saw several of my friends, but nobody was able to tell me anything especially interesting or helpful;

the consulate was not only cut off from the State Department, but could not even communicate with the embassy in Brussels. The vice-consul agreed with me, however, that we were a great deal better off than those Americans who had rushed away at the first sign of trouble and were now somewhere along the open roads, where they would be overtaken by the advance of the German army, under conditions a great deal more difficult and dangerous than anything we had had to pass through. After all, it was reasonable to suppose that within a relatively short time we should be able to get permission from the German military authorities to return to America via Berlin.

Walking back toward the center of town, I watched for some little time the passage of hundreds of field gray trucks, carrying gray-uniformed soldiers, gray anti-tank and anti-aircraft guns, heavy artillery, baby tanks, munitions, supplies, in an unending variety that spoke volumes for the thoroughness of the German preparations.

They were already using a considerable volume of confiscated motor transport. Many of the trucks which passed bore the names of Dutch firms and cities, and had not yet been repainted. I realized then that the German army was getting a large part of its transport as it went, though I had little notion as yet of the proportions which this was to assume. During the course of the day, I learned that every form of transport which appeared on the streets was being promptly confiscated by the Germans. If an automobile owner were incautious enough to drive through the streets, he was stopped and made to turn the car over to the soldiers. Even bicycles—the chief mode of transport in the Low Countries—were confiscated on sight.

The streets were crowded with civilians and soldiers,

and many of the smaller shops had already reopened. As I passed one of the large banks, I saw that the door had already been forced, and soldiers were inside. The block in front of the Century Hotel, the finest in Antwerp, was closed to traffic, and reports had it that the German high command had taken up its quarters there. Army signal corps men were stringing rubber-covered cables along the streets for the military telephone service.

Although there were no signs of hostility on the part of the German soldiers, I did not try to talk to any of them that afternoon. I returned presently to the hotel, and learned that no Germans, as yet, had put in an appearance there.

While we were still sitting over our evening meal, a Belgian police officer arrived, with a group of ten German soldiers. The policeman, looking rather frightened and harassed, informed my hotel proprietress that she must give them a warm meal; there was a strong emphasis on the "must." A long table was arranged for them, and such food as was available was made ready. While they were still eating, a billeting officer arrived to inquire about the number of soldiers that might be quartered there that night. The young officer in charge of the group already there stepped outside, and informed him that the hotel was full, as he and his men had already been assigned rooms there by the authorities; this was news to us, but the billeting officer, satisfied with this assurance, went away.

I fell into conversation with the soldier sitting nearest to me, and learned that they were engineers, all of them Saxons from Dresden or near by. The man himself proved to be a worker from a Dresden factory where I had several close acquaintances, and he talked to me quite freely. He showed me snapshots of his wife and small children, and his home in Dresden, and told me he was very glad that the war would soon be over; all he wanted was to get back to his family and his job. Several of the others concurred in this sentiment.

The group ate hungrily, and ordered beer and wine lavishly with their meal. They assured the proprietress that she need not worry; everything would be paid for. At the end of the dinner, the officer in charge of the group remarked to us that he was completely unable to understand why a small, apparently peaceful country like Belgium, should have been so foolish as to attack Germany. Upon being indignantly told that Belgium had *not* attacked Germany, his face assumed an expression of complete incredulity. "Do you mean to say," he exclaimed, "that you know no more than that of what has been going on? Then I'll tell you!" He then launched into the story, which was soon to become very familiar to us, of how Belgian divisions had, on the morning of May tenth, tried to invade German soil, and of how the Leader, with reluctance and sorrow, had been obliged to give the order to his men to throw them back and protect the fatherland. There had been *no* bombing of Antwerp and Brussels on the morning of May tenth, before the outbreak of war; we were obviously deluded and mistaken about that; if there had been any bombing, it had been a British provocation. At the moment of the senseless and cruel attack on Germany, Belgium had already been full of British and French divisions; our protesting reply that Allied troops had passed through on the *evening* of May tenth was met with a smile of pitying incredulity; of course, they admitted, we could scarcely be expected to know better, with our censored radio and one-sided press—only in Germany were the newspapers and the wireless free to speak the truth. However, they informed us magnanimously, they realized fully that the Belgian people had not been to blame for the aggression against the Nazi empire. Debased democratic politicians were entirely at fault; generously corrupted by British gold, they had sought to use Belgian divisions as the spearhead of an attack upon the peace-loving Germans. After these had borne the brunt of the drive, British and French troops would have taken over.

As it was, by direct orders of the Leader, the battle to free the Belgian people from their British oppressors had been conducted with exemplary and unparalleled consideration. German soldiers had never fired unless fired upon first; they had scrupulously spared civilian objectives and the civilian population, even when to do so cost the precious lives of German soldiers. The Leader's *orders* were that they must come as "friends and deliverers" of the Belgian people, not as enemies and conquerors.

I am aware that all of this, set down in cold print, must seem almost incredible; it was far more so when spoken, with heated conviction, by an otherwise intelligent young officer. Within a very short time, however, we became quite accustomed to this point of view, and rarely wasted our breath in a futile effort to convince German soldiers that Belgium had not been the aggressor nation.

Several other soldiers came into the restaurant that same evening, and hundreds of them in the days that followed. Our conversations with them followed a pattern so standardized that there could be no doubt whatever that they were acting under precise instructions. In practically every case, the soldier or officer, as soon as he was settled down comfortably after unbuckling his belt and holster, would open the conversation with an ingratiating smile and an unvarying first question: "Well, what do you think of it all?"

Necessarily, a question as vague as this produced an equally vague reply. That was all he was waiting for; since you were not really aware of the situation, he would enlighten you. He then launched into an interminable monologue, of a pattern so stereotyped that I soon knew it by heart—telling of a Germany oppressed by France and England, even ruthlessly attacked by a militaristic Belgium. Then the Leader had given orders to deliver the Belgian people from their yoke of bondage. Now, the armies were moving further afield, and the French people, too, would soon be delivered.

Never was there the slightest word of hatred, or even antagonism, toward the Belgian people, or even the French. Every ounce of hatred and vituperation was reserved for England; on that subject, he could not say enough. There was no talk of "delivering" the British people; *they* must be annihilated in order that there might be a free Europe. Only fifteen days, at most, would be required to complete this task; once Belgium and France had been occupied and liberated, England would be forced to accept Germany's harsh conditions of peace, and then they would all be able to go home. For a thousand years, there would be no more war in Europe.

That same evening, before our first group of billeted soldiers had gone upstairs to sleep, I learned that not all German soldiers, notwithstanding, were so fanatical and one-sided in their thinking, despite years of propaganda and isolation from the truth. I strolled outside after din-

ner with the factory worker from Dresden. His manner
was unaggressive and even amiable, and I managed during the conversation to mention casually the six years
which I had recently spent working for the Soviet film industry in Russia; I was curious to see what effect, if any,
this would have upon his attitude. He refrained from any
direct comment on the matter, but his manner became, if
anything, more confidential and friendly. I did not push
the conversation too far into dangerous channels that evening, but it was clear that he had little sympathy for the
Nazi regime and its program of ruthless expansion, though
he had not dared to show this in the presence of his officer.

During all of the first few days of the occupation, it
should be mentioned, I permitted all of the German soldiers who came to the hotel to assume that I was a Belgian. The proprietress of the hotel had herself suggested
this, for our mutual protection; she, on her side, was not
at all sure that it would be a good thing if the German soldiers knew that there were three women alone in the hotel,
and on my side, it was not yet clear what the attitude of
the Germans would be to foreigners caught there by the
invasion. I spoke Flemish with the old lady, French with
her daughter, and German with the soldiers. Most of them
were not sufficiently familiar with the two languages of
Belgium to appraise my accent, and since an American
was about the last thing they expected to find in Belgium
at that time, they assumed that I was the proprietor and a
Belgian.

The hotel, "In the Shadow of the Cathedral," consisted
of two buildings which had been converted into one. The
restaurant occupied the ground floor of both buildings, and
stairways at each side led to the upper floors of the two

structures. I had been living in the right half, where most of the "guest rooms" were located; the left side was mainly occupied by the proprietress' family.

On the first evening of the occupation, when Elvire showed the group of soldiers upstairs, she was still somewhat nervous about the matter, and failed to make clear to them that one room was mine. They were very tired, and went to bed early. When I went up, somewhat later, I found my room occupied, and the door locked. It seemed pointless to awaken the sleeping soldiers—it was more than a week since I had slept in my own room—so I went across to the other building and took possession of one of the vacant rooms.

In the morning, as soon as the soldiers were down at breakfast, I went to my room for a rapid check-up, though I was not seriously concerned; however, I had left in my room, well concealed, a considerable sum of money which I had not wanted to carry about with me, and I just wanted to be sure that everything was in order.

I felt reassured upon entering the room; they had left it tidy and in good shape—but it only took a few moments to discover that the money was gone. My valuable camera equipment was intact, and a rapid verification showed that the only other items missing were a few rolls of color film (on which the guarantee date had already expired) and a lipstick from my photographic makeup kit.

I hurried downstairs, but the group of soldiers had left. The officer, who had occupied my room, had signed a note for the rooms and meals; this later proved to be invalid, since he had signed a false name and given incorrect particulars concerning the regiment and company numbers. I eventually found out that the company had deserted during the fighting in Holland, then, after the danger was past, had come to Antwerp to look for their regiment, pretending to have become separated from it during the confusion of battle. This was the only occasion on which the hotel was not paid for the billeting and feeding of German soldiers.

During the first few days of the occupation, I learned that I was by no means the only person to have suffered from German looting. Two thousand bottles of wine were stolen from a restaurant, "The Golden Rose," near my hotel; the proprietor had been absent the day the Germans arrived. A valuable camera was taken from a near-by store; the same day, a soldier walked into a liquor shop and took several bottles of cognac at the point of a gun.

However, if a few of these cases took the form of armed hold-ups, most of them occurred in shops and homes from which the tenants had fled. The café on the corner near my hotel was locked and empty when the Germans arrived, the proprietor and his family having left for France the day before. The building was broken into and taken over by the group of sentries guarding our neighborhood; these lads, who were somewhat boisterous, proceeded to make themselves very much at home. The house was well stocked with provisions, and they promptly installed two women, whose character was not even doubtful, to make things homelike. They confiscated an automobile, and for two days this drove up at frequent intervals with loads of loot; then they smashed up the car with their reckless driving, and its battered carcass stood for several days in our square, until it was hauled away for scrap iron.

Such incidents were typical of the first two days of the occupation, but within forty-eight hours the situation was fully under control. Large notices were posted in every street by the German command reminding soldiers that looters would be instantly shot—nor was this grim threat idle talk. Several cases came to my attention in which soldiers caught looting were executed on the spot by their officers; the only item which they were permitted to take, in case of necessity, was food. An officer to whom I reported the theft of my money offered to shoot the guilty man before my eyes if I would furnish the necessary particulars. I pointed out, however, that what I desired was not to have the man shot, before my eyes or elsewhere, but to recover my money; the officer agreed that the one did not necessarily entail the other, and I dropped the matter.

A feature of the German soldiers' character, revealed from the outset, and which rather surprised me, was their lack of courage except when banded together in large groups. During the first few days, soldiers with whom I walked through the streets were frankly "jumpy" with fear of civilian snipers or British sharpshooters who were, they believed, still hiding in Antwerp. I tried to reassure them with the argument that if the Allied armies had voluntarily handed over the city to spare the lives of the civilians, despite the military drawbacks of retreating such a distance, they would scarcely provoke what they had sought to prevent by stationing snipers in the city; the Germans, however, refused to be reassured, and affirmed that I knew nothing of the treacherous British character.

The question of *franc-tireurs,* or irregular soldiers not in uniform, has apparently been an almost hysterical obsession with the Germans ever since the Franco-Prussian War in 1871. Many German soldiers told me that their losses in the Polish campaign in 1939 from this cause were terrific; an intelligent and otherwise reasonable officer told me, with cold-blooded satisfaction, that whenever a German soldier had been killed from ambush in Poland, eighty Poles had been arrested at random and machine-gunned.

In Belgium, the Germans were haunted by the same fear, but their methods were more subtle. In Oude-God, where I worked, two German soldiers were shot in the street during the first night of the occupation. Next morning, the German military police rounded up one hundred male citizens of the community, chosen at random, and led them to the square before the City Hall. Here they found awaiting them a machine-gun, a gunner and an officer. The men were lined up along one side of the square, opposite the automatic weapon. After a wait sufficiently long to reduce their nerves to pulp, the officer made a speech, informing them of the killing of two soldiers, and ended with the warning that if one more German soldier should be shot, every tenth male person in Oude-God would be executed. He then released the hundred, and up to the time of my departure, there had been no further shootings in the community.

It would be interesting, but probably fruitless, to speculate on the reasons for this German obsession regarding *franc-tireurs*. I suspect that it is due in a large measure to the fact that to the Germans any method of making war is justified (so long as it seems to have a chance of helping to win the war), and they tend to attribute to their enemies the same mentality. Then, too, since a large part of the German military effort is directed against the civilian population, the army has particular reason to fear reprisals from civilians.

A feature of the German methods which caused bitter comment among the Belgians was apparent abuse of the Red Cross symbol. I heard several stories from alleged eyewitnesses claiming that the Germans had painted the Red Cross on the roofs of buildings containing munitions and other war material; I did not see any of these, but during the period of fighting I saw Allied ambulances and other Red Cross vehicles which had been riddled with machine-gun bullets from the air, and during the occupation I saw thousands of German army vehicles bearing the Red Cross of which a great many certainly had no connection with the medical service. A considerable proportion of officers, too, had the Red Cross painted on their automobiles, though their insignia were not those of the medical service. This, I am sure, came under the heading of "subterfuges which were justified if they helped to win the war," and if the French and British were "fools enough to respect the Red Cross, they deserved to lose." Also, I think, the Germans seem to have believed quite sincerely that the Allies would naturally make the same use of the Red Cross as they, and that they, the Germans, were therefore quite justified in firing on any building or vehicle bearing this symbol; at any rate, the soldiers were made to believe this, and therefore felt no particular compunction about the matter.

Within a day or two of the Germans' arrival, increasing numbers of timepieces in Antwerp began to be set to German Summer Time, two hours ahead of Greenwich time and one hour in advance of the Daylight Saving Time then in force in Belgium. So far as I knew, there was never any official German order regarding this matter, nor any compulsion. Everyone knew, however, that German Summer Time had been imposed on the inhabitants of the other subjugated regions, and assumed that the same would happen in Belgium; also, since the German soldiers were living according to their own time, it simplified matters to bring all timepieces to the same hour. When I left, this same time was to continue throughout the winter, so that the blackout would begin at as late an hour as possible.

A conspicuous feature of Antwerp life was the famous set of chimes in the cathedral tower, which could be heard all over the city. All through the summer, in peacetime, concerts were given on the chimes two evenings a week. In addition, each quarter hour the chimes automatically played one of four Flemish folk songs.

During the German occupation, from 1914 to 1918, the Belgians had put the chimes out of action and during the entire four years the Germans had never managed to put them into operation again. Hence, the chimes had a certain symbolic significance for the residents of Antwerp, and when the Allied armies evacuated the city, this time the cylinders which controlled the chimes were taken away.

The Germans had not overlooked even this; as the Belgians often said, bitterly, "They had thought of everything." With them came new cylinders for the chimes, and within a few days of their arrival these were ringing again as merrily as ever. The melodies were not quite correct; presumably some German musician had transcribed them from memory, and had made a few mistakes, but the effect was all that the Nazis desired. The only source of satisfaction to the Belgians was that the clock hands on the tower, and the time as indicated by the chimes, were one hour

INSTALLATION OF FIELD COMMUNICATIONS

The German army arrived in each community prepared to find all public utilities destroyed by the retreating Allied armies, and had everything in readiness for rapid resumption of services. As soon as a town was occupied, army electricians began stringing cables along the principal streets for military telephones and other communications services. Those shown above are installing wires for loudspeakers, to broadcast news and propaganda to the occupation troops and civilians. These cables, suspended along the fronts of buildings and sometimes lying on the ground, offer saboteurs their greatest opportunity to harass the Germans, and are frequently cut during the night. Nazi reprisals for this have been becoming more and more severe.

(Photo from German Railroads Information Office)

DISTRIBUTING BREAD TO THE CONQUERED

The German caption on this photograph states: "In dense rows the civilian population gathers at a distribution post of the ration trains, with which the NSV assuages the first need." The obvious impression which the picture seeks to convey is that the Germans are feeding the occupied areas. The author describes such a distribution of bread in Antwerp, which lasted until the photographer had the required pictures. Some of this largesse was probably a part of the policy of "making friends" with the conquered peoples, but the gesture was of brief duration. The caption neglects to state that at the moment the Nazi relief organization was distributing a few loaves of bread, thousands of huge motor trucks were already speeding to Germany with the food reserves stored in French, Belgian and Dutch warehouses.

(Photo from German Railroads Information Office)

FLEMISH WORKERS LEAVE FOR GERMANY

The German caption on this photo states: "A number of trains have arrived in Germany with Flemish workers who have found remunerative work in the Reich. The men can now confirm, with their own eyes, what shameless lies have been spread regarding social conditions in Germany. The picture shows Flemish workers before the departure of their special train from the station in Brussels."

Much publicity of this sort was given to the migration to Germany of workers from the occupied countries, some of them enthusiasts for the Nazi regime but the greater part unemployed men and women who saw no other chance to obtain work. No publicity was given, however, to those who returned to their homes; the author talked to some of these, and their version of "social conditions in Germany" was somewhat different from what was presumably anticipated by the smiling workers shown above.

(Photo from German Railroads Information Office)

GERMANY HAS PLENTY OF POTATOES

The original caption on this propaganda photo states that the vegetable crop in
Germany last year was a record one, and adds: "Near a potato-flour factory
tower great mountains of potatoes, brought by the railway."

Although Germany does not produce enough food for her own needs, potatoes are one of her best crops. Recent reports of acute potato shortages in
Norway and Belgium raise the question, however, as to whether the "mountains of potatoes" in Germany are all a part of Germany's own crop, or form
part of the vast quantity of foodstuffs seized in the occupied countries.

(Photo from German Railroads Information Office)

RAISING FOOD—FOR WHOM?

This German photo is captioned: "Under the protection of the German military might, the peasants in Belgium and France till their fields."

The author describes in the text the manner in which workers and peasants have clung to their toil in grim desperation, as the only thing they have left. The photo does not indicate, however, whether the food which this farmer is preparing to raise will be used to feed the hungry civilian population, the occupation troops, or Germany. In the background is seen one of the myriad small flying fields mentioned in the text. Should the R.A.F. single this out for one of its day or night raids, the farmer may have some doubts regarding the efficacy of "the protection of the German military might."

(Photo from German Railroads Information Office)

BOMB 'EM—THEN BEFRIEND 'EM!

This obviously posed propaganda photo bears the caption: "Thus they now learn in France to know the 'barbarians.' Soldiers as assistants at a relief station of the NSV in France."

Photos and posters of this sort were widely used in an attempt to convince the civilian populations that the Germans were there as "friends and deliverers." Perhaps only a few days before, these same children were crouching in a cellar while Nazi bombs and shells burst overhead; even now they do not seem too reassured.

Throughout France were displayed posters showing a German soldier with a French child in his arms, and across it the caption: "Have confidence in him." A friend of the author, an American working for the Red Cross in the repatriation of refugee children, entered a French village accompanied by a Belgian boy of seven, whose leg had been blown off during an attack on civilian refugees. The boy saw one of these posters, and before the American could stop him he had torn it to shreds.

(Photo from German Railroads Information Office)

out of step, and up to the time of my departure the Germans had not managed to put this right.

The minute thoroughness of the German preparations can scarcely be conveyed to one who has not seen them; truly they *had* thought of everything. I had a striking illustration of this during one of the first days of the occupation. An army surgeon, with a fine, sensitive face, came to my hotel for dinner. He was feeling lonely and depressed, and remained talking to me for several hours. I took advantage of this to find out a little about the organization of the medical service, and two of the points which he called to my attention seemed especially worth notice:

One of the fundamental problems in military medicine is that of infection in wounds, due to dirt, which often reaches critical proportions before medical aid reaches the wounded man. Inside the lower left-hand corner of each German soldier's tunic is a long, narrow pocket in the lining. In this pocket is an emergency bandage, which has been soaked in an antiseptic particularly suitable for this purpose. A wounded soldier has no need to open his kit; if he has strength enough to pull this bandage from its easily available location, and can apply it to the wound, the danger of infection is greatly reduced.

A second grave problem is that of loss of blood during the often considerable delay, until aid reaches the wounded man, which makes blood transfusions vitally important, and usually the more quickly they can be performed, the better the chances of recovery. Under ordinary circumstances, precious minutes are lost while the surgeons determine the blood group to which the wounded man belongs, and more valuable minutes pass while they find a donor of a suitable blood group. All of this has been eliminated at one stroke in the German army by the simple device of placing on each man's identity tag not only the number of his *matricule* but his blood group. Thus the surgeon knows instantly what sort of donor is needed, and he may order the nearest available man of a suitable group, even if it be a high officer, to submit to the operation at once.

This same meticulous thoroughness is applied to every item of the German equipment. Compared to the Belgian helmet, which was virtually of sheet-iron, the German headwear was a masterpiece of engineering. Although this mushroom-like helmet is unpopular with the German soldiers, who are convinced that it produces baldness, they have the greatest confidence in its protective qualities. Scores of them showed me the helmet with great pride; made of the best steel, it will withstand a bullet at close range, yet is surprisingly light in weight; a leather skullcap "floats" on the inside in such a way that the weight is evenly distributed and the shock of a blow well amortized.

Unlike the helmet of 1914, the new one no longer displays the famous "God with Us," but this motto now adorns the belt buckle. Hitler may not approve of the Deity, but he is not willing to neglect any device which may help to give his soldiers confidence.

Another instance of the ingenuity which the Germans have used to save precious minutes when every minute counts was the manner in which many of their anti-tank guns were mounted. These were trailed, barrel pointing forward, behind a small, very fast motor truck, in which the gun crew rode; truck and anti-tank gun were connected by a peculiar swivel joint. In action, the truck was driven at top speed toward the oncoming tanks. When almost within range, the driver veered to the right violently, and slammed on his brakes. This sudden turn uncoupled the gun, which moved straight ahead and came to a stop. At the same moment, the gun crew leaped to the ground, and within as little as seventeen seconds from the moment the turning maneuver was executed, the gun was firing its first shell.

If, however, the German equipment showed a high level of intelligence, I was frankly astonished by the degree of almost bovine stupidity shown by the faces of most of the German soldiers. At first I thought I must be imagining this, but as time went on, and I saw more and more of them, the impression deepened. I sometimes watched a column of several thousand soldiers march by, and a face reflecting some trace of intelligence and animation was so uncommon that it attracted instant attention. I have seen, one time or another, marching soldiers of most European nations, but I have never seen a similar spectacle of apathetic stupidity.

This is so widely at variance with the usual estimate of Germany's intellectual level that it seemed to me there were only two possible explanations: either the general opinion of German intelligence in the past has been based on German intellectuals and has left out of consideration the great mass of peasants and workers—or else less than a decade of the Nazi regime has sufficed to reduce a large part of the population to the level of unthinking machines; I leave to others the choice between these two hypotheses.

Most unpleasant of all to watch were the forced marches of German soldiers coming back from the front in Flanders, while the fighting was still not far from Antwerp. More like reanimated corpses than like men, they shuffled

forward mechanically, their faces covered with blood and
sweat and dirt, their backs bent under the load of their
equipment. Gaps everywhere in their ranks spoke elo-
quently of their heavy losses, so vehemently denied by the
Propaganda Ministry. A few stragglers, too far gone even
to try to keep up with the others, came far behind. One
evening, I watched several thousand such battle-weary soldiers pass along the Avenue of Italy. Not one looked at
the crowds of civilians along the sidewalks; I doubt if
some of them even realized that they had arrived in a city.
Suddenly one soldier, amid the gray mass, turned and
tried to smile at a group of soldiers standing on the sidewalk—and his twisted grimace, with an agony of horror
and weariness still in his eyes, was terrible to behold; I
shall never be able to forget it.

Fresh troops on the march were a different matter. They
sang almost continuously on the way, day or night; orders
were orders. Singing made a good impression on the civilian population; no doubt it helped the morale of the soldiers, too, though they must have grown very tired of it at
times. Nevertheless, they sang very well, and their assort-
ment of marching songs was, in its way, excellent. I
learned that the Propaganda Ministry had studied the
marching songs and folk music of the entire world in order
to select the most effective melodies for this purpose. One
I recognized as an old Russian folk song; another was a
Sousa march; all of these had been given suitably martial
lyrics. Very often they sang, "It's a Long Way to Tip-
perary," with new, anti-British words which would have
infuriated any Tommies who might have heard them. One
song, especially popular with the soldiers, was apparently
original; called "Erika," it was a nostalgic and haunting

ballad about a girl back in the homeland, with a curious rhythm and a melody so haunting that even anti-German Belgians caught themselves humming it at odd moments.

Most frequent of all, however, was the German marching song, "Wir fahren nach England," expressing musically the vituperative hatred felt by the German soldier against everything British.

This anti-British phobia appeared at every turn. If a church had been destroyed during the fighting, the British had done it; if there were civilian casualties among the refugees, the British had done it; in short, the British were responsible for every scrap of damage, sabotage, looting, arson and killing in the whole of Europe, and it was not usually wise to try to argue with a German about that.

As I have already mentioned, this hatred did not extend to the French, who were somewhat scornfully regarded as an inferior race, but towards whom there was no bitterness. Many German officers of the more snobbish type did their best to speak French in the restaurant of my hotel, and paraded their knowledge of French wines and cuisine ostentatiously, and usually with lamentable results.

A remark often employed by the more arrogant officers and soldiers was: "I don't see why the Belgians show so little enthusiasm for us. Why, in Holland we were greeted by the inhabitants with flowers!"

As relations between the two neighboring Low Countries opened up again, I had the opportunity to talk with many Dutch citizens, and I asked them about this. They told me that the favorite remark in Holland had been: "I don't see why the Dutch show so little enthusiasm for us. Why, in Poland we were greeted by the inhabitants with flowers!"

I have little doubt that in France the boast was: "Why,

in *Belgium* . . ." At any rate, the statement showed well the wishful conviction of the German soldiery that the conquered peoples had been delivered from slavery, and had every reason to feel enthusiasm for their saviors.

If it be true that the citizens of Holland, despite considerable pro-Nazi sympathy before the invasion, received the German troops coldly and even with hostility, no doubt one of the major reasons was the Nazi bombardment of Rotterdam from the air, which had brought about the capitulation of the country.

I first heard the story of this attack from a colonel in the German medical service, who was proud of the achievement which it represented. A few days later, one of my closest friends gave me a first-hand account of the damage done. I later talked with Dutch refugees who had gone through the bombardment, and relief workers who had helped to aid the victims. Reports from these widely different sources checked remarkably well, and I believe, therefore, that the following account is completely reliable:

Five hundred German bombers, with virtually no opposition, showered high explosive on Rotterdam for forty-five minutes; during that time, thirty-nine thousand persons were killed, and twenty-five thousand families rendered homeless. In the center of the city, which incurred most of the damage, an area four kilometers long and two and one-half kilometers wide (about two and one-half miles by one and two-thirds miles) was so flattened out and pulverized that in all that space it was almost impossible to find a piece of building material as large as your fist; it was as though the entire heap of ruins had been painstakingly shattered with sledge-hammers. To illustrate the property damage: one wealthy man, who owned seventeen restaurants in the city, had one small establishment left in operable condition after the raid.

There were few air raid shelters, and the inhabitants of Rotterdam had taken to their cellars. Knowing this, the German had used retardment bombs, which passed through several floors and exploded in the basement.

After accounts of this raid, German soldiers never failed to point out how generous they had been to spare us in Antwerp the same fate; privately, I felt that the German desire to use Antwerp as a military and naval base was far more responsible than any feeling of generosity or compassion. Rotterdam was less important to them as a future base for operations against England, so they had selected it as an "object lesson" for the people of the Low Countries.

The Germans were greatly vexed, during the first three days of their occupation of Antwerp, by their inability to cross to the other side of the River Schelde and follow the retreating Allied armies. They had, of course, anticipated the blowing up of the tunnel, and arrived on the first morning with everything necessary to build a massive pontoon bridge. They requisitioned a considerable number of barges and a great quantity of lumber, and set to work. When the bridge was nearly completed, and the officers were rubbing their hands and chuckling with satisfaction, a battery of Allied artillery, which had been left behind to delay the German advance, opened fire with deadly precision, and a few neatly placed shells reduced the bridge to splinters.

German planes made every effort to locate this battery, even using an observation balloon on the third day, but each time the bridge reached nearly to the other bank, it was blown up again, always with considerable loss of life.

The Belgians openly gloated over their conquerors, and the fury of the Germans grew by the hour. Members of the high command took up residence in a mediocre water-front hotel, to push the work along more rapidly. A British plane flew over and tried to bomb this temporary head-quarters, which was very near my hotel; the bomb missed its objective and killed several civilians in an adjoining house.

I watched the work going on, from as near as I could get, and I saw officers, red-faced and apoplectic with fury, cursing and kicking their men. The arrival in Antwerp had been behind schedule, according to the von Epp plan, and now they were falling further behind; no doubt quarters higher up were putting considerable pressure on them.

At last, unable to succeed directly, the Germans built a new bridge during the night. Commencing at dusk, they reached the other shore before dawn, and by morning the German army was following the retreating Belgian, French and British armies.

If the Allied high command had known how to use effectively the three-day respite won for them by the "suicide squad" which remained behind to man a battery of artillery and check the German crossing of the Schelde, the subsequent course of the Battle of Flanders might have been very different.

VII

The Way Back

ONCE THE RIVER SCHELDE HAD BEEN BRIDGED, AND THE
Germany army resumed its advance in the direction of
Ostend and the Channel ports, the citizens of Antwerp
began to take stock of their situation, and to make an effort
to readjust their lives to the new order of things. For several days, whole German divisions passed through on their
way to the front; a large portion of their transport consisted of Dutch motor vehicles; other detachments arrived
on foot and departed in requisitioned Belgian vehicles,
which were hastily repainted in field gray. These assault
regiments were followed by garrison troops, to hold Antwerp until the regular occupation units arrived. These
later arrivals were older men, for the most part, and many
of them had served in the First World War. Not a few of
them had taken part in the occupation of Belgium at that
time, and remembered fragmentary bits of the Flemish
language. Less aggressively pro-Nazi than the first shock
troops, these older men were quite prepared to make the
occupation as agreeable for themselves and for the citizens
of Antwerp as their officers would permit.

The first thought in the mind of every Belgian at that
time was to stock up on as many of the basic necessities of
life as possible. No one believed that the war would be a
short one, and every adult knew of the scarcity and privation which had accompanied the German occupation in the

171

last war. Everyone knew, too, that the Nazi authorities were already emptying all the warehouses in Antwerp, and that when present stocks in the stores were exhausted, there would be little to follow. During the first few days, therefore, people spent a large part of their time in shopping. Although somewhat hampered by the theft of most of my ready cash, I spent a large part of what I had on hand for soap, toothpaste, razor blades, tobacco, paper, shoes, and a few such items which would eventually be unobtainable, or nearly so.

Food was already rationed; the Germans had lost no time in lowering the allowances of each commodity, so there was little possibility of hoarding viands of any sort. A few things were not yet rationed—tinned foods, chocolate, tea, sausage, to give a few examples—and those householders who had any money on hand purchased every bit of suitable merchandise which they could find. Many persons, of course, had little money in the house—banks were closed—even the postoffices were closed, so small depositors who kept their funds in postal savings accounts could not touch them. Those who received German marks from the soldiers (so-called "occupation money") had no desire to save any of this "hot money," for no one believed it would have any value after the war, regardless of the outcome.

During the week of active fighting, sandbags had been placed over the fronts of buildings in all parts of Antwerp, and nearly every window was covered with crisscrossed strips of paper to prevent flying glass if the pane were shattered. One of the first efforts of the Germans, in their attempt to restore the appearance of "business as usual," was to persuade people to remove all traces of these measures of passive defense.

"The war is over, for you," they assured the citizens of Antwerp. "You are now under the protection of the German army, and no one can or will touch you."

Only too eager to believe this comforting assurance, nearly everyone hastened to remove paper strips from windows, carry away sandbags, take down boarded shop fronts, and otherwise to restore everything to its normal appearance. Shop signs, all of which had been removed in some districts by overzealous Belgian police determined to prevent the conveyance of useful information to German parachutists, began to reappear. At the same time, blackout measures, under German pressure, were made much more severe than they previously had been.

Gas, light and water services were restored after a few days of German occupation. For some little time, however, it was necessary to boil the water before drinking it, as the filtration plant was still in doubtful shape—but after several days with no source of water whatever, save for a few wells here and there, no one was disposed to be critical. The greatest difficulties were caused by the gas plant. For many weeks, the pressure continued to be very low, and at the peak hours was so slight that cooking with gas was almost out of the question. Thousands of families found it practically impossible to prepare a hot meal.

Meat was a particularly difficult problem during the first week or so. The city storage facilities were equipped with electrical refrigeration. When the power stations were wrecked by the retreating armies, and there was no electric current for several days, the refrigeration ceased, and the meat began to spoil. When the Germans took over, they decreed that since it was through no fault of theirs that so much meat had spoiled, there would be no further butchering until the Belgians had eaten this tainted meat. So far as I know, there were no cases of actual poisoning from this—after all, the meat was not *very* tainted—but during the first week or so, meat was not a very appetizing article of diet.

Prices had been fixed by the Germans at the level prevailing at the moment of their arrival; the exchange rate of the German mark was also promptly fixed at ten Belgian francs (about forty cents) for one Reichsmark (about twenty-five cents if it had possessed a value corresponding to the peacetime rate); a few weeks later this was to be altered to twelve and one-half francs to the mark, an even more ridiculous figure.

Soldiers continued to be billeted at my hotel nearly every night, but there were no repetitions of the unfortunate experience with the first group, which was never paid for, because unauthorized. Within a few days, a central billeting office had been organized; soldiers were then obliged to report first to the local *kommandatur*, which assigned them to quarters and gave them an official document to that effect. Bills were then rendered monthly by hotel-keepers and householders to the *kommandatur*, which authorized payment for all approved lodging and meals—by the Belgian municipal authorities.

The first group to remain at my hotel for an extended period consisted of ten members of the military police, or field gendarmerie, who were waiting to be assigned to an occupied Belgian community. The military police must not be confused with the Gestapo. The word "Gestapo" is an abbreviation of the German name, Secret State Police; its members work in civilian clothes. The field gendarmerie,

on the contrary, is exactly like the military police of any
army; its members wear normal army uniform with special insignia. In the occupied areas, the military police
collaborates with the local police authorities in the regulation of traffic, watching the streets at night, enforcing
blackout regulations and other measures put into force by
the German command, checks up on price-fixing and prof-
iteering—in a word, it performs very much the duties
which any civilian police would normally do. Most of the
officers of the German military police are men who in civilian life are city police officials. Even the minor members
of the force are selected for appropriate special qualifica-
tions, and are therefore markedly different from the great
mass of common soldiers.

This group of ten Germans remained at my hotel for
three weeks, and the experience was a pleasant change for
all of us. With one or two exceptions, they were little interested in politics, and had no strain of fanaticism in their
makeup. Few of them had any enthusiasm for the war; all
were prepared to be friends, and to make the whole unpleasant business as agreeable as possible. Some of them
helped to prepare the meals in the kitchen, and even to
serve them; all of them made up their own rooms in the
morning, to save Marie the trouble. One, who was a truck-
driver in the army, was a painter in private life, and an
excellent one, as attested by a dozen postcards which he
carried in his pocket, with reproductions of some of his
paintings. The last time I saw him, he was planning to buy
a box of water colors and to try to paint a bit. Another
had been in Spain during the civil war, and told me, privately, that his sympathies had been heartily with the
Spanish people in their struggle against Franco and fas-

cism. The highest officer of the group had been a police official in a German harbor city, and he and I took pleasant walks through the port on many evenings, while he talked for hours of criminology, police methods, his home and family, and many things far removed from the conflict then going on. All of them talked more of things "back home" than of dreams of conquest, and the three weeks they remained at my hotel were perhaps the pleasantest (I use the word in a relative sense) of the whole occupation.

The only jarring note was an eleventh member of their group, who arrived about a week after the others. He came directly from Poland, and being a fanatical Nazi, he was furious with the orders of the high command to treat the population of the occupied city with civility and courtesy, and to make friends in every way possible. In Poland, he had been accustomed to a regime of fire and blood, and he felt that the moderate policies applied in Belgium signified a decline of German military authority. He was pleasant enough to us—orders were orders—but his smoldering indignation often made itself felt.

At that time, nearly the whole of normal life was completely paralyzed, and I was faced with the problem of what to do. My credit would not last forever, and there was still no indication that I would be able to resume work at the factory. It was imperative that I obtain some source of income, and that fairly quickly. My first thought was of some sort of photographic or motion picture work, for which I was best qualified—but it was clear that this would have to be in co-operation with the German military authorities. I felt no enthusiasm for that idea, but I had little choice in the matter. Through the secretary of the Belgian firm for which I had been working, I met Captain Fraunhofer, then connected with the photographic service of the army and previously connected with the Central European sales branch of the Belgian company.

Captain Fraunhofer received me amiably, and though he was extremely busy, took some little time to discuss with me the possibilities of my situation. He decided that my best hope for work, under the circumstances, would be to make documentary films, and suggested that if I would prepare a letter, he would see that it was sent to Berlin by the field post. I drafted such a letter, setting forth my experience with documentary films in various countries, and Captain Fraunhofer sent it off. I never received a reply from the ministry, and in the light of subsequent happenings, this was just as well.

The captain also sent me to Lieutenant Perlt, whom I have mentioned elsewhere, who was in charge of all motion picture activities in Belgium, but before anything had come of this, I was able to resume my own work.

Almost the only business which was thriving at that moment was that of the street photographers, who took one's portrait and developed it within a few minutes. Three of these men were set up in the square in front of my hotel, and they were busy from morning to night taking portraits of German soldiers against the background of the old cathedral. They were literally coining money, and if I had not been able presently to resume work in my own laboratory, I should very probably have joined their ranks with an improved process which I had in mind.

The German soldiers were "photograph conscious" to a degree difficult to convey. At least one soldier in three, it seemed, carried a camera, and used it on everything in sight. Many of those who did not have cameras when they arrived in Antwerp, took advantage of the low exchange rate to buy German cameras for far less than they would have cost at home. Even high officers, passing the cathedral, stopped their luxurious cars while they gravely photographed its majestic façade. I recall one cavalry officer, passing on horseback, who whipped out his Leica and photographed the cathedral from several angles; as he could not stop his regiment for so frivolous a purpose, he twisted round in the saddle and nearly fell off his horse in getting the last picture. Civilians were not permitted to take photographs in the street, except in special cases, such as the "minute-photo" makers, who received the necessary authorization.

For some time after the German attacking forces had swept on west across Flanders, we had little military news. The Germans assured us every day that "the war would be over in fifteen days," but the Belgians merely laughed at them. We continued to listen, quite openly, to London and Paris, and the Germans made no attempt to stop this, merely prohibiting citizens from repeating to others that which they had heard from foreign stations.

The first major event of which we were aware, after the occupation of Antwerp by the Germans, was the capitulation of Belgium, the occasion for a great deal of revelry and drunkenness on the part of the occupation troops.

At that time, with my information coming chiefly from the British Broadcasting Corporation, I was furiously indignant, and felt that King Leopold had betrayed the cause of the democracies. I was somewhat taken aback, therefore, to discover that practically no one in Belgium agreed with me, so far as I could discover. Instead of sharing this indignation, the Belgians were delighted that they were officially out of the war, and overjoyed that their fathers, husbands, brothers and sons, nearly a million of whom were with the Belgian army, were no longer exposed to the ruthless assaults of German tanks and dive-bombers, and would, they supposed, soon be at home again. I had many violent arguments on the subject, but I never found a Belgian who agreed with me. (As time went on, both extreme positions were modified somewhat. I eventually realized, after talks with a great many returned Belgian soldiers, that no other course had been possible or even thinkable, and that the only question had been one of time; the Belgians, in turn, came gradually to a feeling that the capitulation had been a bit hasty, though it would have had to come sooner or later.)

For the moment, the Belgians were filled with a wave of enthusiasm for their king which amounted almost to idolatry. Pictures of Leopold appeared in every window; people talked of nothing else but their gratitude to him for several days.

Leopold had a residence in Antwerp which he practically never occupied in peacetime, a fact due, it appeared, to his fear of assassination by pro-German elements among the Flemings, who considered him far too openly pro-French. (I mention this otherwise irrelevant fact here because it is not without bearing on the contemptible libel launched by a few political adventurers who have dared to accuse Leopold of collusion with the Germans; the fact that these calumniators do not, themselves, come into court with clean hands should be enough to dispose of their charges, but these have, unfortunately, received wide publicity in certain American magazines carrying a sufficient weight of authority to mislead many persons.)

Immediately after the capitulation, floral offerings began to appear before Leopold's Antwerp residence, which was in one of the principal avenues of the city. As the days went by, the number mounted. I immediately suspected that this was the work of the German Propaganda Ministry, and I still believe that they had a hand in it at the outset—but within a few days the entire space in front of the palace was covered with such a mound of floral tributes, from elaborate wreaths to humble bouquets of wild flowers, and so many persons were massed before the house from morning to night, that it was impossible longer to consider it anything save a spontaneous expression of gratitude and affection.

Remember, too, that the Belgian government had fled; however excellent the motives of its members, the people felt deserted in their hour of great need—and the fact that King Leopold, who might easily have found refuge elsewhere, had chosen to remain with his people, a prisoner in the hands of the Germans, made them feel that he was the one man upon whom they could count; subsequent events have proved that that popular intuition was not mistaken.

When Belgian soldiers began returning to Antwerp, I felt confident that they, at any rate, would share my indignation at the capitulation. I was wrong. They were no less happy than the civilian population that the vain resistance had been brought to a speedy end, and their idolatry of Leopold was no less complete.

I can pretend to no inside information concerning the capitulation. However, I do know what the Belgians

PRISONERS ON THE MARCH

Captured French soldiers being led to work in the port of Rouen. These men will be obliged to labor for the Nazis until the end of the war.

(Photo from P. Guillumette)

thought of it, soldiers and civilians alike, and in one case I talked with a returned soldier—an officer of the association of veterans of the previous war—who visited Leopold on an official mission after the capitulation. The following account, therefore, may or may not represent the final truth of the matter, but I believe that it represents a fair statement of the affair as it appeared in Belgium; it is not what I felt about the capitulation at the time it occurred, but the view to which I came after discussing it with a great many of the persons most affected by it:

Within a very few days of the beginning of the invasion, it became clear that the striking power of the German army had been badly underestimated in Allied quarters. It became equally clear that the French and British were, despite all their promises, not yet in a position to offer any serious resistance to the German offensive weapons, and particularly to the German air power. Most of all, it became clear that the chief target of the German attack upon Belgium was the civilian population and not the army.

By means of parachutists dropped behind the lines, the Germans were able to start the mass migration of refugees moving across the Low Countries toward France, independently of operations at the front. Then a terrific blow at some point in the line by a German mechanized column, backed up by Stuka dive-bombers, compelled the Allied armies to fall back—with their retreat rendered almost impossible by the congestion of refugees in all highways. Once started, this tactic gained in effectiveness as the days went by; each time the Germans wished to render difficult or impossible a particular movement by the Allied armies, a near-by aggregation of refugees was bombed and machine-gunned, so that its members began fleeing in the direction which the Germans wished to block. Then the German mechanized column broke through, scattering confusion, causing more civilians to join the panic-stricken mass of refugees, cutting communications and making it still more difficult for refugees to flee and Allied armies to move.

During this time, the Belgian armies in the field were experiencing a curious German tactic. Except for a few days of furious fighting along the Albert Canal and around the Belgian forts, the German army conducted itself as though orders had been given to push the Belgians back, but not to harm them any more than was absolutely necessary. A Belgian column on the march was invariably accompanied by scores of German planes, flying at low altitudes directly over them—but not a bomb was dropped, nor a machine-gun bullet fired; then the fliers would reach a French or British unit in the same column, and would unleash everything it had, blasting the group to bits.

One close friend of mine, with a Belgian artillery regiment, told of firing for two days straight into the German lines, less than two miles away, without ever receiving a shell in return. Yet the Germans knew well the location of the battery, for planes flew over it from morning till night, diving straight at it and zooming up again, but never bombing or machine-gunning the position. During all this time, the Belgians subjected the Nazi machines to constant machine-gun fire at point-blank range, but the bullets merely bounced back on their heads from the protective arrangement of rubber, leather and wire netting on the bottom of the black ships. Some months after the occupation, oddly enough, in company with this friend who had related the story, I met a German artilleryman who had been in the lines opposite; he admitted that the effect of

the Belgian artillery fire had been literally murderous, but
that the German batteries had had orders to harass the
Belgians without causing any more casualties than necessary.

This peculiar policy gave the Belgian soldiers the feeling that the Germans were literally playing with them as
a cat would with a mouse; dozens of them used this very
expression in describing the campaign to me. The vital
factor in creating this state of mind was the complete command of the air by the Germans. There were Allied planes
in Belgium at that time—as I have mentioned, we saw perhaps half a dozen in Antwerp—but I have never encountered a Belgian soldier or officer who had, during the whole
of the eighteen days, seen a single French, British or Belgian airplane. In consequence, the Belgian soldiers felt
completely at the mercy of the Germans, who could wipe
the former out at any moment without interference from
the Allies.

No reliable figures have been prepared concerning the
number of casualties in Belgium during the eighteen days
of the campaign, and it will never be possible to do so,
but the most truthworthy estimates which I have heard
place the total number of dead at between forty and
seventy-five thousand; of these, it seems safe to say that
one-third occurred in the army and two-thirds among the
civilian population.

This situation placed King Leopold in a particularly
difficult dilemma. As commander-in-chief of the armed
forces, he found himself at the head of an army still practically intact, but hopelessly outclassed and outnumbered
by the invader, and not receiving effective aid from its
allies. He found himself the ruler of a country in which

the civilian population was receiving the heaviest of the enemy blows, with the army incapable of protecting it.

On the eighteenth day of the campaign, half a million refugees were encamped around the historic Belgian village of Bruges. On that day, Leopold attended a meeting of the Allied command—a meeting at which, if we may believe reports, the serious lack of co-operation between the French and British was acutely evident, as was also their impotence to check the German advance in any effective way. Returning to his own headquarters, Leopold received an ultimatum from the Germans: immediate capitulation, or the village of Bruges, with its half million refugees, would receive a visit from the Luftwaffe exactly like that made to Rotterdam, from which few of the half million would escape. The capitulation followed.

I tell this story for what it is worth; it may or may not be exact in all its details, but it is the story which is believed by practically the whole of the Belgian population, and as such is of interest. I personally feel that it is, at least, very close to the truth, and that it represents fairly the situation as it existed at that moment.

The Belgian army could have fought on, perhaps for another week or ten days; what the results would have been in military terms it is difficult to say, but the result in terms of casualties and suffering among the civilian population is not difficult to imagine. As commander of the Belgian forces, Leopold's duty was to fight on so long as his army could offer any effective degree of resistance— but as king his duty, and I think a greater one, was to protect the people over which he ruled, and to spare them any suffering which seemed futile and unlikely to alter the ultimate outcome. It was perhaps unfortunate that the two functions were combined in one man, but since they were, I scarcely see how he could have made a different decision.

No doubt the capitulation had a disastrous effect on French morale. Aside from that, however, there is nothing in subsequent events to indicate that the prolongation of Belgian resistance for a few days would have materially changed the outcome. The Battle of Flanders and the Battle of France were lost five years before, when the Allied commands and governments decided that mobile mechanized armies could be checked by static fortifications. The French met the Germans in 1914 with the methods of 1871; in 1940, they apparently assumed that the Germans would use the methods of 1914. Yet if the Allied military observers in Spain had been on the fighting front during the civil war, as was the American military attaché, instead of sitting in club armchairs in Madrid, they might have seen the development and tryout of the whole totalitarian technique that was later to smash the Allied defenses in the Low Countries and France. First a powerful blow by a column of highly mobile tanks, used in an entirely new way; assistance by units of military co-operation planes, gunning and dive-bombing positions which the tanks could not take alone; then the break-through by other mechanized units and the mass of infantry; all timed to co-ordinate with savage attacks on the civilian population. At that time, the French and British ruling classes—the first concerned with smashing the Popular Front, which had dared to prove that decent working conditions could increase production in the antiquated sweatshops of France, and the other chiefly worried about its Rio Tinto mines, which "that fine, Christian gentleman, General

Franco," had sworn to protect—in those days, Britain and France lost the battles of Flanders and France.

If Leopold had any fault from a military point of view, it was that he was perhaps too humane. A professional soldier, unmoved by slaughter and suffering, would no doubt have been willing to fight to the last private's life, as happened so frequently in 1914-'18. History has not judged too kindly the generals of the last war, who, in their dotage, hurled millions of men into a useless sacrifice, not justified by any military expediency. I do not think that Leopold need fear the verdict of History on the decision which he made when faced by the choice between the shame of capitulation and the senseless crucifixion of a brave people. It will not be forgotten, I believe, that having delivered his people into a bondage already inevitable, he chose to remain with them—nor will it be forgotten that thereafter he refused, despite threats and pressure, to lend his name and newly augmented popularity to a Belgian puppet government set up by the Germans.

This last fact is probably the reason, or more accurately, the excuse, for German non-fulfillment of the promise made at the time of the capitulation that Belgian prisoners would be set free. At the time of my departure, not only the men taken prisoners during the eighteen days of fighting, but also a large share of those who laid down their arms, were still held in Germany. There were German promises almost every week that these men would be returned to Belgium in the near future, but few persons continued to take such promises seriously.

As a matter of fact, there was an astonishing amount of confusion in the German policy in regard to Belgian prisoners in the period immediately after the capitulation. Within a few hours, the Nazis began disarming the Belgians and marching them toward Germany. They first received an issue of rations—some of the Belgian soldiers, in the general breakdown of supply lines, had eaten practically nothing for several days—and they were given a taste of German discipline. Worn with fatigue, they were obliged to march thirty miles and more a day, with German guards marching beside them, and from time to time opening the breech-blocks of their carabines and significantly showing their prisoners that the guns were loaded with real bullets.

Thus far, the German attitude was clear-cut and consistent. As the first columns of prisoners began to reach Antwerp, however, the Germans seemed unable, for several days, to decide just what they did want to do with them. Some groups were simply set free, and given twenty-four hours to resume civilian clothes; if found in uniform after that period of time, they would be rearrested. Others were liberated if they were met en route or upon arrival by relatives bringing them civilian garments. Still others were taken to barracks in Belgium, where lists of their names were posted, and relatives were given a period of several days to claim them, and take them home. Far more, however, were taken directly to Germany, and it was months before some of their families had any news of them. The whole question was handled in extremely haphazard fashion, and it was some little time before any settled policy appeared to have been reached.

As soon as word spread, with the lightning rapidity of the grapevine telegraph, that Belgian prisoners were beginning to pass through Antwerp, practically all other activity ceased for more than a week. Tens of thousands of persons lined the streets along which the troops must pass, and each brought his contribution of cigarettes or chocolate to be tossed at random into the rapidly moving mass of khaki-clad men. After the first day or two, practically all of the prisoners passed through in motor trucks, and they were driven at high speed through the streets—so rapidly as to make recognition impossible, and even to render it difficult to hurl into the passing vehicles gifts of tobacco and food.

I was in the Avenue of Italy the evening the first group arrived. The Belgian prisoners were wedged tightly in the trucks, and many of them were obliged to stand. They were gaunt and pale and weary, their faces unshaven and dirty, their uniforms ragged and misshapen—but they still had one quality which contrasted them sharply with their German guards: they could still smile.

Many thousands of civilians lined the avenue; from all sides others raced to the scene. As each truck passed, a great roar of cheering rose from the crowd, hats flew in the air, packets of cigarettes rained on the vehicle. An uninformed observer, watching the scene, would have supposed that they were the conquerors, not the vanquished. The world was calling them "quitters," and even "traitors," but to the Belgians they were just menfolk who had passed through a great trial, and had come home again.

As the days passed, the trickle of prisoners became a flood that blocked the streets from morning till night. At the exit from the foot tunnel under the river, at the end of the pontoon bridge, along the principal streets, at the field *kommandatur,* and wherever the men were likely to pass, crowds gathered and stood for hours on end, scanning each passing face, hoping and waiting. No casualty lists had been published since the commencement of fighting; no one knew what might have happened to his or her kin among the million men who had gone away. Now and then, a man or woman would rush forward to embrace someone whom they had miraculously found in the sea of marching men; or, sighting a comrade of their missing soldier, would run alongside to demand news of him— sometimes to learn that they need no longer wait.

During this time, Charles, the son of my hotel proprietress, returned. He was clean-shaven, and wearing civilian clothing, but was badly in need of a haircut, and his garments fitted him only in approximate fashion. Taken prisoner by the Germans immediately after the capitulation, he had been with a column of marching men for two days. Toward dusk on the second day, passing near a small forest, he had profited by a moment's inattention by the nearest guard to slip into the woods. Here he had waited until the column had passed, then made for the nearest farmhouse. A peasant woman had given him a suit belonging to her own husband, also away with the army, and had burned his uniform. Next morning, he had set out on foot for Antwerp, still a hundred miles away, avoiding German patrols and sentries by every possible artifice.

A considerable number of Belgians managed to escape in this way, including a few of my colleagues, and it would seem likely that the German sentries deliberately closed their eyes to these flights by the more daring of their prisoners, content so long as a reasonable number of hostages remained.

The night after his return, Charles came to my room after the others had gone to bed, and remained until three in the morning, talking incessantly and at times incoherently of the campaign. Fatigue made his voice hoarse and rasping, but he could not sit down, and paced back and forth, now coming within the little circle of light cast by the black-shaded lamp, now disappearing again into the murky shadows. Hour after hour he went on, bitterly describing the story of the eighteen days of confusion and despair. It was not a pleasant story; immediately after his last unauthorized visit to the hotel, his regiment had been sent to the Albert Canal. Almost immediately after, Holland had collapsed, leaving Belgium's weakest front wide open, and the retreat across Flanders had begun. Each day, the officers had promised that on the next day the Belgian army would counter-attack, and each time, next day had seen a further retreat. Supply lines had quickly become disorganized, and after the first few days, they only had to eat what they could find in abandoned houses and shops. All through the day, Nazi dive-bombers flew over, dived at them and zoomed up again, circled round them making circles of smoke for the German artillery, to fix their position. During the night, the enemy guns would fire just often enough to keep the defenders on the alert and prevent rest. Next morning, the planes would start again. When the regiment moved, it moved in broad daylight, completely at the mercy of enemy bombers and artillery. There had been no front, properly speaking, but only scattered units, so that often one group could not see the units occupying positions to the right and the left of it— and when the German planes dropped leaflets saying, in effect: "Your army has surrendered; why do you fight on?" the soldiers often wondered if it were perhaps true—perhaps they alone were still resisting the German advance.

Always and again, he insisted, the officers had lied to them about the military situation; lied so clumsily that none believed his superiors, and none had any further confidence in anything they might say.

Most of all, he was crushed in spirit by the looting which had taken place toward the end. "They taught me to steal," he said, hoarsely, clutching my shoulder in fury and despair. "To steal! I never stole anything in my life before. We broke into houses—we had had nothing to eat for four days, except a little stale bread—but the others didn't only take food. I took some cigarettes—I hadn't smoked for days—but some of the men took silverware, and jewelry and money. What will those Belgians think of their army when they return home?"

At times, his voice, coming out of the darkness, became almost hysterical; his eyes, as he approached the light, burned with the memory of things he had seen. At last, calmed by this outburst, he went upstairs to his room and to bed.

Next day, the question arose of regularizing his status. Each Belgian soldier must receive a discharge from German field headquarters before he could consider himself even provisionally free, and Charles had no document whatever. This was during the time that ten members of the German military police were living in the hotel, and we were not too sure what they would do. We need not have worried, however, for none of them reported him, and after a few days one of the officers accompanied him to the field *kommandatur* to try to obtain a discharge for him. This attempt did not succeed, but it served a useful purpose, inasmuch as it could no longer be claimed that he had failed to put in an appearance at the German headquarters. A few days later, Charles heard that a group of prisoners was being discharged in a village near Antwerp; he spent the night there, introduced himself among the prisoners next morning, and by noon had received the necessary official document and was on his way home.

Simultaneously with the return of prisoners from the front, the first scattered groups of refugees began trickling back into the city. These were mostly persons who had left just before the German arrival, and who had not gotten far before being overtaken by the armies, but some had come from greater distances on German army vehicles. For eighteen days the Germans had made the life of the refugees an inferno; once Belgium had capitulated, the Germans applied themselves with no less zeal to the task of befriending these same refugees. For weeks, nearly every German army vehicle returning from the front brought a few refugees back to their homes. Others returned on foot, or on bicycles. Although at that time the German soldiers were confiscating all other bicycles met with in the highways, no refugee's vehicle was touched. (One elderly laundress of my acquaintance went about freely on her bicycle during the entire period, by the simple ruse of always having a few ragged bundles tied on at the back, wearing old clothes, and announcing to any soldier who stopped her that she was a refugee.)

The condition of many of these refugees was pitiable in the extreme, and as the days went by, and they came from farther and farther away, their state grew worse. I recall one woman, accompanied by a son of fifteen or so, who had pushed a baby carriage through Holland, across Belgium and into France, while the boy pulled two other children in a toy cart. Her feet were bloody and raw, so

that she could scarcely take another step; a German soldier stopped her in the street and brought her into my
hotel. He then summoned an army doctor, who bandaged
her feet expertly and gently. She wanted to continue on
her way immediately, but the proprietress of my hotel insisted that she remain the night. Next morning, she was up
soon after dawn, and after a little breakfast, hurried away
with her children, only one thought in mind—to see
whether anything remained of the home she had left behind. She did not talk much about her own experiences—
few of the refugees were able to, I discovered—but she
did tell us of a Belgian family which had been executed
before her eyes—men, women and children—because they
had sheltered two French soldiers in the house. She told
of this without emotion, her voice flat and her face expres-
sionless, just as a young girl of eighteen told me, a few
days later, of seeing crowds of refugees run over by a
column of tanks, so that the road was spattered with brains
and blood; like this girl, she had exhausted all capacity
for feeling any emotion whatever.

One woman, an acquaintance of mine, returned without
her eight-year-old son; they had become separated in
Calais, he had gone on to Paris, looking for her, and she
had been cut off and forced to return to Antwerp; four
months were to go by before he returned, and she was one
of the lucky ones. One of the worst things she had seen,
she told me, was the plight of the thousands of abandoned
dogs and cats roaming the streets of Calais, with nothing
to eat save each other; she had brought one of these stray
dogs back with her, and three months later she was still
unable to step from one room to another without being
followed by him, so afraid was he of being deserted again,

and so vivid his memory of the terror of being alone.

Infinitely sadder, however, was the situation of the thousands of stray children, separated from their families in the mad flight, many of them too young to give their names or tell from where they came. One woman stopped at our hotel with eight such children whom she had found along the road, ranging perhaps from two to four years of age.

Another woman, living across the square from us, brought back with her a seventeen-year-old French girl, whom she had found abandoned in a French farmhouse. The girl was an illegitimate child left with the *Assistance Publique,* and farmed out to work; as such, she literally had no name and no right to identity documents of any sort. After a few days the woman, who could ill afford to keep the girl, went to the Belgian police for help. The police officer who listened to her story informed her curtly that she needed only to have left the girl where she was; my usually meek neighbor told him exactly what she thought of such an attitude, took the girl back to her home, and before I left, had found a good place for her with friends.

The mere relation of a thousand such stories could not, however, give any notion of the panorama of misery and sorrow which passed by our door for months. The story has been told elsewhere, many times, and perhaps as well as it can be told, but no account can convey a fraction of the reality; those who did not see and experience it cannot possibly visualize what it meant—and in that they are, I think, rather fortunate; they do not have to try to forget it.

For many months the chief concern of the Belgian Red Cross was the repatriation of the thousands of children who had become separated from their parents, or orphaned, during the mad flight. These were scattered throughout occupied and unoccupied France, and the task was a heart-breaking one.

Military news was, of course, uniformly bad during this period. After the capitulation came Dunkirk, and the success of the British in avoiding annihilation; then the crumbling of French resistance, the entry into Paris and the French armistice. All of this seemed almost incredible to the Belgian people, but it did not alter their conviction that Germany would lose the war—or the irritation of the Germans at Belgian obstinacy and stupidity in believing anything so ridiculous.

The collapse of France created a path across German occupied territory to nominally neutral Spain. This led to the hope that the Germans might permit Americans to cross to Portugal and return home, and the consulate requested the passports of all Americans wishing to do so. This was at the beginning of July, and represented the first effort by the American diplomatic or consular authorities to do anything whatsoever about our difficult position.

After a few days, I was advised by a German official close to the situation that I would be wise to get my passport back and make individual application in Brussels to the German High Command for Belgium and Northern France. He assured me that I would have no difficulty, in that case, in obtaining permission to leave, whereas the group application included the names of several persons not favorably viewed by the German authorities. A friend at the American consulate in Antwerp told me, quite off the record, that this was probably correct, so I decided to go to Brussels and make the attempt.

A private bus-line had opened, and I took this to the

capital. I visited German headquarters, where I was received with the utmost courtesy; I explained my case, and was told that if I would bring my passport with a letter from the American Embassy requesting a permit to depart, I should almost certainly receive this within ten days of my application. As I already had the possibility of transport for a considerable distance into France by motor truck, offered me by the factory, this put an extremely optimistic light on the situation, and I hurried to the embassy. Here I saw Miss Willis, the secretary, who had been extremely helpful on two previous occasions. She informed me, regretfully, that such a matter would have to be decided by Ambassador Cudahy, to whom she would present the matter.

I learned from her that the embassy had been given seven days to leave the country, as had all the other embassies and legations in Norway, Holland, Belgium and Luxembourg. Later, an additional three days' grace was granted. Consequently, things were in a turmoil at the embassy. I later was told, although not by Miss Willis, that a German officer had called at the embassy, seen Ambassador Cudahy, and that a conversation somewhat as follows had ensued:

Q.—Who are you?

A.—I am the American ambassador to the government of Belgium.

Q.—And where is the Belgian government?

A.—Why—in London, I believe.

"Then," concluded the courteous German officer, "you have seven days in which to join the government to which you are accredited. Your place is by its side."

This situation probably did not facilitate the granting

of my request; in any event, a few days later, I received
a letter from Miss Willis, informing me that in view of
the fact that my name was included in the group application already pending, it was not felt possible to put forward another request for me, until a reply had been received to the first demand.

That reply was not to be received until three months
later, and in the meantime there was nothing further that
I could do. My hotel bill had already reached enormous
proportions—I was borrowing money for incidental expenses—and I could not resume work at the factory because the head of the department with which I collaborated
was in unoccupied France, unable to return, and without
him no one at the plant could take the responsibility for
continuing my work. Thus ended, for me, the second month
of the occupation.

VIII

Life Must Go On

By the middle of august, 1940, after three months of German occupation, life in Belgium began to settle down to a more or less stable pattern. Despite war, despite the presence of Nazi troops in every community, despite the absence of a large part of the population which was still in German prison camps or among the refugees in France, daily life had to continue. Hitler had failed to keep his promise to lead his troops into London on August 15, and for the first time a few of them began to admit, cautiously, that perhaps the war would not be over in fifteen days, after all. The Belgians, on their side, began to be increasingly confident that Hitler could not win before winter, and therefore would not win at all.

This led to a general acceptance on all sides of the fact that the present situation was likely to continue for a long time, and that within this framework daily life must be reorganized as best it could be.

The Germans decreed that all commercial establishments must reopen, and must take back all of their former employees. There were exceptions to this drastic rule, but it was generally complied with, and it resulted in the return to work of a considerable number of persons. These, in turn, began to have money to spend, and commercial life was correspondingly stimulated. The reopening of the banks and postal savings accounts was also an aid in the

resumption of business, even though the amount which
could be drawn each month was limited.

The German army itself employed a considerable number of Belgians, as interpreters, office workers, chauffeurs
and the like; these wore a yellow armband bearing the
Wehrmacht insignia. Some of the out-of-work dock labor-
ers were engaged to unload munitions arriving by boat
from Germany; they were paid one dollar and sixty-five
cents a day for this, on the strict understanding that the
Germans had no liability for compensation in case of acci-
dent. Only the neediest accepted this work. Soon, several
of the docks, located in densely populated neighborhoods,
were piled high with explosive materials. Another munition dump was in a residential district, a fact which created no little unfavorable comment among the Belgians.

The Germans also hired a large number of civilians to
drive army trucks. At the beginning of the invasion, these
extra drivers were mostly Dutch, but as time went on, so
many of them were killed in occasional R.A.F. "hit-and-
run" raids on columns of vehicles that it became difficult
for the Germans to find willing candidates in Holland. At
the time I left, considerable inducements were being
offered to Belgians for this work.

For many months after the invasion, there was no means
of transport in the occupied countries except motor vehicles and, in certain districts, barges. The wholesale destruction of railway bridges by the retreating Allied armies
made it impossible to run any trains whatever in Belgium
and northern France. In Holland, there was far less destruction and railroad service was quickly restored; to
the south of Paris, in France, the same was true. Thus,
supplies for the German army had to be brought as far as

Holland by rail, then distributed throughout Belgium and northern France by motor truck; the same vehicles, on their return journey, were filled with confiscated supplies for transportation to Germany. By the middle of August, not a great deal remained in Belgium to be seized, but material from France continued to provide cargo for thousands of trucks which passed through Antwerp each day.

There was not the slightest indication, at that time or even later, that the Germans were short of gasoline, or that they were trying to conserve it. They had seized vast supplies in Holland, Belgium and France, and it was issued to army drivers with a lavish hand. Civilians, it is true, were not allowed to drive private cars of more than seventeen horsepower, but those who owned the light cars so common in Europe had little difficulty in obtaining gasoline. Business firms were allowed ample supplies for commercial needs. Many of the German officers whom I knew went off for days at a time on completely unnecessary pleasure jaunts, covering thousands of miles, through the occupied areas; for these trips they received gasoline without the slightest trouble. It seemed obvious that either Germany had gasoline sufficient for all needs, or else that she felt completely confident of winning and ending the war before her reserves could be exhausted.

A network of private buslines covered Belgium at that time, but these were overcrowded and expensive. It was obviously essential to restore train service as soon as the right-of-way could be repaired, if life were to resume something of its normal character.

The first step in this direction was to repair the blown-up bridges and lines, and to this end large detachments of the Nazi *Arbeits Dienst*, or Labor Service, arrived in Bel-

BOOTY FROM DUNKIRK

French workers, supervised by Nazis, hoist from the Channel one of the motor
trucks abandoned by the British in their retreat from Dunkirk.

(Photo from European)

THE AGE OF PROGRESS

With the prohibition of private automobiles, Parisians turn to contraptions such
as this home-built trailer attached to a bicycle.

(Photo from P. Guillumette)

gium. Every German youth is, in principle, obliged to
serve for one year in this organization before commencing
his military service. Its members wear military uniform,
but instead of field gray, it is khaki.

Their arrival in Antwerp did not improve the general
situation. During the first few days of the occupation, there
had been a certain number of younger soldiers among the
shock troops who were political fanatics and had made
themselves extremely disagreeable to everyone. After that,
nearly all of the occupation troops had shown a reasonable
desire to get along with the civilian population with a
minimum of friction, and there had been few unpleasant
incidents.

Not so with the Labor Service youths. They had known
nothing but Nazism, and their arrogance was tempered by
no broader culture or education. They pushed civilians
off the sidewalk as they passed, they insulted women, made
themselves as obnoxious to everyone as possible, and even
treated with disdain the older German soldiers. The results
were not long in making themselves felt: the Belgians
boycotted them, and the German soldiers knocked them
down in street fights and café brawls with a frequency
alarming to the German command. In one instance, in a
free-for-all fracas in a café near the Central Railway Station in Antwerp, Belgian civilians and German soldiers
joined together in hammering into unconsciousness a group
of these young Hitler hoodlums who had sought to show
the superiority of the one hundred per cent Nazi youth.

I had seen this same mentality at work years before in
Italy, when, during the making of a film, my company
had been obliged to engage a guard of young Fascist
Blackshirts, nominally to "protect us from interference by

the crowds." Actually, we never had the slightest trouble with Italian crowds, which were good-humored and docile, but we had a great deal of trouble with the Blackshirts, who thought everything was permitted to them.

The same gangster mentality was to be found in the Nazi Labor Service battalions. Superficially viewed, the idea back of the Labor Service organization is a principle both admirable and democratic: this being that every boy, whether his father be a bank president or a coal miner, must engage in manual labor for one year, so that whatever his later career, he will understand and respect the working man. However, if the principle be sound, the results obviously depend upon what is taught—and the results in the case of the Labor Service youths who passed through Antwerp were the most damning indictment of the Nazi system which I have seen, and the most appalling indication of what the future of Europe will be if the Nazis are not smashed.

Working under the supervision of German engineers, and aided by Belgian civilian labor, the *Arbeits Dienst* battalions did, at any rate, put some of the more important bridges rapidly into usable condition, and after their departure the job was continued with local workers. The new bridges were of wood, but they were strongly built, and bit by bit the railways began to run occasional trains. A line from the Dutch border brought troops to the East Station in Antwerp, making connections at the frontier with Dutch lines already functioning. Other lines connected the principal Belgian cities, and a through line to Paris was provisionally repaired so that one train a day could be run over it at greatly reduced speed. As trains began to move again, another uniform appeared in the streets—the dark blue of the German railway workers. These men were practically all of middle-age, and at least one was on each train which ran, and in each railway station.

The resumption of even partial train service made possible the beginnings of postal delivery; many Belgians received in September letters and parcels which had been lying in various postoffices since the invasion, early in May.

Civilian, commercial transport was improved by the fact that many owners of Belgian buses and trucks which had been confiscated by the Germans now received them back, the invaders having replaced them with others taken in France. Compensation boards began to function, and those persons whose property had been confiscated were awarded payment—in occupation money if the amount were small, in bonds payable eventually by the municipality if the amount were large.

Newspapers and magazines were by this time appearing regularly, under German control, and their number was augmented by new German-language publications for the army in the field, such as the "Brüsseler Zeitung."

During all of this period there was not the slightest item of news about King Leopold, his whereabouts or his well-being, and the Belgians began to feel a certain amount of anxiety on that score. The political magazine "Pourquoi Pas?" dared to appear with a cover illustration showing an empty throne, and over it a large interrogation mark. The number was confiscated on the stands, and publication suspended by German decree.

(Only a few weeks before, an issue of the same magazine had carried a cover portrait of Mussolini, and under it was a line from one of his recent speeches concerning Italo-German amity: "Good friends will always fight for each other." On two newsstands where I saw this displayed, someone had scratched out with a pencil the word "for.")

As part of their campaign to restore the appearance of normal life, the Germans reopened every possible establishment. Schools opened as usual, though many youths of sixteen and over were still in France. Museums were reopened to the public, though without the old treasures of Flemish art, which were left in safe repositories, and only modern works were displayed. The small admission charge made before the war was entirely removed, presumably to show that the Nazi policy was to encourage a love of art. The museums were visited in considerable numbers by German soldiers, as were all the important public monuments. Each group of soldiers arriving in Antwerp went about, often with guidebooks and lecturers, on an educational tour of this sort. Somewhat later in the autumn, groups of Hitler Youth youngsters began to arrive for similar educational tours.

Daytime life in the cafés took on its accustomed air, though much of the clientele was German; after dark, only a few of the larger cafés attracted any important number of civilians. The "Ancient Belgium," a vast café-concert, reopened its doors, with its previous international range of vaudeville acts replaced by purely local talent.

Night clubs of various types have been an important feature of Belgian life for many years, owing to the fact that only beer and light wines may be served in public cafés and bars; hard liquor may be sold in bottles over the counter for consumption at home, or served in private clubs. The natural result has been that practically all Belgian night establishments have borne the name of a "club" or "circle"; becoming a member of one of these select and exclusive organizations usually involved the payment of five francs (about fifteen cents) and a delay of two or three minutes while a membership card was filled out.

Many of these clubs sought to reopen as life climbed back to something like its habitual level, and the German authorities seemed unable to make up their minds what to do about them. For a few days, business went on in the "night spots" as it had before the invasion, with music, dancing and drinks. Then the German police decreed that all female employees, taxi-girls, entertainers and all, must undergo a medical examination each week, and carry the same sort of card that they were issuing to prostitutes. Soon after, another German decree proclaimed a month without music in places of public entertainment in Germany and all the occupied countries, "in honor of the war dead." This was severely enforced, and without music and dancing the night establishments starved. Presently, the ban was modified, and music was permitted until nine-thirty, but with dancing only two nights a week until this hour.

At the time I left, this matter seemed to depend largely upon the discretion or whim of local authorities. Anneesen Street, in Antwerp, for example, was on the boundary line between two military police districts; as a result, establishments on one side of the street were permitted no music after nine-thirty and were closed at midnight, while those on the other side remained open till morning—with music. In general, small cafés were supposed to shut their doors at midnight, but in practice most of them closed when the last German soldier in the place chose to go home, which was usually about four in the morning. All of this fluctuated, at different times and in various communities, with variations in the curfew regulations. At one period in Antwerp, cafés might remain open until midnight for the soldiers, but no civilians were allowed on the streets after nine P.M., so that when closing time came the café employees and waiters did not, theoretically, have the right to appear in the streets on their way home. Gradually, all of these inconsistencies were ironed out, but a café proprietor's life was not an especially happy one until they were.

Factories continued to reopen during this period, although large numbers of industrial workers were still prisoners in Germany or refugees in France. The plant with which I had been connected opened its doors, work being on something less than a half-time basis, and I was permitted to complete a limited amount of unfinished research in my laboratory. This brought only slight relief to my acute financial situation, but it was better than remaining idle.

By this time, the German authorities, and such Belgian civil functionaries as were still at their posts, had apparently accomplished all that was possible for the re-establishment of economic life—and the most pressing problems in Belgian national life became the return of soldiers held prisoner in Germany and refugees stranded in France. Since the return of prisoners was wholly at the caprice of the German authorities, public attention centered about the more immediate problem of repatriating the refugees.

Just how many of these unfortunates there were will never be known with any degree of accuracy, but it is

highly probable that in the middle of August a million
Belgians were still in France, and the number may have
been considerably higher. Many had returned on bicycles,
and even on foot, but those who had automobiles were,
ironically enough, much worse off: they could not obtain
gasoline for the return journey. The Belgian newspapers
were filled with the clamor of demands that something be
done about this. Though the newspapers were severely controlled by the Germans, there was little doubt that this out-
cry corresponded to a strong wave of public opinion
throughout the country.

The situation at that time was a confused one; it seemed
as though someone was still missing from nearly every
Belgian family—a soldier, who might be a prisoner of the
Germans, or wounded, or killed; a boy of sixteen to
eighteen, who might be in England or in France, occupied
or unoccupied; a relative, who might be in Portugal, in
France, in England, or might have been killed in one of
the savage attacks on refugees during the invasion. The
Red Cross and the newspapers made all possible efforts to
establish lists of prisoners and lists of those in various
encampments in France, but these covered only a small
fraction of the missing persons.

Some of the newspapers chartered large motor coaches,
and began evacuating refugees from France systemati-
cally, if not on a large scale. Then a civilian organization
was set up, which proposed to charter buses and trucks in
great number, and evacuate everyone. Matters were
speeded up when the Vichy government decreed that all
refugees must quit unoccupied France by September 15.
Somehow, those with automobiles obtained gasoline; buses

evacuated others, and by October most of the refugees were at home.

As soon as trains started running between France and Belgium, many refugees were returned by this means, relieving the pressure on motor transport materially. The first to profit by this were the Belgian political prisoners who were being held in France—German-born Belgians suspected of being Nazi agents or spies, Belgian Fascists, Flemish nationalists and other dubious elements, who had been rounded up by the Belgian police immediately after the invasion.

One of these was a mechanic employed at the factory in which my laboratory was located, who had built much of my experimental apparatus. He had been held in a camp at Cerbère, on the Franco-Spanish border, from which he was to have been taken to Morocco. The tale he told of the suffering and privation endured was a gruesome one, and while I felt little sympathy for most of the persons involved, some of them had been arrested merely as a preventive measure, and certainly did not merit the bestial treatment which they had received. My acquaintance, who had been a robust person, was almost a skeleton upon his return; for some time, he was obliged to remain in bed, and it was weeks before he could eat a regular meal. At that, he had been one of the more fortunate ones; his description of the ravages of dysentery in the concentration camp would make nauseous reading. Despite every aid which the German authorities could give them, the railway journey from the Spanish border to Paris had required nine days, and that from Paris to Brussels, six days. On one occasion, they had passed over a hastily repaired bridge, beneath a locomotive which had been blown into the air by a mine, and still hung suspended in the twisted wreckage of the old bridge. The train was bombed on several occasions; at times, the train would be obliged to back up for several hours, then try another line, because a right-of-way which had been in operating condition the day before had been blown up by the R.A.F. during the night. Despite my desire to return to America as quickly as possible, he strongly urged me not to risk the journey across France.

The pro-German Flemish newspapers made the utmost capital of the hardships undergone by these political prisoners—so much so that in the end, I almost regretted that the former Belgian government had not done what any totalitarian government would have done in the same circumstances, and executed them without formality. Among the returned prisoners was Leon Degrelle, leader of the Rexists, or Belgian Fascists. This fact was a source of some little embarrassment to the pro-German newspapers; for some months, they had made political capital of the fact that the former Belgian government had brutally had Degrelle shot, and here he was, alive! There was no indication, up to the time of my departure, that Degrelle was having any more success than previously as a political leader, despite every encouragement by the Germans. There were window displays, with his picture exhibited beside that of the King, giving the impression, quite unwarranted, I believe, that the King approved of the Rexist movement, and appealing for volunteers for a Belgian Storm Trooper organization, but the public paid little heed. It was highly unlikely that the Germans would allow such organizations to be armed—and without that, there was little appeal to the gangster element.

Considerably more important, for me, was the fact that early in September the head of my department at the factory returned from near Lourdes, in unoccupied France, where he had been stranded with his entire family since May, unable to obtain gasoline for the journey back to Belgium. With his return, I was able to resume work on a normal and even an intensified basis. My immediate material worries were solved, but there was still no serious indication that the Germans would permit me to return to America, and no certainty as to how long the factory would be able to remain open.

During all of this time, soldiers came and went at my hotel. Some were frankly disagreeable, others were reasonably amiable, but with none of them did we become as well acquainted and as friendly as with the group of military police officers quartered there early in the occupation.

Often there were groups of aviators, mechanics, wireless operators and other members of the flying and ground staffs of the German air force, and these were usually the most unpleasant of all. At some time during that period— I did not note the date—Goering paid a visit to Antwerp, and I saw him riding down Keyser Avenue in his huge automobile, in the back of which was mounted a machine-gun with its attendant gunner. There was, I am glad to report, no cheering from civilians at his passage.

It was at this period that raids by the R.A.F. on the coast cities began, and the result was an intensification of German effort in the construction of air raid shelters in all parts of the town and an increase in the number of anti-aircraft batteries and searchlight units.

German officers talked a great deal about "Germany's secret weapon"—talked rather too much, it seemed to me, to make the whole thing plausible. This "weapon," which had been tried out in France with tremendous success, so they claimed, could be employed in seven ways. The implication was that it was some sort of deadly ray—perhaps super-sonic waves—and it was claimed that when directed at an enemy soldier, up to a distance of three hundred feet, he promptly fell, stone dead. When officers talked to me of this, I usually replied that if Hitler really had such a weapon, I was astonished that so much time and money and trouble were being expended on the construction, or even the transport, of more tanks and airplanes and cannons; this, in most cases, ended the discussion of "Germany's secret weapon."

A great deal of public indignation was stirred up, at this period, by the tales brought back from France by returning refugees. All of them were disgusted with the lack of cleanliness in France, Belgium being, in tidiness, not far behind Holland; many of them told of the greatest suffering and privation. I talked with many of these, and it did not seem to me, on the whole, that most of them had any just cause for criticism. All of them had received ten francs a day from the French authorities, plus the same amount of food available to the French civilian population. This was not a great deal, but they could scarcely expect to receive more than the French had for themselves. Many of them had undoubtedly lived in miserably inadequate surroundings, but, after all, no one had ever advised them to flee, or told them that they might find a haven in France, and taking as a whole the stories which I heard, I believe the French people did a very great deal for them, in view of the total dislocation of life in France at that time. By no means all of the refugees abused the French, but, unfortunately, the discontented ones made far more noise than the others, and a good bit of bad feeling against the neighbor country was created among the general public, which the Germans naturally did not try to discourage.

Public sentiment toward Germany and the Germans was taking a divided course. The shortage of food was beginning to make itself felt acutely, and there were few, even among the most pro-German citizens, who did not blame Germany for this. Thus, on the one side, there was increased feeling against Germany, but, at the same time, friendliness with the German soldiers was in no way declining, and had perhaps even increased. After all, most of them were behaving themselves well toward civilians, and not all of them were arrogant brutes. Many of the soldiers in Antwerp had been stationed there for some time, and hoped to remain until the end of the war—which was no longer to be "in fifteen days." As a result, they inevitably formed acquaintanceships, and even friendships, among the civilian population.

At first, this fraternization, in public and in private, by Belgian civilians with the men who, only a few months before, had been bombing and blasting them, seemed to me somewhat repugnant. As time wore on, I was not so sure. The citizens had to live with these soldiers in their midst, and were, in fact, completely in their power; it is doubtful whether any really useful purpose would have been served by boycotting the invaders. On the contrary, I began to see that association between German soldiers and the Flemish-speaking Belgians was beginning, however slightly, to put notions into the soldiers' heads not at all to the liking of the Nazis. In France, the language barrier made fraternization more difficult, even by those who were willing to do so.

Belgian women, particularly, never hesitated to criticize the Nazi regime in talking with soldiers, and many statements which the latter would not have tolerated from a man thus went unchallenged, and constant repetition was having its effect. In spite of themselves, the German soldiers were acquiring a new conception of democracy and freedom.

After the last war, Belgian women who had associated with German officers or soldiers had their hair unceremoniously hacked off by the population, so that for years after, short hair was a mark of shame. The memory of that was still vivid in 1940, and for a time most Belgian women were extremely chary of being seen with the invaders. As the occupation went on, their diffidence in this respect began to diminish, and by the time I left, some of the women who had been loudest in their protestations at the outset were associating openly with German soldiers.

This was a natural consequence of the increasing degree of fraternization between soldiers and civilians, and had been further increased by the fact that a large number of Belgian men were still prisoners in Germany; of the men who were at home, a great many were unemployed, or had had their incomes so reduced that social activities were out of the question.

The German soldiers, on the contrary, had more money than they sometimes knew what to do with; not only were they well paid, but those in civil service posts, for example, also received each month a sum sufficient to make up the difference between their military and civilian pay. Those who did not eat in barracks received an ample cash allow-

ance for this purpose. This enabled them to entertain generously, and it was perhaps not surprising if they had little
difficulty in finding recipients for their lavish attentions.

From the very outset of the invasion, the young girls of
fifteen and sixteen showed no hesitancy whatever about
associating with the Germans; Belgian young men were
still away with the army, and the few who were not had
no money, but there were good times to be had with the
invaders, and the girls proposed to have them. There was
no lack of soldiers to exploit this willingness, and few
who had any scruples concerning the inexperience and
even ignorance of these 'teen-age girls. What the results
will be in terms of the illegitimate birthrate in 1941, one
can only speculate, but it was already evident when I left
that it would be high. One hotelkeeper of my acquaintance,
who was doing a thriving but unwelcome business in rooms
for temporary occupancy, frequently protested when Nazi
soldiers sought to take young girls who were scarcely more
than children upstairs, whereupon the soldier would re-
mind him that he was a German, and that no Belgian had
the right to tell *him* what to do. Parental control had completely broken down in this situation; many of the girls'
fathers were still in prison camps, and their mothers dared
not protest, for there was a general feeling that if a girl
were to tell a Nazi soldier that her mother had forbidden
her to associate with Germans, the mother would probably
disappear in the direction of a concentration camp. The
Germans were prepared and willing to be friendly toward
the Belgians——but Heaven help the Belgian who did not
accept that friendship!

Individual German soldiers, however, could and did on
occasion display a friendliness less hypocritical. Not long

before my departure, there was a period of several days
during which it was literally impossible to find the smallest quantity of potatoes. My hotel proprietress confided to
the soldiers billeted there that on the following day she
would be obliged to close the restaurant, her chief source
of income, unless she could find potatoes somewhere. That
afternoon, the soldiers brought her several hundred pounds
of them—in a German army truck, which meant no small
risk if they were caught.

While the Gestapo made its hand felt on occasion, its
activities in Belgium during the first half year of the occupation were not as extensive as might have been expected;
less, for example, than was the case in Holland, where a
civil administration under the traitor of Vienna, Seyss-
Inquart, had been set up. King Leopold's repeated refusal,
despite a reported visit from Hitler, to collaborate with
the Germans in the formation of a puppet government kept
Belgium under military rule. Many of the reserve officers
with the occupation army, who were charged with the actual administration of affairs, were men who, in private
life, held important commercial and professional posts in
Germany. They were neither political fanatics nor military
martinets, and when one had to deal with such a man, one
was reasonably sure of the fairest treatment possible in
the circumstances.

How long the Nazis would tolerate the continuance of
this absence of a puppet government was difficult to say.
An intoxicated Gestapo man told me one evening, at my
hotel, that King Leopold was to be confined in an insane
asylum, and that he was worried as to the possible reaction
on the part of the Belgian people if they ever learned of
it. No great importance should be attached to a remark

made under such circumstances—but it was perhaps significant that a Gestapo agent should have been thinking along that line.

In addition to the occupation troops, a considerable number of German soldiers were in Antwerp for medical treatment. Most of the hospital facilities in the city had been taken over by them, and many wounded men were brought back after the battles in France. I saw many of these patients, but a point which struck me as curiously in contrast to military hospitals during the last war was that I never saw a maimed or crippled soldier. I was not alone in noting this, and I heard on several occasions—and even from Belgian hospital workers—that the German army doctors had strict orders that any man who was maimed or crippled so badly that his appearance later would have a depressing effect on military morale, was not to get well. It was, naturally, impossible to confirm this, but it was very generally believed, and the continued and consistent lack of any crippled patients lent color to the accusation. An army doctor, whom I knew slightly, committed suicide; the story told at the time was that he had received orders to give a lethal hypodermic to any badly maimed patient, and that being a conscientious doctor and a devout Roman Catholic, as well as an obedient soldier, he had gone to a priest for counsel in this dilemma. The priest told him that as a doctor, it was his first duty to help the patient so long as there was any hope of saving life. Unable to reconcile this with his deep instinct to obey orders, the story goes, he shot himself.

Whether this accusation is true or false is impossible to determine; it would, in any case, be promptly denied; but it is thoroughly consistent with the general Nazi policy, which considers that anything is justified so long as it helps to win a war. Large numbers of the German dead were burned after the battles of Flanders and France, so that there should be no huge cemeteries as in 1914, to discourage the soldiers and, incidentally, to reveal to the world the falsity of Nazi claims concerning the number of casualties in these battles. A considerable number were thus disposed of in the furnaces of a factory near Antwerp. Belgian soldiers being marched back as prisoners immediately after the capitulation, saw no German corpses en route, and few graves, even in areas where there had been heavy fighting only a few hours before.

During August and September, I kept in frequent touch with the American consulate, but there were no encouraging developments in the matter of obtaining permission to leave. After a considerable period of inertia, the matter was placed before the German authorities, who replied that the war would soon be over, at which time all foreigners could return home if they wished. There matters stood for a time, until one of the vice-consuls took the question up with the authorities in Berlin, where he had gone with the diplomatic pouch; he made some little progress toward a solution, but his untimely death in a collision between his car and a German railway train again left the matter suspended in midair.

The research work for which I had remained in Belgium had been carried about as far as it could be, and while there was still work to be done, it was not at all certain that the factory would be able to remain open indefinitely. Furthermore, if America did come into the war at some future date, a belief very common in Belgium, I would automatically be sent to a German prison camp for the duration of the war, as British and French males from sixteen to sixty had been—and I had seen the appearance of Belgian prisoners who had returned in a state of collapse after only six weeks in such a camp! In short, I felt that I should be happy to shake the dust of Belgium from my feet, at least for the duration of the war, but the chances of so doing seemed extremely unpromising.

IX

What a German Soldier Thinks About

WHEN THE GERMANS ENTERED ANTWERP, AND I BEGAN TO come into daily contact with them, at my hotel and elsewhere, my chief interest was not in their military equipment and preparedness, but in their state of mind. What a German soldier thinks of the military and political situation in Europe is, in a large degree, the measure of the real success of the Nazi regime; his morale will have an important bearing on any eventual attempt by Great Britain to invade the Continent and smash the Nazi power. To attempt to rebuild a Europe at peace, if it is to be stable, his beliefs and convictions must be taken into account. My visits to Germany before the war, and my many contacts with Germans through my work, had prepared me for a depressing degree of fanaticism on the part of a great number of them. At the same time, I knew that there were, here and there, intelligent Germans who were not deceived, and I was curious to see whether or not I should find men of this stamp in the army.

I have told, elsewhere in this book, of the unusually favorable circumstances under which I came in contact with large numbers of soldiers, billeted at my hotel for one or more nights and eating many of their meals in the restaurant. Here we often had groups remaining long enough for us to become well acquainted with them, and when their superior officers were absent, they often talked

freely and without restraint. On other occasions, the officers themselves talked with a frankness that astonished me.
It is perhaps worth remarking that my hotel was noted in
Antwerp for its cuisine—a fact which explains why many
of the Germans returned again and again to the restaurant,
and in the end, talked to us much more unreservedly than
they would have to a casual stranger. A full report of all
my conversations, here, on the street, in cafés and elsewhere with German soldiers would easily fill an entire
volume, and would perhaps be more confusing than helpful. I shall, therefore, in the following, select those things
which seem most typical, and which strike a note which
recurred frequently in conversations with many different
men.

It is important to bear in mind that the German soldier
is not merely a pawn in a military chess-game—he is also
a human being away from home, and, in most cases, has
been away from home for a very long time. A great number of men have undergone their period of military training, then been stationed for several years in Austria, in
Czechoslovakia, have gone through the Polish campaign,
then the Dutch, Belgian and French campaigns—and the
dominant, constantly recurring theme in all of their conversations is their desire to go home. Let me state clearly
at the outset that I am not suggesting that Hitler's army is
practically ready to revolt; that would be wishful thinking
of the most harmful sort. At the same time, it would be
equally stupid to lean too far in the other direction and to
assume that this fact has no military importance whatsoever. The Germans are a people to whom family life means
a great deal, and family ties are strong. Nearly every German soldier to whom I talked for more than a few minutes

proudly showed me snapshots of his wife and children, or his fiancée, or his mother, and expressed in no uncertain terms his hope that soon the war would be over and he would be able to rejoin them in a Europe at peace. As members of Hitler's army of conquest they have had their good moments; their leader has given them an almost unbroken sequence of successes; life has been very comfortable at times in some of the occupied cities—but none of these things gives any enduring satisfaction to a man away from his family, and one who sees several of the best years of his life going by while he makes no progress whatever with his job or career in civilian life.

Immediately after the invasion, when every German soldier believed that the war was nearly at its end, this desire to go home was not important. It seemed very clear to them that they would soon be able to do so, and the matter was not worth worrying about. As the months went by, and one postponement followed another, they were not so certain; if Hitler fears a long war, it is perhaps more because of this than of the question of material reserves. Time is on the side of the Allies, not only in a material sense but because the Germans have been taught for years that the war would be a short, sharp struggle—a Blitzkrieg, or lightning-war—whereas Churchill has been shrewd enough to warn his people from the outset that the war would be long and difficult.

One other factor must be borne in mind, however: so long as the German soldier believes he is fighting to protect his family, he will put up with a great deal, no matter how lonely he may be or how much he would like to return to that family. I remember, on one occasion, the attempt of a friend of mine to explain to a group of German soldiers why Frenchmen with five or more children had been excused from military duty. The German soldiers were bewildered, and completely unable to understand this. "But," they said, "if he has five children, why doesn't he want to fight to protect them?" So long as the German soldier has this feeling, he will submit to a great deal.

The most important factor of all, no doubt, is the German soldier's opinion of Hitler, and to illustrate that, I can think of nothing more typical than a conversation which I had in Paris, in November, 1939, with a French army surgeon, when I went there to move my personal effects to Antwerp. A German plane had been shot down behind the French lines, and this surgeon had been called in to attend the badly wounded aviator. A rapid examination showed him that there was no hope whatever, and that the most he could do was to give the patient something to ease the excruciating pain. He did this, then told the flyer as gently as possible that there was little he could do as a doctor, but that if the dying man had any messages or last wishes which he would like to have conveyed, he, the doctor, would see that they were sent off. The badly wounded man nodded weakly, raised himself on one elbow with a desperate effort, and said: "May God bless and protect Adolf Hitler!" That attitude, however incredible, is practically universal in the German army. Never, in all my conversations, did I hear a word of criticism of the German leader. Even those not in sympathy with his regime, and who openly attacked it, believed that Hitler was, himself, sincere and had the good of the German people at heart; believed, too, that he had accomplished a great deal for Germany, whatever might be the outcome.

Any propaganda effort which ignores that fact is, I believe, foredoomed to failure. The leaflets dropped over Germany by the R.A.F. early in the war, for example, which carried a direct attack on Hitler, could not, I am sure, serve any useful purpose whatever—at any rate, not until things become a great deal worse than they have been up to date. It would be far more skillful to take the line that Hitler's sincere and earnest plans for the benefit of the German people have been betrayed by corrupt politicians around him; it is a venerable principle of argument that one must start off with a statement with which the opponent will agree, then, step by step, proceed to a point with which he was not in sympathy at the outset. An atheist who wished to shake the faith of a devoutly religious man would make little headway if he started off with scurrilous attacks on the Deity; direct criticism of Hitler is, to the mass of the German people at the present time, just that.

If, however, practically all of the German soldiers idolize Hitler, it does not follow that the same is true of the Nazi regime. In far more cases than I would ever have anticipated, German soldiers told me, in effect: "Hitler is honest and sincere, but he is surrounded by a gang of crooks, and it is they who have gotten us into the present mess." Again and again, I heard the most bitter criticism of Goering, of Goebbels, of Hess, Himmler, Ley and von Ribbentrop; again and again, German soldiers charged that these men were growing rich at the expense of the German people—that they were corrupt and unscrupulous. It is along this line, obviously, that any successful propaganda effort must be directed; Hitler is, for the present, as good as invulnerable, but many men around him are admirable targets, and the German people are already more than half disposed to react favorably to criticism of them.

Any plan, such as that of the British appeasers to make a private deal with Goering at the expense of Hitler, was foredoomed to failure; if necessary, the German soldiers would fight almost to the last man for Hitler and against Goering. Surprisingly enough, every German seems to have heard the story—which I had previously heard both in London and in Berlin—that Goering, as a former member of a religious sect practicing voluntary sterilization, submitted years ago to an operation which made it impossible for him ever to have any children other than the son by a former wife whom a Swedish court took away from him (curiously enough, this story seems practically unknown in America); many Germans assume, therefore, that the widely publicized and photographed children of his present wife are not his, and this does not increase their respect for him, nor give them any particular love of him. When the first child was born to Emmy, and was given the name "Edda," a widely repeated witticism went the rounds in Berlin to the effect that "E-d-d-a stands for *Emmy dankt dem Adjutant.*" Many German soldiers believe, too, the tales to the effect that Goering obtains a substantial amount of graft on all contracts for military material.

There is somewhat more respect for Goebbels, for it is an incontestable fact that at the time of the early Nazi putsch and other uprisings, Goebbels did, despite his physical infirmity, display a great deal of personal courage, charging in the face of machine-guns at a moment when, as one eyewitness described it, "Hitler was lying on his belly on the pavement, howling with terror." However, the frequent amorous scandals in his private life of recent years have not heightened his popularity, and he

NAZI BOOKSHOP IN BRUSSELS

Window of one of the many propaganda bookstores opened by the Germans throughout the occupied areas. The German caption states that this innovation was greeted
with great satisfaction, not only by the occupation troops but by the subjugated
civilian population. The author failed to note any signs of this "satisfaction" on the
part of the latter.

(Photo from European)

could not succeed independently of Hitler. As for the other Nazi leaders, I saw no evidence that any one of them occupies any considerable place in the affections of the German people. I seriously doubt whether any one of them could successfully carry on after Hitler's death, as Stalin did after the demise of Lenin, for the emphasis in Germany has been far more on the Leader and less on the Party than was the case in Russia.

The German people have very little love indeed for the rank and file of the Nazi political machine. Many German soldiers complained to me bitterly of the constant extortion of money, in their civilian lives, in the form of so-called voluntary contributions to various Nazi causes. One German officer of considerable rank, occupying an important civil service position in private life, told me, with almost undisguised resentment, of how, when a list was circulated in his neighborhood for Winter Help, or one of the many other money-raising campaigns, his name would already be written in at the head of the list, and opposite it the sum which he was required, not requested, to give as a fitting example to his fellow private citizens. Superficially, he was better off than he had been before the days of Hitler, but in reality, when allowance was made for all these various forms of tribute, there was not much difference at the end of the month. The German people do not forget that the Nazis have never given an accounting of the use to which these enormous contributions have been put, and a great many Germans feel that the Nazi party as such is chiefly a machine for the financial exploitation of the German people.

(I should like to mention here an incident which, though it does not directly belong to the subject of this chapter, throws an interesting sidelight on this matter of Nazi funds. A British associate of mine was in Berlin the last winter before the war. While he was seated in a café, a collector for the party came to his table, held out a contribution box, and said: "Winter Help? Winter Help?" Then, leaning over, confidentially, he added, in a low tone: "For cannons!")

Not infrequently, the bitterest criticism came from men who had themselves been members of the Nazi party in the days of its early struggles. These men often felt that they had fought for something very different from the present Nazi regime, and though they still idolized Hitler, they felt that he, as well as they, had been completely betrayed. A great deal of their admiration for Hitler, I believe, springs from the German's antipathy toward disorder and confusion. There was a great deal of this in government affairs in Germany during the period before Hitler came to power, and while it is not my purpose here to go into the reasons for it, nor to try to fix the blame, the fact remains that most of the German people badly wanted some sort of order brought out of the chaos then reigning. Since it happens to have been the Nazi party which accomplished this, however questionable the means, a certain measure of gratitude on the part of the German people goes to Hitler for that reason. Democracy, in the sense in which we think of the word, seems to a considerable proportion of the German people to be merely weakness; any future government which is to follow the Nazi regime in Germany must give the appearance of strength and order, or it has no hope of succeeding.

Most important of all, probably, is the fact that the average German, rightly or wrongly, feels that he is in a material sense better off than he was before Hitler came to power. Such privation as there has been, he attributes not to Nazi militarism but to British oppression of the German nation. It is not my purpose in this book to discuss at length the Nazi political system, or to give an opinion as to its soundness or sincerity; I am only dealing here with the result in terms of public morale. In that connection, the one thing which counts to the German people at the present time is the fact that Hitler has succeeded in giving them the feeling, or at any rate the illusion, of economic well-being and security. They have seen the elimination of unemployment, and the majority of them do not bother to analyze the means by which this has been achieved; they have seen wage conditions apparently improved, and they do not probe deeply into the question of the real value of those wages. The Strength Through Joy movement has given them vacation and travel opportunities which many of them could never have afforded, and they accept this at its face value. The people feel that their old age is provided for, and that their children are assured of the best of care.

Take, for example, the case of a German private in the army. In addition to his keep, he receives a sum equivalent, in Belgium, to about thirty cents a day, a figure far higher than in most European armies; while actual fighting is going on, he receives the equivalent of sixty-five cents. It matters little to him if this be paid in "worthless" paper money which costs the Nazis nothing, so long as he can exchange that money for things which he wants.

I leave to the economists the task of determining how long all of this can continue; I am concerned here with what the German soldier believes *now,* not with what may

be the economic breakdown of tomorrow. It would be difficult to exaggerate the importance of the fact that the German soldier *believes* that Hitler has given him economic
security. I have watched the effect of this conviction at
work for years in most of the totalitarian states, and I am
certain that an increasing number of persons in the world,
if obliged to choose between political freedom and economic security, would prefer the latter. They would rather
have both, but of the two, they would sooner sacrifice something of their freedom and enjoy the assurance of employment and stabilized social conditions, rather than enjoy
complete liberty of thought and expression in a world as
economically unstable as that following the First World
War. Propaganda efforts aimed at the German people,
offering them a restoration of their political freedom, will
have little effect unless linked with some assurance of an
order in Europe which promises them some sort of economic stability.

Practically all German soldiers believe, of course, that
Germany is completely justified in fighting this war. This
is not solely due to the propaganda which they have been
fed since Hitler came to power. The stories which Hitler
has spread—of the German military victory in the First
World War, the betrayal of it by dishonest politicians at
home, and the "iniquitous" Versailles treaty—would not
have succeeded so easily if they had not corresponded to
something which a large proportion of the German people
already believed. After the last war, no useful effort was
made by the Allies to win the support of the German people for democratic ideals and peaceful collaboration between European nations; German schools went right on
teaching the same glorification of military triumphs and

the soldier that they had taught before the war. Even a well-educated, "reasonable" German is almost incredibly ignorant of the most elementary facts concerning the last war and the period immediately following it. The German people believe that for decades they have been cheated of their rightful place in Europe, and they see this war as a righteous and completely justifiable means of winning that place. Their hatred of the British is, naturally, closely linked with their feeling of deception and frustration. The one irreconcilable enemy of the German people, they feel, is Great Britain. They see England as a "bloated financial octopus," and tell you, with a satisfied smile, that when they have taken all of England's gold and all of England's colonies, it will no longer be Germany which is the "poor, have-not nation." They do not make a distinction in their hatred, as the Russians do, between the British government and the British people. A very special brand of hatred, however, is reserved for the man whom they describe as "Germany's greatest enemy," Mr. Winston Churchill; Germans now firmly believe that he is a Jew. Again and again, as early as the summer of 1940, German soldiers told me smugly that they had positive information that a special airplane was in readiness, day and night, to take Churchill to Canada; the situation in England was becoming too dangerous for him, and he was preparing to leave the British nation to its fate. This was, of course, the story being spread assiduously by the German radio at that period. The German soldiers make no secret of the fact that, if they ever do set foot in England, there will be no question of fraternization and "friendly" treatment such as there has been in the Low Countries. Their hatred of England has been cultivated for so long and has grown so intense that I doubt whether their own officers would be able to restrain them from a display of savage brutality such as has not been seen in western Europe for centuries.

The soldiers' attitude toward America is chiefly one of indifference. They do not like the United States, and they feel that America's intervention in the First World War was a barbarous and unjustifiable attack on the peace-loving German people, but the hatred is a passive one, with more contempt than anger. The cocksure fanatics told me, with unwavering certitude: "America won't come into *this* war—there are no profits to be made from it!" The thinking German, however, was not so sure, and he merely told me: "I hope America won't come in this time; after all, it's none of her business." On the whole, their attitude toward the American people is considerably less hostile than toward the British people, owing at least partly to the fact that so many of them have relatives somewhere in the United States, and they know in many cases that those relatives are well off and reasonably happy. Some German soldiers even asked me, quite frankly—if American demo-plutocracy were as bad as their leaders assured them—how it was possible for people in America to be so prosperous, while they in Germany, working a great deal harder, had less; unfortunately, such men were the exception rather than the rule. All of them have a certain respect for American industrial capacity and mass production methods, but they are equally sure that no American machine could be as good as its German equivalent. Few German soldiers realized, at the time I left, the extent of current and proposed American aid to Great Britain. Their newspapers have played up conspicuously the anti-administration speeches of, for example, isolationist senators, often giving them almost as much prominence as speeches by leaders of the Nazi government. In a similar manner, they have given great importance to the activities of American organizations opposing aid to Britain, and at the time I left, German-controlled newspapers were stating flatly that no more material would be manufactured for the Allies in America, because American manufacturers were convinced that the war would end in Germany's favor so shortly that there was no point in fulfilling further orders. The newspapers made it quite clear, too, that the American public was solidly opposed to any sort of aid to Britain.

Viewed collectively, the German soldiers' attitude toward propaganda is difficult to comprehend unless one has encountered it at first hand; even now, I find it impossible to explain. In the month of June, 1940, they were told that London had been bombed on a colossal scale and practically destroyed; they believed this, and neglected no occasion to repeat it. Two months later, they were told that the first intensive raids were being commenced against London; this flat contradiction did not seem to worry them at all, nor did they even seem aware of it, and they believed the second story as enthusiastically as they had the first. If a report on Tuesday were the exact opposite of something announced with equal conviction on Monday, they altered their opinion accordingly but expressed no surprise at the discrepancy.

A recurring note in scores of conversations which I had with German soldiers was their almost hysterical fury at nocturnal British air raids. They, the Germans, were not cowards; they went to drop bombs in the daytime, in courageous and gentlemanly fashion—why couldn't the British play the game, and conduct themselves in the same way?

German bombs were dropped in daylight on specific objectives; the British came over in the dark and merely
threw bombs about at random. When the Germans, too,
began making night raids, this was, naturally, only a legit-
imate form of reprisal for British barbarity. The soldiers
were not so much worried about air raids which might
affect themselves; they were far more concerned about
the danger of bombs being dropped on their families back
home. This fear has almost become an obsession with the
German soldiers, and if anything ever leads them to lay
down their arms, it is very likely to be the feeling that
their families are exposed to grave danger from which the
Nazis are no longer capable of protecting them. From a
long-range point of view, aerial bombardments within
Germany are probably more important and more far-
reaching in their results than bombardments of troop concentrations in the occupied areas. The Germans, incidentally, have a very considerable respect for British pilots
and planes. On many occasions, I have heard German
fliers, anti-aircraft gunners and others, speak highly of
the ability of British pilots and the fire-power of R.A.F.
machines. Many members of the Luftwaffe also praised
Britain's ground defenses. They worried a great deal more
than might have been expected about the balloon barrage;
they told me that special planes went over at a great height,
directly before each important raid, to locate these bal-
loons and to bring some of them down, if possible. They
also seemed to feel that the British anti-aircraft gunnery
was a force to be reckoned with, both in quantity and
quality. One young pilot told me: "I have been over England seven times, and I don't know how it is possible that
I am still alive. Flying over England is horrible! It is ex-

actly like flying your ship against a steel wall." The German pilots spoke admiringly of British fighter planes; they would never admit that they were the equal of their own Messerschmitt 109 and 110, but British ships were, notwithstanding, adversaries worthy of their steel. The German fliers were convinced, however, that Britain did not have nearly enough planes, and that as time went by, she would have less and less as the Luftwaffe destroyed all of her manufacturing facilities.

The mechanicians, ground crews, radio operators and others were very much like any of the other German soldiers, and were often just as friendly and agreeable. The German pilots, however, were in a class by themselves; not so many of these came to our hotel, for with their high pay and extra bonuses for each flight, they were able to afford the best hotels and usually went there. I did, however, meet a considerable number of pilots, at one time or another, and arrived at the conviction that practically all of them were at least slightly mad. Most of them were taciturn and moody, and frequently, when they did talk to one, their conversation quite literally did not make sense; often I had the impression that their minds were definitely unbalanced. I am not suggesting that they were drugged, as has often been charged, for I have no evidence of that, but if they were not, one can only suppose that the nature of their training and activities has undermined in a large degree their mental stability. However, and this I can vouch for personally, they consumed limitless quantities of alcohol. When they were billeted in my hotel, they came downstairs already drunk in the morning, consumed a breakfast largely alcoholic, continued to drink during the day until it was time for them to report for duty, they returned intoxicated and continued to drink during the rest of the evening until they went to bed almost unconscious. Army regulations dealt severely with drunkenness among the soldiers, but I never saw a military police officer who dared to apply disciplinary measures to a flier. During the fighting in Belgium, I was told on several occasions, bottles of brandy were frequently found in the cockpits of planes that had been brought down. Whether this was true or not I cannot say, but I should not find difficulty in crediting it. Army fliers have never been noted for sobriety, in any country, and it would not be surprising if men whose work obliges them to bomb civilian objectives and machine-gun defenseless women and children should feel the need of an artificial stimulus. Politically, the pilots were probably the most rabid fanatics in the entire German military organization. With many of the German soldiers, one could argue quite intelligently and say pretty frankly just what one thought of the Nazi regime without any particular bad feeling on either side, but I never encountered a case of this sort among the fliers. Somewhat similar were the tank drivers, who, like the fliers, were a highly selected and trained group, no doubt chosen at least partly for their political reliability. I did not encounter many German pilots who appeared to be less than twenty-five or twenty-six years of age, despite many stories to the contrary. Some of the gunners, wireless operators, and the like, are much younger, and the presence of such youths in planes shot down over England may have given rise to these reports.

The general opinion of the great mass of the German soldiers about the war during the summer of 1940 was, I think, well summed up in the statement made to me by one of them: "Holland was a gift. For Belgium, we had to pay a small price. France has been expensive. As for England—well, I don't know what it will cost!" This I heard again with slight variations on several occasions. German soldiers were practically unanimous in asserting that the Dutch campaign had been literally "a walkover." They attributed this, on the one side, to the efficacy of their propaganda and Fifth Column organization, which had practically delivered the country into their hands, and on the other, to the unequaled striking power of the German concentrations of dive-bombers, against which, they confidently asserted, nothing on earth could stand up. The only exception to this opinion which I encountered came from a member of an armored train crew, with whom I talked during the first week of the occupation. Armored trains had played an exceedingly important part in smashing a breach in the Dutch border defenses, and this man told me that it would be a mistake to suppose that the soldiers on the Dutch frontier had not resisted valiantly. "Why," he exclaimed, admiringly, "I was forced to machine-gun some of them at a distance of fifteen feet from me; they wouldn't give in!"

After the Belgian campaign, the German soldiers expressed a certain amount of disillusionment; as soldiers, they admired the stubborn resistance which Belgium had put up in 1914, and they were somewhat astonished that the same army in 1940 had opposed them with relatively less determination. They showed no surprise at the outcome of the French campaign, since the whole object of the movement through Holland and Belgium had been to crush France, and they felt no astonishment that an offensive so carefully prepared should have succeeded; how-

ever, their remarks made it clear that the campaign had
been far less of a "walkover" than the rate of advance
might indicate and that their casualties had been many,
many times heavier than the official German announcements had claimed.

Faced by the possibility of having to make a direct attack on England, many of them felt, for the first time, I
think, a certain element of doubt. They were confident
enough of winning in the end, but they felt pretty certain
that the price would be a heavy one. Many of them hoped
that the submarine warfare and aerial bombardments
would bring England to her knees without the necessity
of an actual assault upon the island fortress.

So much for the generally held opinions expressed to
me by the great mass of German soldiers as I came in
daily contact with them during a period of five and one-
half months. There is nothing in them not already familiar, I realize, to anyone who has read the outpouring of
the German propagandists. They are not, however, the
whole of the story. What is infinitely more important, I
believe, is the difference between what the German soldiers
believed in May, 1940, and in October of the same year.
There were many such differences, and their significance
seemed to me very great.

As I have mentioned in other parts of this book, the
Germans entered Belgium in May with the unshakable
conviction that the war would be over in fifteen days. Military operations in France took somewhat longer than they
had expected, but peace was still just around the corner.
When, after the French capitulation, England failed to sue
for peace, they admitted that there would be a little delay,
since preparations must be made for the invasion of the

island, but the war would be over by August fifteenth. When that date, in turn, passed without the achievement of victory, I began to detect, for the first time, signs of weakened confidence by the German soldiers in their Leader. By September, there was no longer any mention of an end of the war "in fifteen days," and an increasing number of soldiers and even officers and pilots admitted to me that the war would not be finished in 1940—a revolutionary contrast to their attitude at the first moment of their arrival. This had a definitely unfavorable effect upon morale, for the great majority of the men wanted nothing so much as to go home. Some soldiers said to me, grimly: "If the war isn't over by winter, we'll go home and let the politicians do the fighting!" Again I must stress that I am not trying to create the impression that Hitler's army was, or is, ripe for rebellion—but the fact that even a few German soldiers made remarks of this nature represented such a sharp change from anything which had been said in previous months that it was definitely significant. Men began much more openly to criticize the Nazi regime, if not Hitler.

Somewhat surprising to me was the case of a German propagandist whom I met in September. Every unit in the German army and navy has directly attached to it its own press correspondent, newspaper photographer, motion picture cameraman, and radio commentator—a system which other armies might perhaps be well advised to emulate— and these men were not outsiders, but active soldiers or sailors with the specific assignment of carrying on their specialized work for the Propaganda Ministry. This propagandist, whom I met at the factory, expressed the greatest disgust with all things connected with the Nazi régime, except, as usual, Hitler, and made no secret whatever of his contempt for the German propaganda. On one occasion, while examining a recent German magazine, I called his attention to a remarkable photograph purporting to show a British ship being sunk by a torpedo. He looked at the photo indifferently. "After all," he said, "there is nothing whatever in the picture to prove that it was taken in 1940 —and not in 1914."

In September and October, I heard a constantly increasing number of expressions of lessened confidence in the Nazi régime and dissatisfaction on the part of the soldiers. The reasons for this were many and varied. The fundamental one, which I have mentioned, was that most of the men had been away from home too long, and had had enough. I am not a specialist in military questions, but I believe there is a very old principle, the soundness of which has never been questioned, to the effect: "Never leave your soldiers too long in a foreign country with nothing to do." Many historians feel that Napoleon's downfall really came, not at the Battle of Waterloo, but during the years when he left his men too long in Spain. It is fatal for soldiers to begin to ask themselves why they are fighting, and occupation troops have far too much time on their hands for the good of their own morale. Hitler is, in this sense, faced with a grave problem: if he leaves a regiment too long in one place, its members become much too friendly with the local population. To circumvent this, he moves them about frequently, but many of the men are specialists of various sorts, some hold key administrative positions, and once they have become familiar with conditions in a particular community it is inefficient to shift them elsewhere. A considerable proportion of the soldiers in Antwerp consisted of men who had been there since the beginning of the invasion, and who had formed many local friendships. From these Belgian acquaintances, they had learned a great many things not taught them by the German propaganda, and were no longer as certain of the indisputable rightness of the Nazi cause as they had been at the time of their arrival.

Another important factor was at work: life in Belgium was not as comfortable in October as it had been in May. Cafés were beginning to serve *ersatz* coffee, there was no longer chocolate to be found in the shops, nor any of that range of merchandise (such as they had not seen in years) to be bought with their easily-earned money. True, they still received good army rations, but the little extras that had made life so comfortable—more comfortable than many of them had ever known in civilian life at home— were no longer available. Winter was coming on again, and, surprising as it may seem, the German soldier's uniform protects him very poorly indeed against cold weather; many told me that they had suffered excruciatingly during the severe winter of 1939-'40.

So long as Hitler could give his soldiers one success after another, and so long as he could give them more material comfort than they had known in civilian life, their desire to go home remained in the background. When August fifteenth came and went without the promised victory, and then other dates for which the same promise had been given, their confidence wavered. So long as there are countries in Europe to be plundered and the booty distributed among the soldiers, so long can they be kept quiet and contented, but with the exception of Sweden and Switzerland, there is not a great deal left in Europe. A brilliant victory in some area or another would, of course, pull confidence up again, but I have the firm conviction that the morale of this German army can never be brought back to the exuberant point of the summer of 1940. There is not room here to detail all the evidence which I saw, in later months, of that drop in morale, but there was no question in my mind that it was genuine and serious.

Much more vital, of course, is the question naturally raised by such a statement: Will the German army revolt? It would be rash to give an uncompromising answer to that question, but there are definite signs that, given certain conditions, it might very well revolt. It is even more difficult to say what direction that mutiny might take. A young German naval officer said to me, one evening: "Do you remember where the trouble started in Germany in 1918?" I replied that so far as I could remember, it had started in the German navy—Kiel, wasn't it? "Yes," he replied, "and that is where it will begin *this* time. I don't know how far off it may be, but I can see it coming. Remember that a considerable proportion of the men in the German navy are from the peacetime merchant marine and passenger ships. They are men accustomed to traveling about the world; they know something more than what has been told them by the Propaganda Bureau. Except for the submarine crews, these men are getting nothing whatever to do, and idleness is always dangerous." I mention this for what it is worth; it proves nothing, but I had many such conversations before I left, and however remote revolt may be at the present time, it is significant that any German soldiers or officers think about it, and dare to say so.

Another opinion which I encountered with surprising frequency was typified by the unsolicited statement made to me by an officer one night in a café. He was of a rank somewhat higher than one usually encountered in public, and we fell into conversation when he lit my cigarette for me (my lighter having gone dry). Our talk consisted chiefly of the usual polite phrases about the war, until he startled me by saying, quite calmly, "Oh, Germany will soon be Soviet." Since I knew him only slightly, I did not press the matter further, to inquire exactly what he meant by this, but I encountered the same apparently sincere opinion on a number of occasions before my departure. After all, there is little in German character or history to justify a belief that any revolt which did occur in Germany would be in the direction of capitalist democracy in the western European sense. Whatever may be Hitler's motives for the initiation of socialist institutions in Germany, and for creating a hatred of capitalism among the masses, he has succeeded too fully to make it possible for another government to turn back.

If the British can prevent further spectacular successes by the Nazis, and win at least a few victories in some sector, time will continue to undermine the morale of the German troops. The Germans are behind the war because they believe that war pays; the moment they become convinced that this war, at least, will be unprofitable for them, their attitude will change. At the time I left Antwerp, the morale of the army was slowly declining; how far and how fast it will move, the future will tell. On one occasion, not long before my departure, some two hundred German soldiers were marched through Antwerp en route toward Germany, with hands manacled behind them. In such cases, we didn't ask indiscreet questions, but there was little room for doubt that these few men, at any rate, had already revolted; there were instances in which pilots at the Antwerp air field refused to go up and were shot by their officers. Such events were infrequent and their importance should not be exaggerated. In a few cases, fliers were accused of circling out over the North Sea, dropping their bombs, then returning and reporting sensational damage done in England; special flights began to be made by officers to check up on results reported by pilots.

More important, because much more widespread, was the fact that during several weeks before my departure, the German soldiers stationed in Antwerp were beginning to drink much more than was good for them. The regulations concerning drunkenness in public were brutally severe, and during the early months of the occupation it was rare to see an intoxicated soldier on the street. Before my departure, this situation had changed sharply, and on such evenings as I was out-of-doors in the blackout, I passed dozens of noisy, drunken soldiers, and even in the daytime one occasionally encountered them. During the first few months of the occupation, nearly every German soldier carried an automatic pistol, but from September, they were forbidden to carry sidearms in the city without special permission, which was granted only in case they must return home late at night along a route considered unsafe. A week before my departure, as I came out of a motion picture theater toward eleven o'clock at night, an excited German military police officer shoved a gun in my stomach and flashed a light in my face, then exclaimed, disgustedly, to another: "Never mind, Hans, it's only another civilian!" The implications were obvious.

The fact that so many German soldiers were beginning to drink heavily was, of course, a clear indication of their inactivity and its attendant state of mind. However, there was one other indication which I began to notice with increasing frequency before my departure, which seemed to me the most significant sign of all of a weakening in the morale of the Nazi military machine: an important number of the soldiers who came to my hotel began to listen to London on the radio. At first, this began as a joke; they wanted to listen to London merely to hear the ridiculous lies spread by the British Ministry of Hate; soon, however, they made no excuses, but simply listened in silence to the German-language broadcasts from London. It would be a great exaggeration to say that they believed everything that they heard; they did not, but they were beginning to compare what their own Propaganda Ministry had told them with what the enemy claimed, and they had taken the dangerous first step toward thinking for themselves—something very far removed from their state of mind when they had entered Belgium in May, 1940, confidently believing that a little nation of eight million inhabitants had brutally attacked the great German Empire.

X

Bombs in the Night

BRITISH BOMBERS FLYING OVER AT NIGHT, HIGH ABOVE
Antwerp, were something to which we were thoroughly accustomed by the autumn of 1940. During the first, static
phase of the war, R.A.F. pilots passed over the Low Countries frequently en route to Germany.

When Britain had recovered breath after the debacle in
Flanders, and began to raid German cities with something
more incisive than propaganda pamphlets, R.A.F. planes
flew straight across the water to Antwerp and on to Germany. With the Schelde, or Escaut, river forming a deep
harbor the city was easily recognizable from the air and
formed a convenient landmark, despite the blackout.

Not unnaturally, the Germans decided that Antwerp was
the place to try to stop the British fliers, before they could
reach German territory. Since all of the raiders flew over
at night, save for an occasional lone reconnaissance ship,
German planes could do little to stop them; for that matter, the German air force then had few pilots trained in
night flying.

Hence the burden fell entirely on the anti-aircraft gunners, and Antwerp was surrounded with what men in that
branch of the service assured me was the largest concentration of anti-plane artillery ever set up. I can well believe it.

Batteries ranging from machine-guns and quick-firing

three-quarter-inch pieces up to five-and-one-half-inch cannons were mounted in every available spot. (These are
approximate equivalents of the metric figures; the pom-
pom projectiles were twenty millimeters in diameter, and
the caliber of the heaviest pieces was one hundred and
thirty millimeters.) In parks, fields, gardens, courtyards,
in every section of Antwerp—on the city's lone skyscraper,
on the central railway station, near the barracks along the
canal—guns were mounted and searchlights put in place,
many of them material captured from the Belgians and repainted field gray. It sometimes seemed to me that loca-
tions in the immediate vicinity of schools, churches and the
like were especially favored—but perhaps that was only
coincidence!

In some cases the batteries were in plain view, in others
they were hidden with remarkable ingenuity. There was a
heavy gun near my hotel which frequently entered into
action at night; one could not mistake its nearness, from
the concussion and simultaneous flash which accompanied
each burst, but we never managed to locate it.

At first the gun emplacements were hastily improvised
affairs, only slightly camouflaged, but as time went by they
assumed an air of increasing permanence.

In general, a battery of guns and a group of searchlights
were mounted near each other. A typical unit was that
near my laboratory, in an open field between an apartment
house and a church. (The residents of the apartment house
were not very happy about it.) The searchlight was surrounded by a pyramid of earth, with a shaft in the center
which was covered over in the daytime, rendering the
whole extremely inconspicuous. The guns were housed in
a vague wooden structure, which had been erected for the

purpose, and might have passed for an abandoned shed. Inside it were two five-and-one-half-inch pieces and several pom-poms. The roof drew back at night. At the back of the field, perhaps seventy-five yards away, was a sort of observation tower not unlike the judges' stand at a country fair racing meet—a boxed-in platform supported at a height of some twenty feet. In the center of the field was a low wooden building, serving as headquarters for the battery, and admirably camouflaged.

So far as I was able to see, the men serving the guns— about twenty-five in the case of the battery I have described —had no bomb shelters whatever. Perhaps this was to discourage any thought of abandoning their posts when bombs began falling uncomfortably near.

During the month of August the number of these batteries seemed to increase constantly, and in the daytime one saw thousands of men of the anti-aircraft service on the streets of Antwerp, with their insignia of silver wings on a background of rose tabs. The guns rarely entered into action in the daytime, but one could never be sure what they would do after dark.

By an eerie coincidence, British bombers usually passed over at night just as I was listening to the London radio news bulletin. Sitting in my darkened room, shades drawn and door locked, with the radio turned up just loud enough to distinguish the words, I would suddenly become aware of the familiar faint purring sound of planes far overhead, on their way to Germany.

Sometimes they came and went without any sign of life from the anti-aircraft batteries; on other occasions, guns would burst into noisy activity on all sides at once, while searchlight beams crossed and recrossed the sky.

This depended in a large measure upon the visibility. On an overcast night, when it was doubtful if the planes could see Antwerp at all from the altitude at which they were flying, the guns often remained silent; as often as not, the searchlights remained dark; probably the intention on these occasions was to refrain from giving the R.A.F. pilots an indication as to their whereabouts. On a night relatively clear, or with clouds and patches of clear sky, and with moonlight, the passage of the "pirates" was greeted with a pyrotechnic display that must have made serious inroads into Hitler's "Winter Help" funds.

On such nights, as soon as the sound detectors indicated that the British "devils" were approaching, anti-aircraft guns of all calibers began putting up a wall of steel in the sky, firing at random in the general direction of the oncoming machines.

Meanwhile a score of powerful searchlight beams explored the heavens, some sweeping back and forth at random while other crept along the sky slowly and meticulously, with particular attention to patches of cloud which might hide the enemy.

The purr of smoothly running British engines, with a slight throb due to their being set just out of synchronism to keep dangerous vibration at a minimum, became louder and died away again. At short intervals my room was brightly lit for a split second as the nearest battery fired another shell, followed almost simultaneously by a dull, violent explosion which shook my windows, then, after a longer pause, came the dry sound of bursting shrapnel. Through it all continued the calm, correct accents of the B.B.C. announcer describing the raids of the previous night. Before the bulletin was finished, the bombers had departed and the guns were silent, sometimes for the rest of the night, sometimes to burst into deafening activity again as further waves of British machines passed over. Before dawn, they usually came over again, flying homeward. Lightened after the completion of their night's work, they flew higher than ever, and the German barrage was usually a brief and desultory affair.

Actually, at that time the best of the British bombers were able to fly more than a mile higher than the extreme range of the best German anti-aircraft guns (and higher than the German bombers, incidentally), so the only result which this furious expenditure of munitions had was to oblige the R.A.F. pilots to fly very high while approaching the coast. Under certain meteorological conditions this might be important, but there was no instance of a plane being brought down at night.

At that period the only real danger to residents of Antwerp was from falling bits of shrapnel, or from shells which failed to explode in midair and sometimes went off upon hitting the ground. The German anti-aircraft fire took no account whatever of the fact that what goes up must come down, and twice I was caught in the central street of the city with bits of shrapnel falling like rain, with the difference that as they struck the sidewalk sparks of fire flashed for an instant. A doorway was adequate shelter, but at such moments one did not feel especially friendly toward the German gunners who were thus sprinkling us with bits of jagged metal which fell back to earth with substantially the same velocity as that which they had when leaving the muzzle of the cannon.

In a few cases fairly serious damage was done to property by shells which exploded after falling back to earth, but there were no reports of any casualties.

Then, during the month of August, bombs began occasionally to fall in Belgium as well.

A paper mill near Antwerp, engaged in manufacturing cellulose for the Germans, was paid a nocturnal visit, and as an extra night shift was working to take care of increased orders, the number of casualties was rather high.

The Antwerp airport, being more than doubled in size and given a concrete surface to support the heavily laden German bombers, was raided repeatedly, though without great effect.

In a village near by, a British machine dived down in daylight and scored a direct hit on an anti-aircraft battery, killing the crew.

Several factories in Holland were heavily bombed, and bit by bit people realized that Antwerp's turn might come at any time.

Then came an incident which provided a topic of heated conversation for days: during one night, early in September, a bomb was dropped in the center of Brussels, beside the Bourse, killing a number of civilians and doing considerable damage.

The German-controlled press and radio made a great fuss of this newest example of the "savage barbarity of Mr. Churchill's pirates," pointing out that it would have been difficult to find a spot more remote from any possible military objective.

This was true, but, somewhat unexpectedly, proved too true for the Belgians to believe. My own immediate reaction when I heard the news was that after all, there was no proof that the bomb was British, and that it would have been quite in keeping with the methods of the Nazis, from the Reichstag fire onwards, to release the bomb themselves (perhaps from a captured British plane) in order to create unpopularity for the R.A.F., for which the Belgians were showing much too much enthusiasm. I learned, incidentally, that German soldiers had carefully gathered up and removed all telltale bomb fragments, immediately after the explosion and before daylight.

I did not say much of that suspicion to others, but to my surprise, nearly every Belgian I talked to during the day advanced the theory of a Nazi provocation.

That evening, a particularly offensive German sergeant, who was trying to get even drunker than he was in the restaurant of my hotel, said to me sneeringly:

"I suppose you think that that bomb was dropped on Brussels by the bad Germans?"

The complications which resulted from my reply are another story, which I have mentioned in Chapter Three, but it struck me as peculiar that a German under-officer, with no provocation on my part, should have made a statement of this sort.

There was no mention by the B.B.C., on the day following the bombing, of any raid on Brussels, so the whole matter remained rather mysterious.

A few days later, a similar incident occurred in Antwerp. A single plane, flying low, dropped a bomb in the direction of the central station. The explosive missile failed to hit the railway terminal and landed in the Jewish quarter just behind it, causing a number of casualties.

Again the same public reaction followed. Rightly or wrongly, Antwerp opinion was practically unanimous in declared that a German bomber was responsible.

Probably this was ridiculous; certainly there was no

proof that it was not the work of the R.A.F. The only fact perhaps a bit peculiar was that when this particular plane went over, not a shot was fired at it, though it passed directly over an anti-aircraft battery located on the roof of the station.

However, the significance of these two incidents lay, not in the truth or falsity of the accusations of Nazi provocation, but in the fact that so many Belgians were beginning to think the worst of the Germans, despite all efforts of the latter to win the friendship and confidence of the vanquished population.

At about this time, the German air force began to receive intensive training in night flying, a fact I learned from several of the pilots who frequented my hotel. It must be remembered that the great majority of the German fliers had a training which, if excellent in quality, was most limited in range. Most of the planes and pilots were intended for co-operation with the army in the field; these men were trained in short-range daylight flying but not in navigation by instruments.

When, therefore, planes began to circle the sky frequently at night, wing-lights illuminated to warn gunners on the ground that they were German, it was fairly clear that there would soon be night raids over England.

At about this time, early in September, I decided to move from my hotel near the waterfront to a location closer to my work. I cannot pretend that this decision was dictated by any occult powers on my part, though later events caused some of my Belgian friends to wonder if I did not perhaps have inside information.

My reasons were simple. I was spending an hour a day in the streetcar, going to and from work, and I needed this extra hour for the supplementary work caused by the absence of my staff. Originally, I had decided to live in the center of Antwerp, despite this long trip to the factory, because I did not relish the idea of spending my evenings in the little suburban town around the plant. Now, however, the blackout had ended the advantages of being centrally located in the evening; one practically never went out, and if one did, there was little to do.

The house on the corner near my laboratory, which had been struck and badly damaged on the morning the German invasion began, had now been repaired. I engaged a room there, and arranged to take my morning and evening meals with the proprietress of the bakeshop on the ground floor, as did several employees of the factory. I knew from them that she was well stocked with provisions, and food was becoming really scarce.

My first night was spent in a room in which two persons had been killed on the morning of May 10, my own room not being quite ready. I was not displeased, next day, to move into my own quarters. These were on the side of the building facing Antwerp, and along the skyline I had a clear view of the city, the harbor and the airport.

I moved away from the waterfront on September 8. On the night of September 13 came the first bombardment of the port of Antwerp.

I returned to my room that evening about nine o'clock, as usual, and sat down to work on a book on dyestuff intermediates which I was then writing. At about eleven o'clock there came the familiar droning of British airplanes flying high overhead—so familiar that I paid no attention to it, but went on working.

Gradually I became aware that the noise was not dying

away in the distance as it always had in the past. The planes were still there, and seemed to be circling about. Perhaps, I reflected, they were German, after all; this thought irritated me, for like everyone else in the war zone I maintained that I could recognize the sound of a British plane and distinguish it from that of a German ship, which always seemed to make a rather ragged sound; experts asserted that this was impossible.

I went to the window. The planes were invisible, and the blue-white beams of a dozen searchlights were exploring the sky.

As I watched, I became aware of an exceptionally bright star—bright enough to be a planet, but in the wrong part of the heavens at that hour. Staring at it, still thinking more of my chemistry than of this strange astronomical event, I gradually became aware that it was moving very slowly downwards.

I suddenly realized that I was watching a parachute flare drift slowly to earth, spreading a dazzling light. At that moment the German anti-aircraft batteries began a furious effort to shoot out the flare, and every searchlight in the sky swung over sharply to the area above it, seeking the plane which had let it fall.

The staccato bark of the pom-poms could be heard from all directions, and the black sky became alive with balls of fire—red, green, blue, yellow—which seemed to float lazily upwards like feathers in the breeze. Then the heavy guns joined in, and the earth shook with the fury of their explosions, each followed, as always, by a second burst, quite different, as the shell exploded in midair.

Still the parachute flare drifted slowly to earth, and before its light had burned out it was joined by a second, which seemed much closer.

It was clear now that Antwerp was about to be bombed —but where? Just across the street was the factory, a factory not working for the Germans—but did the R.A.F. pilots know that? A short distance away was the former automobile plant, now used for the overhauling and repair of Messerschmitts; would that be the target?

The sensible thing to do, I realized, would be to go down to the basement, the least sensible would be to continue to stand by the window—but the spectacle of the black sky pierced by the silvery beams of the searchlights, the blinding glare of the falling lights, the graceful curved lines of gaily colored tracer bullets drifting lazily up and disappearing in midair, and, near the horizon, the red flashes as the anti-aircraft guns fired again and again, all this was so overwhelmingly beautiful that I remained at the window. Forgotten for the moment were the shell fragments falling over the city and the explosives waiting to be loosed on our heads—I was watching a fireworks display that filled the whole of the heavens with a display more vast and lovely than any I had ever seen.

I thought of the pilots flying far out of sight, playing a desperate game of mathematical chance with the thousands of projectiles being sent in their direction, seeking to identify the target which would presently be centered in their bombsights. Idly I wondered if any of my friends were up there—several were in the R.A.F., including one of my fellow directors of the British color film company for which I was in Antwerp.

Then the horizon near the port was lighted up by a red flash, brighter than before, and there was a new noise—an ominous, rumbling burst, not followed by a second explosion in midair. The bombing had begun!

As I watched, the flashes came closer and closer together, and the sound of the bursting bombs became a continuous roll of thunder. The earth shook with the concussion as the anti-aircraft batteries redoubled their efforts,
all firing blindly toward that part of the sky whence the
bombs were falling. Here and there the persistence of the
red glow showed that incendiary bombs were getting in
their work.

Then the noise of the explosions ceased, the planes disappeared in the distance, the anti-aircraft batteries fell
silent, the projectors were extinguished, and only a flicker-
ing glow in the sky here and there remained to show that
the raiders had passed that way.

I seated myself to continue work, but before I had
reached the bottom of a page, the performance was resumed. Again flares drifted downward and tracer balls upward, with the fan-like projector beams waving slowly
back and forth. Again bombs rained on the harbor, somewhere near the spot where, only five days before, I had
been living. How many waves of bombers came over, I do
not know. At about two o'clock the noise ceased again. By
three o'clock I decided that they would not be back that
night, and I went to bed.

Next day, there was not a great deal of work done in
Antwerp. Everywhere, there was but one topic of conversation: the raid.

Sentiment that day was largely anti-British. Many persons had been pretty badly frightened, and the general
feeling was that night raids were a cowardly and brutal
form of warfare. A considerable number of civilians had
been killed, with little damage to military objectives, so

far as could be learned.

In the afternoon, I decided to take a walk through the district most heavily bombed—at the end of the Avenue of Italy, Naples Street, London Street, the Promenoir—provided that the Germans would let me.

I set out on foot from the center of Antwerp, fully expecting to find cordons of soldiers blocking entrance to the more seriously damaged quarters.

This was not the case, and for an hour or more I wandered freely along the waterfront and through the near-by backstreets which had suffered most heavily.

In Gas Street, a large house had received a direct hit and thirty-five civilians were dead. Here and there the roof of a house was blown away, sometimes the whole upper story was missing.

In the port itself, the amount of damage done was disappointingly small, and certainly out of all proportion to the size of the raid.

There was broken glass everywhere; scarcely a windowpane or a glass sign remained intact along the whole of the waterfront. People were beginning to sweep this up, and here and there were vast heaps of broken glass and rubble.

A few buildings had been seriously damaged. A bomb had burst just outside my favorite waterfront café, the Atlanta, smashing in the front. Another had struck a near-by apartment house, and in front of many buildings people were loading their worldly belongings onto handcarts and drays, unwilling to face the possibility of another such night of inferno. I knew many residents of this neighborhood; some of them had had miraculous escapes; two of my friends had not escaped.

As for the harbor itself, at which the attack had presumably been directed, there was no evidence of any damage whatever. All the important buildings were intact, with the occasional exception of missing windowpanes. Nowhere was there any serious evidence of explosion or fire. Even the warehouse, which had, out of sight on its roof, the largest concentration of anti-aircraft guns in the port, was unscathed.

There were rumors that five river barges had burned; if this were true, there were no traces remaining, and every section of the port was filled with hundreds of river craft of every description, some loaded with merchandise for Germany, others ready for the attempted invasion of England.

Continuing my walk, I saw a large number of German naval craft lying along the shore. At the Promenoir, I saw for the first time the five great German ships loaded and ready for the invasion attempt. Not one of these vessels bore the slightest indication of any damage.

My net conclusion was that if this were a fair sample of their marksmanship, there was not a great deal to be said for their night raids. So far as property damage goes, I had little reason later on to alter that opinion.

The description of the raid given that day from London by the B.B.C. was exaggerated and inaccurate in the extreme. Perhaps it was honest—perhaps, to the pilots flying miles above, that was the way it had looked—but Belgian listeners knew that it did not correspond to the truth, and their confidence in the British broadcasts was not strengthened.

These bulletins did make clear, however, that England realized what every person in Antwerp knew—that Ger-

many was about ready to try to invade the island kingdom
—and to that extent the Belgians admitted that the object
of the raid was a justifiable one.

That night the R.A.F. came again, and practically every
night thereafter for a week. After that the raids became
irregular, though fairly frequent. It is unnecessary to describe these other raids, for they all followed pretty much
the same pattern. Sometimes they came at ten o'clock in
the evening, sometimes at four in the morning—sometimes
once during the night, sometimes at long intervals.

The objectives were various—often the harbor, now and
then the airport, army barracks and the like—but nearly
always civilians and civilian property remained the chief
sufferers.

Some people were badly frightened by these raids, but I
never got the impression that their number was large. If
the bombs began to fall very close indeed, only a fool
would not be frightened, but most persons soon became
accustomed to the nightly visits and took them calmly.

The Germans had, by this time, constructed a considerable number of public air raid shelters, and some people
began to make it a practice to sleep in them nightly; these,
however, were only a very small portion of the population.
Others went into their own cellars during each raid. I never
did; once I had verified in what quarter the bombs were
falling, I went on working on my chemistry book. Looking
now at the notes I was writing, I find them surprisingly
neat and orderly, but here and there the pen has jumped a
bit, indicating a burst a bit closer than usual.

On one occasion I jumped right out of my chair when a
terrific explosion shook the whole house. It had been very
close indeed, and for a moment I thought of descending to

the cellar. However, there were no more near-by bursts, and I eventually went on working.

Next day, I learned that a British plane, caught in a searchlight beam and evidently hit, had jettisoned the entire contents of its bombrack at random. The bombs, apparently about a dozen in number, had struck a house in our neighborhood; fortunately, there were only three occupants.

My failure to take shelter was perhaps imprudent, but there was a considerable advantage in carrying on with work which absorbed almost my whole attention. After a little time, I really minded the raids very little. The most annoying was that one got to sleep very late, for there was little point in trying to sleep until the night's visit was over.

Curiously enough, the worst nights were those when the raiders did *not* come. Usually, they appeared at some hour between ten P.M. and three A.M., and since they rarely returned the same night, one could then go to bed and sleep. On the nights when they failed to appear, one waited impatiently until two or three o'clock, wishing to have it over with. Then one went to bed, but it was not easy to sleep, for one's ears were still listening for the faint droning sound that would herald another bombardment, and sleep was fitful and restless.

Each night, of course, other waves of bombers continued to pass over on their way to Germany, and one could never be quite sure when one heard planes, whether their goal was Antwerp or elsewhere. In either case the noise of the anti-aircraft fire made sleep impossible, and the room was brilliantly lit up by the glare of the explosions.

The most disquieting occasions, of course, were moments when a parachute flare was released directly over our heads, as sometimes happened. It did not necessarily follow that bombs would come after, but there was always the uncomfortable thought that the pilot might mistake us for something else. At such times, shrapnel would be bursting directly overhead, and the "flaming onions" would be curving upward to a point exactly above us, and I kept well back from the window. Not infrequently there would be bits of shrapnel in the street next day, and here and there a broken window in the neighborhood.

After the first resentment created by the raids had died down, public sentiment took a less anti-British turn. It must be remembered that at that time Germany was raiding England almost exclusively in the daytime, and while there were probably good reasons for the fact that the R.A.F. operated almost solely at night, the impression created at first was that the British lacked the courage to appear in daylight.

Gradually, however, the Belgians became aware of the obvious fact that they were being bombed because of the gray army in their midst. As they had no very high opinion of the bravery of the Germans, who shielded themselves behind the civilian population on every possible occasion —guns in front of churches, munition trucks in school playgrounds, supply wagons in public parks, tanks placed overnight near hospitals—they were less ready to criticize apparent British lack of courage. By October, one frequently heard Belgians express the hope that the R.A.F. would come often and hit hard, so that the war might end that much sooner.

The violently pro-German elements of the population of course lost no opportunity to condemn the "barbarity of the British," but such views became less and less common, and the majority of Belgians, while hoping that the raiders would "stay on the other side of town," were on the whole sympathetic to the R.A.F. At any rate, England was finally doing something, though disappointment was frequently expressed at the small amount of damage done.

Now and then a military objective was damaged. Official secrecy made it impossible to learn much about this, and the German-controlled newspapers gave only reports of civilian casualties and property loss. On one occasion, it was reported with fair reliability that a barracks had been hit, causing the death of several hundred German soldiers; on another, it was certain that a munition dump had been blown up.

The cumulative effect of the raids upon the German soldiers stationed in Antwerp was considerable. They had looked upon the occupation as a "soft assignment"; one soldier whom I knew had refused, shortly before the raids started, to take his leave in Germany because he felt so much safer in Antwerp. But all that was ended, and the occupation soldiers—many of them older men, with little taste for this war—now found themselves under fire. They did not like it very much.

One German acquaintance of mine was on sentry duty in the port the night of the first raid. I talked with him next day, and he was still jittery as he described to me the hail of incendiary and explosive bombs which had seemed to be falling everywhere at once.

Particularly affected were the young artillerymen serving the anti-aircraft batteries. While others took shelter they were obliged to remain beside their guns, knowing full well that every round betrayed their exact location to the enemy overhead. On one occasion a gunner from the battery near the factory—he could not have been more than eighteen—came into the bakeshop on the morning after a heavy raid, and tears streamed down his face as he described the horror of the night. I do not pretend that that case was typical—he was of a temperament which should never have been in so dangerous a branch of the service—but there were frequent instances which showed that the nerves of the troops were definitely affected.

Most of all, however, the German soldiers worried about the effects of British bombardment in Germany. Most of them had families, and this bombing of Antwerp made uncomfortably vivid to them the realization of what those at home were going through. They saw for themselves that civilians were the heaviest sufferers in night raids—and in Germany, those civilians might well be members of their own families.

On the Saturday night before my departure from Belgium, a German soldier billeted in the house next door to me blew his brains out. He had been home to Germany on leave, and there he had found that his wife and baby had been killed by British bombs and were already lying in their graves. With conscientious Germanic sense of duty, he had rejoined his regiment that day, and in the evening, with his service revolver, ended a life which no longer seemed to him to have a meaning.

Taken as a whole, I feel pretty certain that the most important result of the raids—perhaps the only important result—on soldiers and civilians alike, was the lack of sleep. I have been under bombardment by the German Luftwaffe and the British R.A.F. I did not go through anything comparable with Rotterdam or Coventry, but I saw enough to convince me that aerial warfare, taken by and large, is a most inefficient method of destruction, and that night bombing is an almost futile method of wrecking important objectives.

I do not pretend to be an expert on the matter, and I can only judge by what I have seen, but three points seem to me to be reasonably clear:

1. Bombing from a fast-moving and unsteady plane must in any case be far less accurate than artillery fire from a firmly anchored gun.

2. When the bomber is forced by anti-aircraft fire to operate from a height of several miles, the accuracy is greatly diminished. The best bombsight in the world will not seriously change this fact, since the effect of air currents and of refraction in strata of air of unknown temperature cannot be precisely allowed for.

3. When, in addition to the foregoing, the bombing is carried out at night, with accompanying loss of visibility, the accuracy becomes virtually nil.

There has been a good bit of hypocrisy on this matter. Even Mr. Churchill has pretended, in one of his excellent speeches, that R.A.F. pilots are obliged to descend to a reasonable distance from the ground before loosing their load of sudden death, so as to avoid hitting innocent civilians. I do not for one moment doubt that Mr. Churchill believes this, but I can assure him that it is very, very untrue. I wish it were not.

The chief sufferers from night bombing raids are civilians, and will continue to be civilians. I admit that this has been inevitable, but I should like to see a bit less pretending on the score of the results. Night raids are the most brutally barbarous weapon that the mind of man has ever conceived, and nothing will alter that fact.

Mathematically considered, the most effective form is that practiced by the Germans: large numbers of bombers flying in formation, dropping bombs at regular intervals over a wide target area, without consideration for individual objectives. Obviously, civilians are again the chief sufferers, but the mathematical probability of hitting important military targets would seem rather better. The German method is more coldly barbarous in its conception, since there is no effort or desire to spare the civilian population, but the results are much the same. Dive bombing apart, it seems to me the only method which causes a property damage proportional to the expenditure in explosives.

I have had the opportunity to discuss this question with refugees, both native and American, from Holland, Denmark, Germany, France and England—and all of them have told pretty much the same story: property damage sometimes serious but rarely commensurate with the quantity of bombs dropped and never more than a fraction of that claimed by the enemy bombing force; damage and casualties heaviest among the civilian population; in rare cases important results in terms of temporary hold-up of transport or closing of a factory for a week or two.

All of these refugees agreed on one thing: that the result of night bombing which most counted, in terms of winning or losing the war, was lack of sleep. Two things contribute to this: the maddening, deafening noise which accompanies a raid, and the expectation, waiting for the raiders to come. Of the two, the latter is perhaps the worse.

The noise and concussion of a raid must be felt; they cannot be described. The combined effect of bombs screaming as they fall, then bursting with an earth-shaking blast,

and the rattle and roar of anti-aircraft guns of every caliber, frays the steadiest nerves. Fear aside, the sheer physical effects are devastating. The man who has been through
a raid is not at his best for work, however great his determination and courage.

I saw this in Antwerp after only a few consecutive nights
of bombing. People were going around with eyes smarting
and red from lack of sleep; the man you talked to looked
at you dully, only half taking in what you were saying;
the man at work went about his duties mechanically, with
lagging steps and uncertain movements; people crossing
the streets just missed being run down by passing vehicles,
so great was their inattention. Translate that into terms of
industrial production, and the result must be an important
one.

The cumulative effects of too little sleep are profound
and painful. The police of many countries have long
known this: the strongest man, placed in a cell where a
powerful light burns day and night and awakened by his
jailers each time he falls into a fitful sleep, will sooner or
later tell everything he knows (and perhaps some things
which he doesn't) if only they will let him slumber peace-
fully.

To obtain the full effects of "air raid insomnia" it is obviously necessary that attacks over a particular district be
continued for a fairly prolonged period—often enough to
keep them awake, irregular enough to keep them lying
awake waiting on the nights the bombers don't come.

For this purpose, the smaller groups of British bombers
are probably as effective as the mass concentrations of German planes, and I believe that in the long run the results
in terms of lost sleep will, in this war of nerves, have

proved to be more important than material damage. So far as temperament goes, I would back the British to hold out longer against this than the Germans.

As for the civilians in the occupied countries, it is not unnatural that they should feel considerable resentment at the fact that they are exposed to the disturbance and danger of aerial bombardments. Whatever the outcome of the war, a great deal of bitterness will be left, directed against both sides. That, unfortunately, must always be the fruit of total warfare.

A point much criticized by the Belgians was the British claim that R.A.F. raids on the "invasion ports" must be carried out at night; the alleged reason being that the distances involved were too great to permit of fighter escorts, and that without these bombers would be helpless in the daytime. The logical Belgian mind pointed out that while this might well be true of R.A.F. raids deep in Germany, it was scarcely valid for a target in the Antwerp area, for example. If, they said, the Germans could take off from Antwerp with fighter escorts to bomb England in the daytime, why couldn't British fliers take off from England similarly protected to bomb Antwerp in the daytime, when they would have some chance of seeing what they were hitting?

There may or may not be a good answer to that question, but I mention it merely as an example of an opinion frequently met with and which British propaganda would be well advised to take into account.

Parenthetically, it seemed to me that all too frequently the British broadcasts to the occupied countries were based on the assumption that the entire population of those nations was dominated by an aggressive enthusiasm for the

British cause; this was especially true of programs directed at France, which made the fatal mistake of trying to tear down Pétain (who, however much his Fascist ambitions may justify such attacks, is nevertheless a popular idol of the French), instead of concentrating on venal politicians like Laval, whom the public know for what they are. I hope that as time goes on, British propaganda will take into account more adequately the real state of mind in the occupied areas.

Particularly vital is the matter of absolute accuracy in all news broadcasts. A great many persons are skeptical of all information given out by either side, though on the whole they attach more credence to reports from London than to those from Berlin; confidence in this respect can only be built up very slowly, but a small lapse suffices to tear it down.

One experience which brought this home to me vividly occurred shortly before my departure. I had remained in town in the evening, but left for home shortly before ten o'clock, while the streetcars were still running. As I came into the Meir, along the central avenue of Antwerp, a storm of anti-aircraft fire broke loose just over my head, and shrapnel began spattering in the street. Diving for a doorway, I watched a lone British plane try to escape from the crossed beams of a score of searchlights. (The Germans had just instituted a new searchlight technique, in which the crossed beams of projectors on all sides of the city traveled across the sky together, forming a brilliantly lighted space from which it was almost impossible for a plane to escape.)

Eventually the machine got away, but by that time the streetcars had stopped running. I set out on foot for the village of Oude-God, and during the hour and a half of stumbling through the darkened streets which followed, there were four raids. None of them was close enough to me to be alarming, but I soon discovered that however illusory the feeling of security indoors during an air attack, it was infinitely preferable to the great open spaces. The spectacle was a majestic one, but scarcely reassuring.

During the last raid, as I neared home, I paused to watch a bomber which had been attacking the port and was caught in the spider's-web of searchlight beams. As it turned and swooped in an effort to extricate itself from this desperate situation, the sky around it glittered with sprays of colored projectiles. Suddenly, as I watched, the entire plane glowed for a second, like a cigar sharply puffed, then dropped drunkenly to earth, its motors racing out of control.

Next day, I listened to London as usual. There was a description of the raids on Germany and the occupied ports, ending with the phrase: "From these operations, all of our planes returned safely."

The effect was unfortunate, whatever may have been the explanation, and I was by no means the only person in Antwerp to see the plane crash and later to hear the contradictory news report. I understand that there has been a sharp change of policy in this respect in London; I hope that this is true.

The Germans, to be sure, have no high regard for truth in their news bulletins, but they do go to considerable length to avoid too obvious contradictions. Planes leaving for raids over England usually take off in small groups from several fields; often a group leaving from one base returns to another. Thus even the pilots taking part in the raids have little knowledge of the extent of the losses, and airport workers practically none. However low the figures announced for the day, it is unlikely that any individual member of the air corps will know they are untrue.

If I have spoken critically of the British propaganda, because I would like to see it bettered, I should not like to leave the impression that it is entirely without effect, or that no one believes it. At the risk of being repetitious, it should be pointed out that great numbers of Belgians, for example, risk concentration camp to listen regularly to London; even if their confidence in the B.B.C. is qualified, they prefer it to the German-controlled stations.

One of the most successful of the British propaganda efforts has been the "build-up" given to Van Dyck, the Flying Dutchman. This war has been almost totally lacking, on both sides, in outstanding individual heroes, and the figure of Van Dyck is one of the few to capture the popular imagination.

When his mother and sister were killed in the German bombardment of Rotterdam, Van Dyck swore that every night, so long as he lived, he would drop bombs on Germany. Escaping to England, he joined the Royal Air Force, and since that time has done his best to keep his vow. He has become an almost legendary figure: when caught in the glare of the German searchlights, Van Dyck illuminates his wing lights, as though to say to the enemy, "Here I am! Why don't you do something about it?" He swoops low and machine-guns anti-aircraft batteries, and flies with a complete disregard for the most elementary prudence. Up to the time of my departure he was, despite his recklessness—perhaps because of it—still safe and sound, with a heavy price on his head. Each morning after a raid he came on the air from London in the Dutch broadcast with a familiar: "Hello, Adolf! How did you sleep last night?"

How Adolf had slept I don't pretend to know, but a good many of Adolf's compatriots had assuredly slept very badly—and I am sure that fact will, in the long run, prove to have been extremely important.

XI

Hitler Misses the Boat

To DISCUSS THE ATTEMPTED INVASION OF ENGLAND BY THE Nazis, as it appeared from Antwerp during the autumn of 1940, I shall be obliged at times to leave the domain of solid, verifiable fact for the more dangerous realm of hypothesis. Many of the facts are clear, but others will only be known after the war. One fact is that an attempt *was* made, in September, 1940, to invade the British Isles; how genuine was the attempt, and how far it got before it was stopped, remain the secrets of the German and British general staffs.

When the British army was encircled at Dunkirk, German soldiers leaped to the conclusion that the war was as good as over. Then the British army slipped out of the trap, escaping the promised annihilation. The German propaganda convinced the soldiers that this was a cowardly retreat and extremely unsporting of the British, who would, nevertheless, soon be compelled to make peace with the new masters of Europe. The German soldiers waited patiently for Great Britain to make peace, and as it soon became evident that she had no intention of doing so, it was necessary to tell them that England would be brought to her knees by other means. So, in a radio address which reached the whole of the German army, Hitler promised them a triumphal entry into London on August 15. Presumably he meant August 15, 1940, but he failed to specify the year. He was also vague about the method to be used, but it was generally assumed that he meant a spectacular invasion of the British Isles.

For some little time the German soldiers in Belgium, who were eager to have it over with and to go home, talked of little else. Men speculated eagerly on their personal chances of being chosen for the army of invasion, and hoped feverishly that they would. Some studied English in their spare time; others read up on English cathedrals and historic spots which they would visit—if it had not proved necessary to destroy them to make the British realize the folly of resistance. Soldiers leaving Antwerp for an unknown destination promised Belgian acquaintances, in all seriousness, to send them postcards from England.

One day during that period I was in a small jewelry shop, having my watch repaired, when a German captain entered and demanded to see diamond rings. As Antwerp is one of the diamond centers of the world, a considerable choice was spread out before him at prices which were, in view of the forced exchange rate, ridiculously low.

Critically he examined one stone after another, trying to bargain for even lower prices. At last he pushed the tray aside, remarking: "Probably I'll be able to do better in London."

There is no point to the story, save the fact that he definitely was not joking. Even an officer highly enough placed to have some idea of what was going on was completely confident of setting foot on British soil in the near future.

As the 15th of August drew near, it became clear that Hitler would soon have failed, for the first time, to keep a promise of conquest to his men. He explained that a great deal of preparation was needed for so difficult a task, and the date was set back to September 15.

By the middle of August, however, it had become abundantly clear that big-scale preparations for an invasion were definitely on foot. The first tangible sign was the mass commandeering of river barges.

These barges have played a vital part in the commercial life of the Low Countries for centuries. Along the canals and rivers and at sea, these great barges have carried a large portion of the imports and exports of Holland and Belgium. The bargee was usually a man who was born and raised aboard the boat, which belonged to his father before him and would pass on to his son when he died. Thus the barges represented something more than commercial craft; they were family estates, and when the bargees found the Germans taking their boats and paying them with paper money for which they would never be able to obtain another, as they believed, they were indignant—and being indignant, they talked.

Thus, within a very short time everyone knew that the Germans were seizing hundreds of barges in Belgium and Holland, and the obvious conclusion was drawn.

Soon there were stories of strange new craft, rebuilt from the confiscated boats. Three barges were placed side by side and fastened together securely at the bow and stern. Then a concrete deck was laid over the whole. The result was a weird contraption, nearly square in shape. In the opinion of the Belgian rivermen, only landlubbers could have imagined that such a boat could have any practical utility, so unwieldy and cumbersome was it.

Reports told, soon after, of extensive maneuvers off Holland, witnessed by German general staff members and intended to establish the value of the new craft. The whole affair was shrouded in the greatest secrecy, but could not be carried out without the help of Dutch rivermen and tugboat crews, and a certain amount of information leaked out, indicating that the results had been disastrous. There had been collisions and one boat had sunk, with loss of life.

Perhaps the unfavorable showing was due solely to the poor navigability of the triple-barges—but it is not unlikely that the Dutch crews had a hand in it. Credence is given to that idea by one incident which occurred during the tryouts, and which I had from a maritime officer:

One of the tugboats towing a barge laden with soldiers, not far off the Dutch coast, became somewhat separated from the others. No particular attention was given to this in the general confusion and disorder which marked the trials, until it was realized that it had disappeared. The tugboat captain towed the barge well out into the North Sea, then cut the hawser and left it to drift helplessly— while he sped for England, where it was believed he arrived safely.

All such stories are slightly apocryphal, under conditions of wartime censorship, unless one has oneself witnessed the events in their entirety. However, my source was a fairly direct one, and if the story be true, the Dutch captain may have had a good bit to do with informing the British of the extent and nature of the invasion plans, resulting in the intensive bombing of the channel ports which began in mid-September.

Early in that month, a sudden increase in the number of German sailors on the streets of Antwerp made it clear that several naval craft had arrived in the harbor. I had no occasion to visit the port for a few days, and it was not

until the R.A.F. raids focused attention on the invasion
preparations that I took a walk through the harbor and
realized the full extent of the German moves. All along
the docks, half hidden by the sheds, were lying small naval
craft. At the Promenoir, tied up at the passenger dock
where the great ships coming from the Congo had once
put in, were five merchant liners. Residents of the harbor
district told me that for days the Germans had been loading supplies, artillery, light tanks, motorcycles, munitions,
machine-guns and military material of every type on these
ships, and that a large number of soldiers were already
quartered on board.

All five ships were camouflaged from stem to stern—
camouflaged in a manner reminiscent of the last war, and
which in this conflict I have not seen before or since. The
sides were painted with huge black and white geometrical
shapes, conspicuous curved and angular areas recalling a
constructivist painting, and, curious detail, on one the silhouette of a whale, spouting a vast jet of water.

There was no effort at concealment of these preparations; the Germans seemed always to go on the theory that
no one could leave Belgium and no one could communicate with the British, so that there was no reason for trying to prevent the civilian population from seeing what
was going on. For the most part, they were probably right.
In modern warfare, and under a totalitarian régime, it is
possible to cut off communication with the enemy so completely that the old need for secrecy does not exist, with
consequent simplification of military moves.

From the latter part of August, "invasion troops" began
arriving in Antwerp in great numbers. My new residence
was on the main highway leading into Antwerp, and each

evening, sitting in a near-by café, I saw thousands of them pass. They were mountain troops, Bavarian and Austrian, wearing the same uniform seen in photographs of the operations in Norway, with a soft, peaked cap. Many of them were in small, fast motor vehicles with wheels and a caterpillar tread, other units were on foot. They came at dusk, when there was enough light for their movements, yet little enough to render the field gray uniforms and equipment almost invisible at any reasonable distance.

By the middle of September, more than 100,000 of these mountain troops were in Antwerp, and we knew that there were large concentrations in other occupied ports as well. A high official of the hotel association told me at that time that more than 20,000 officers, newly arrived for the invasion, were quartered in Antwerp hotels.

The invasion troops had with them a large number of mules, not unnatural for mountain units, and these were put aboard the ships in the harbor.

Billeting facilities were badly strained by the arrival of so many additional soldiers, and many of the Austrians and Bavarians were quartered in my village. They were young, for the most part, and few of them seemed fanatics on the subject of Nazism. Mild-mannered and pleasant, they were very different from the shock troops which had passed through Antwerp at the outbreak of the war in Belgium. They made no secret of the fact that they were there to invade England, but I cannot say that they seemed especially happy about it. On the contrary, many of them felt that they, the vanguard of the invasion, would undoubtedly suffer terrific casualties.

Few of them had ever been in a boat, and the German command obviously realized that seasickness would hit them heavily, for one of them showed me a powder which had been issued to all and which was to be taken at the moment of embarkation as a preventive measure.

Nearly two weeks before the commencement of intensive R.A.F. raids showed that Britain was aware of the situation, an incident occurred in Antwerp which indicated that an invasion attempt might be very near.

On September 1 and 2, "the invasion of England" was filmed for the German newsreels in the harbor of Antwerp, with the bathing beach at St. Anne serving to represent the shores of Albion. St. Anne is directly across from Antwerp, on the opposite side of the Schelde River which forms the vast harbor, and is a favorite spot for excursionists during the summer.

Here, for two days, invasion barges drew in to the shore and men leaped into the shallow water as light tanks and motorcycles sped from the concrete decks to the sandy beach, firing as they went. One of the men in charge explained to me the reason:

"You see," he said, "when we invade England it will be at night, or very early in the morning, and there won't be enough light to photograph it. Since this will be the decisive event of the war, it must be covered for the newsreel—so we're staging it here, exactly as it will be done later on the English coast."

It struck me at the time that in staging this film the Germans were rather leaving out one of the principal actors, and that the British might have something to say about the writing of the script when the time came for the real life drama, but I kept this thought to myself. Very probably the "invasion," as staged at St. Anne, served a double purpose, being as much a dress rehearsal for the military authorities as a convenience for the propaganda department. A considerable number of Nazi generals, with red stripes down the sides of their trousers, watched the entire operation from beginning to end; when it was over, they did not look too happy about it. None of those connected with the affair seemed to feel that it had gone off especially well, or that it promised overmuch for the success of an eventual attack along these lines.

So much for the evidence visible in Antwerp in September, 1940, that Germany intended to attempt an invasion of the British Isles, based on direct observation. It leads, logically, to two important questions, in the discussion of which I must rely on a careful sifting of indirect evidence:

1. Did the Germans attempt to invade England in September, 1940? If so:

2. Was the attempt a genuine, bona fide one?

My answer to the first question would be "Yes," and to the second, "Probably not."

As this will undoubtedly seem a bit contradictory, it will be necessary to consider briefly such elements of the situation as came to my attention before leaving. The most significant were the following:

At a given moment, a large portion of the invasion troops left Antwerp for an unspecified destination.

When I left, there were a great many badly burned German soldiers in the hospitals of Antwerp.

During the first weeks of October, the bodies of hundreds of German soldiers were being washed ashore along the Belgian coast, especially in the vicinity of Ostend. Many of them were so badly burned as to be almost unrecognizable.

ENGLAND IN ANTWERP

The waterfront section of Antwerp. On the opposite side of the Schelde River is seen the beach used to film the "invasion of England" for the German newsreels in September, 1940, as described by the author.

(*Photo from Wide World*)

Many of the invasion barges were missing, although the naval craft and merchant liners were still in the harbor, their number having been increased by fresh arrivals.

None of these facts, taken alone, could be taken as proof that an attempted invasion actually took place. Taken collectively, they all point in one direction. I believe these facts to be exact. I first learned of the burned patients from a Belgian nurse working in an Antwerp hospital; Americans living near Ostend confirmed reports of bodies being washed ashore. Later, I heard these stories scores of times, which proves nothing—but it was extremely significant that reports from the most widely scattered sources were unanimous on one point: that a considerable number of German soldiers had been badly burned.

Later, en route to Lisbon, in Lisbon and aboard the "Exeter," I had the opportunity to compare notes with persons coming from other invasion ports and from England, and putting together all of the corroborative evidence, it seems to me an overwhelming probability that the following took place:

On or about September 16, a considerable force of towed triple-barges set out from a point along the Belgian coast, constituting the first wave of the attack, which was to occupy a strip on the English coast at which liners could put in and disembark the invasion troops.

At a point probably not far from the Belgian coast, they were spotted by the British. Destroyers of the Royal Navy then managed to cut them off, and forced them well out into the North Sea. Here planes of the R.A.F. dropped oil drums with great quantities of oil on and near the barges, then followed with incendiary bombs which turned the whole into a blazing inferno.

Although very probably true, this story leaves a number of points unexplained. The question arises, for example, "What was the German air force doing while this was going on?" However, the same thing happened at Dunkirk; for if the Germans had been able to adapt themselves quickly to an unexpected situation, and had put into the air a concentration of planes such as they could easily have mustered, there would have been no British army to evacuate—but they failed to do so. Similarly, the Germans seemed so certain that by choosing suitable conditions of poor visibility they could land in England unperceived that they failed to make much preparation for the alternative possibility. As the barges were very slow-moving, the planes were doubtless to take off much later, so as to arrive at the coast in time to smash any resistance which the troops might encounter in landing.

So much for the September attempt at an invasion of England. Did the German high command really expect it to succeed? Was the attempt a sincere one? I have already indicated that I do not think so; before I left Antwerp, I came to the conclusion that Germany's real goal lay to the south—in the Balkans and along the Mediterranean—rather than across the Channel. My reasons for that were many.

For one thing, it did not seem reasonable to me to suppose that if the German high command felt that an invasion attempt had any serious chances of succeeding, they would pick for the assault the poorest of their available troops. The Austrian and Bavarian soldiers who arrived in Antwerp for the purpose were among the least warlike in the whole of the German army. As in 1914, the Austrians and Bavarians lack the military temperament; they were already nervous about the outcome when they arrived in Belgium. Since it required no great acumen to realize that British resistance would be terrific, the choice of the mildest and least aggressive of all the German forces to storm the English defenses did not seem to indicate that the high command thought the invasion scheme sufficiently important or sufficiently feasible to risk the picked shock troops which had already suffered so heavily in France.

The soldiers sent to Antwerp, ostensibly as invasion troops, were not only second-rate military material but were of doubtful political reliability as well; enthusiasm for the Nazi cause has never been as high among Bavarians and Austrians as in other sections of Hitler's empire. Their only special qualification was the fact that they were mountain troops, and equipped as such; the choice of such men suggested that the invasion attempt was perhaps to be in one of the more rugged portions of the British Isles, such as Scotland, rather than in the south.

Another element in the situation which seemed to me to indicate that the invasion plan was not serious at that time was the absence of air attacks on the scale to be expected. German officers and Nazi officials, with whom I discussed the invasion, invariably advanced the opinion that the attempt to land in England, when it came, would be preceded by an aerial bombardment on a scale dwarfing anything yet seen in the war, so as to "flatten out" completely a large area for the debarkation of the mechanized units and shock troops. The figure of 20,000 planes was frequently mentioned. Hitler could not put this many first-class ships in the air at one time, but for a raid on such a scale almost anything capable of carrying a few bombs could be mustered into service. The matter of airport facilities for the loading and take-off of so many machines would be more serious, however, and in September, 1940, the Germans were still engaged in laying out new fields and enlarging the old ones.

The arrival in Belgium of two thousand Italian fliers and mechanics also seemed to me significant, coming, as it did, at a moment when German pilots were being transferred elsewhere in considerable numbers. Such a move presumably meant one of two things: a shortage of German flying personnel, or a transfer of Nazi pilots to a theater of war considered more vital than the channel ports. Since there was nothing to support the view that Germany was running short of aviators, despite considerable losses over England, it was far more plausible to suppose that the Italians were taking over to release German groups for service elsewhere. The Germans have no high opinion of Italian fighting ability, and it was highly improbable that they would have been brought to Belgium if really important operations were planned in that sector.

Although the Nazi politicians at that time were continuing to promise the soldiers a speedy and victorious termination of the war, everything indicated that the German high command had no illusions on that score. Large-scale construction of air raid shelters, long-term contracts for military supplies, expansion of certain factories, extensive building operations—all of these, carrying well into 1941 and even beyond, made it clear that the general staff saw no rapid end to the war.

Only two things could have justified a vast invasion move at that time: first, that it be successful, and second, that the war, as a consequence, be brought to an end. The higher German officers were inclined to skepticism on both points.

Concerning the success of the operation, there was a considerable weight of authority in military circles back of the opinion that for Germany, without a navy worth mentioning, to attempt an essentially maritime operation while the Royal Navy was still afloat was to invite disaster. The only factor, they argued, which could perhaps compensate for such a shortcoming would be complete control of the air—and while in September, 1940, the R.A.F. was badly strained, it was by no means a negligible barrier. The coastal defenses of England had been greatly strengthened and her army reorganized; from a military point of view, the difficulty of invasion had increased enormously between June and September.

It seemed clear that an invasion would be a costly operation, in men and material, and it could be justified, even if successful, only if it brought the war to an end—and the German command was becoming increasingly dubious on that point as well. There was still the British Empire, and they were more concerned with smashing that than with wrecking the British Isles.

Faced by the inevitability of a long war, the German militarists were chiefly interested in food and raw materials. The capture of Britain would bring them relatively little, for she herself was dependent on imports. The Balkans and the African colonies were another matter, and I left Belgium convinced that Germany's immediate drive would be to the south. For several weeks before my departure there were heavy troop movements—greater than any since the lull after the fall of France—through Antwerp, across occupied France toward the Spanish border;

other divisions were, it was said, moving toward the Balkans. All of which scarcely indicated an imminent invasion of the British Isles.

Assuming, then, that the invasion attempt in September, 1940, was only a half-hearted one, the question arises: why was an attempt made at all?

The first and most obvious reason was that if Germany did intend serious moves to the south, she would quite naturally try to make it appear that she meant to strike elsewhere. By creating the impression of vast preparations for an invasion, Germany forced England to divert a considerable portion of her war effort to coastal defense, attacks on the channel ports, patrolling of all approaches to the British Isles, and other anti-invasion moves. This tied up a large part of the British sea, air and land forces to protect England against what may well have been only a feint.

Another important possibility is that the whole invasion scheme was carried through because of pressure from Nazi leaders and against the wishes of the military chiefs. Hitler had promised his soldiers an early entry into London, and for political reasons it was highly desirable to keep that promise. He never allows his men to remain idle too long; idle soldiers sometimes began to ask why the war must go on. An invasion attempt would keep many divisions occupied for months.

Perhaps, too, Hitler thought he knew better than his generals, and believing that England could be invaded at that time, forced his generals to make an attempt. There would be nothing surprising in this, for such differences of opinion have been common in the past. If this were the case, the half-hearted nature of the invasion project may well have been due to the conviction of the high command that it was doomed to failure; if so, they quite naturally refused to risk their best troops. The Bavarians and Austrians were selected as "guinea pigs" for the experiment, since their loss would not greatly affect Germany's military strength.

There is ample precedent to support such a theory. Poison gas was tried out by the Germans in the last war against the desire of the general staff and under pressure from the Kaiser. Because the high command was unconvinced and hostile, no preparations were made to take advantage of possible success; after the first gas attack, reports of the German intelligence officers that in several miles of the front not an Allied soldier was left alive were not believed—and Germany lost the chance to end the war. Perhaps, in the same manner, the invasion effort was made simply to demonstrate to Hitler that the scheme was not, for the moment at least, a workable one.

A detail which may seem trivial, but which struck me at the time as significant, was the manner in which the troop ships in the harbor of Antwerp were camouflaged. As I have already described, they were painted in a manner reminiscent of the last war rather than typical of this. Camouflage of this sort was tried out in the early years of the First World War without notable success, and in the present conflict there had been no indication of any attempt to revive the "cubist" manner of painting ships to render them inconspicuous.

The German camouflage was of a very high level of excellence, and when I saw five troop carriers painted in a manner which seemed to heighten rather than diminish their visibility, I could not refrain from wondering whether the German command did not *want* British reconnaissance machines to see them. If the invasion plans were largely a feint to divert a large part of England's war effort in a false direction, it was essential that Great Britain be aware of the preparations, and many details, trivial in themselves, suggested that this was the case.

Even if it be true that a considerable force was destroyed by oil and incendiary bombs, as I believe, it does not inevitably follow that a serious invasion attempt was being made. Nothing precludes the possibility that after the rehearsals held off Holland and in the harbor of Antwerp, further trials were being made at sea to accustom the troops to actual maritime conditions.

If a serious, full-scale attempt at an invasion of the British Isles does eventually come—and it would be highly imprudent to assume the contrary—it will be when the German high command feels that submarine attacks on British shipping and mass aerial attacks on industrial centers have sufficiently weakened the defenders of the island fortress to make possible a smashing victory. Until such a conviction of success exists, Germany will not risk an attempt to storm the fortress; failure of a widespread offensive might easily destroy Hitler's prestige with the soldiers and even bring about his downfall.

In connection with the possibility of an invasion of England at some future date, it is necessary to speak of one matter which would be extremely grave, if true. Conversations with several German fliers and flying personnel during the weeks immediately before my departure indicated a definite possibility that somewhere in the remote regions of Ireland are German aviation bases, submarine bases, and perhaps even a certain number of soldiers ready to aid when the time for an invasion comes.

My first suggestion of this came from a flying officer whom I knew rather well. He dined at my hotel frequently, and for a fortnight or so his visits ceased. When he returned, I asked him, merely to make conversation, if he had been home on leave.

"Oh, no," he said, casually, "I've been living at one of our bases in Ireland for a few weeks."

I treated his remark as a joke, and intimated that he was telling a rather tall story—but he refused to be shaken, and gave a number of corroboratory details. (As I have mentioned, the Germans in Belgium made little secrecy of their movements, assuming that we could make no use of any information they might disclose.)

I dismissed the whole matter from my mind as too fantastic to be possible, but before I left several similar remarks left me wondering whether it were as impossible as I had thought. There was no suggestion of any official co-operation from the Irish government, but the outlawed I.R.A. might well have been able to establish small flying fields in remote parts of the country, which would be extremely valuable to the Germans in spotting British convoys and summoning submarines operating from near-by clandestine bases.

It is to be hoped that the whole story is a myth which has grown up in the German flying corps and among navy men. If not, and if it be true that a small, picked body of German soldiers is already in Ireland, it is obvious that these men could play a significant role in co-operating with an invasion force.

I feel convinced, however, that when I left Europe the chief military aims of Germany were to the south, and that the Balkans, northern Africa and Spain are likely to be the theater of the next stage of the war. The whole matter is too uncertain to warrant a prophecy, but I would not be surprised if one of these—perhaps Spain—should prove to be the field on which the war is finally decided. The fact that the Italian end of the Axis is likely to crack first lends added support to this hypothesis—but it remains a hypothesis only, and there would be no justification for lessening the constant vigil along Britain's coast.

XII

Conducted Tour: Brussels-Lisbon

EARLY ON THE MORNING OF OCTOBER 7, I RECEIVED A
Special Delivery letter dated the sixth, and reading as
follows:

"SIR:
"Permission has been granted by the German Government for
a group of American citizens desirous of returning to the United
States to leave Belgium at an early date. You are urged therefore
to present yourself not later than Tuesday morning, October 8,
at nine o'clock at the American Consulate, 27, avenue des Arts,
Brussels, in order to make arrangements for the journey. It is pre-
sumed that after making the necessary arrangements with a representative of the German travel bureau you will be able to
return to your home if necessary before departing for the United
States.
"It is strongly urged that all American citizens in Belgium
take advantage of this opportunity to go to the United States
since it is probable that no further permission will be granted.
                    "Very truly yours,
                                    WILLIAM H. BEACH,
                                    American Consul."

I did not feel as elated by the receipt of this letter as
might have been expected. I was familiar with the general
progress of the negotiations which the consulate had been
carrying on with the Germans, and I knew the most recent
proposal, which was that the journey should be arranged
by Mitropa, the official German travel agency, and that the
entire trip from Antwerp to New York would have to be

paid in Belgium in American currency. I assumed that this was the arrangement referred to in the latter, and it was of no help to me, whatever. I had pound sterling in London, but no possibility of laying my hands on it—no chance of receiving dollars from America—no legal possibility of buying any foreign money in Belgium—and even the wealthy corporation which owned the factory where I was working could not, with the Germans in control, lay its hands on a single dollar.

My first thought, therefore, was to throw the letter in the wastebasket and go to work as usual. I was very busy just then with the syntheses of some new lightfast dyestuffs, and I had little wish to waste four hours in the train to and from Brussels, and perhaps several hours more at the consulate, on a fruitless errand. I soon thought better of this, however, for the letter offered no real clue to the nature of the arrangement proposed by the Germans, and I decided to visit the Antwerp consulate, where some of my friends would surely know enough to enable me to decide as to the usefulness of carrying the matter further.

A half hour later, I was in the office of Dwight Fisher, the vice-consul, who told me that the Consulate General was as ignorant in the matter as I. A hasty message from the Brussels consulate had given the information which had been incorporated in the above letter; the German travel agent would give further details directly to the interested parties; the consular staff had worked most of the previous day, Sunday, getting the letters out to all Americans in the Antwerp area. I expressed some annoyance at the idea of being obliged to go to Brussels merely to find out the nature of the conditions, which the German travel agency could easily have put in the form of a circu-

lar letter, but Fisher urged me to do so, despite the inconvenience. The German officials had made it pretty clear,
he said, that anyone who did not leave now would have
to remain until the end of the war; no further permission
would be granted.

Not wanting to arrive in Brussels during the lunch hour,
I waited until noon, then took the electric train for the
capital. I arrived at the consulate soon after two o'clock.
The German travel agent, a Mr. Rummelspacher, was just
going out to keep an appointment, but promised to return
at three. I settled down to wait. Just after three, Mr. Rummelspacher returned, and toward four I was able to see
him. The conducted tour would leave Brussels by train in
about ten days, and would be accompanied by an agent
of Mitropa all the way to Lisbon; members of the tour
might take one piece of registered baggage, not too large,
and two small pieces of hand baggage; the price of the
trip, which would include meals and hotels en route, was
payable in Belgian currency only, or, of course, German
occupation money; this eliminated for me the insoluble
problem of raising foreign currency.

So far, so good; the price of the tour, equivalent to
about one hundred dollars, was extremely moderate, and
it seemed probable that I could get it together by Thursday
morning at nine, the three-day time limit fixed for payment. However, there was a complication, and a formi-
dable one: in order to obtain a Spanish visa, one must be
in possession of a Portuguese visa, and in order to obtain
the latter, one must have a reservation on a boat leaving
Portugal. The only means of obtaining a boat reservation,
in Brussels, was through Mitropa. This would be nearly

three hundred dollars, but would be payable in Belgian currency, also.

The list for the Brussels-Lisbon trip would close Thursday morning, and if I wished to be included in that list, I must bring him, not later than Wednesday morning, a substantial deposit. I made a rapid calculation: I would arrive back in Antwerp too late that evening, Monday, to do anything further; I must raise the money during the day on Tuesday, then take the nine-thirty-seven train from Oude-God on Wednesday morning, in order to arrive in time. I was not optimistic about the chances, but I was prepared to attempt anything.

I spent all of Tuesday raising the money for the boat reservation, by means irrelevant to this story; by the time I had closed the arrangements, the cashier's office was shut for the day, and would reopen at nine the next morning. At nine o'clock I was there, waiting, when the office opened —only to learn that the cash-box was brought in punctually at nine-thirty. This made the whole thing pretty hopeless; the station was a brisk twenty minute walk, and the last train which would get me to Brussels under the deadline was due to leave at nine-thirty-seven. However, I could only try, so I waited in an agony of impatience. At nine-thirty, the cash-box was brought; at nine-thirty-two, the money had been counted out, the receipt signed, and I was out the door. I sprinted across back-lots and through back-streets at a rate I had not attempted in years, and arrived at the station at nine-forty-two, just five minutes after the train had, supposedly, pulled out. I dashed into the station—and learned that the train was six minutes late!

The train lost more time before Brussels was reached,

and when I arrived at the consulate, Mr. Rummelspacher had just departed. For a few minutes, it seemed as though my chance of leaving for America had also departed. Then Mrs. Grant, of the consular staff, volunteered that she could give me the address of Mr. Rummelspacher's hotel. He had said he was going out to keep an appointment, but there was just a chance that I might still catch him.

In twenty minutes I was at the travel agent's hotel, and met him as he was just leaving by the front door. He accepted the deposit with good grace, gave me a receipt and placed my name on the list. The first difficult step was "in the bag."

Only the first step, however. This was Wednesday, and next morning I must again be in Brussels with another important sum of money, which I did not yet have, nor did I even have any certitude that I would be able to raise it. So I hastened back to Antwerp—two hours of standing in a train crowded like the New York subway at six P.M.— and continued my efforts of the previous day. I was miraculously lucky—any other phrase would be a rank understatement—and by evening I had the funds in hand for the remainder of the passage money and the conducted tour to Lisbon, though I had had to sacrifice property worth several thousand dollars to raise it.

Thursday morning, I was at the station in comfortable time for the nine-thirty-seven, only to learn that the entire train schedule had been altered overnight, and that the next Brussels train making a stop in Oude-God would be in at ten-thirty. It was too late to get to Antwerp to catch the train leaving there at nine-thirty-two, and I settled down to wait, wondering whether, after having been so lucky thus far, I would still manage to get under the wire, somehow. When I eventually arrived at the consulate in Brussels, I was relieved to find Mr. Rummelspacher still there, and although he was somewhat bad-tempered about the delay, he accepted my application and money. I was on the list, but the date of departure was not yet fixed; everyone was asked to meet at the Brussels consulate a few days later to learn the decision of the German command.

Meanwhile, there was a new complication: Berlin had decided that Belgian currency could not be accepted for steamship tickets, which must be bought in dollars. Transactions in foreign currency were not permitted in the occupied territory, either—so there was no possibility of arranging ocean transport in advance. Mr. Rummelspacher refunded the deposit paid, in return for a signed agreement to book through Mitropa in Lisbon. I had sold a quantity of valuable equipment at a terrific sacrifice to raise the necessary Belgian francs, which were now practically useless to me, since they could not be taken out of Belgium.

Eventually, an arrangement was worked out by which the Americans leaving could buy checks on New York, against blocked funds in America, with their surplus francs. This served to get the money out of Belgium, but meant that I could not utilize it until I reached New York —and my ticket would have to be paid for in Lisbon. However, I had gone too far to turn back; something would turn up. Most of the Americans planning to leave were in a similar situation, and the consulate assured us that an attempt was being made to arrange with an American bank in Lisbon to advance money on the blocked checks. (It was not until I reached Lisbon that I learned that there *is* no

American bank there.)

Meantime, reports concerning conditions in Lisbon were not reassuring. There were, we were told, three million refugees in Portugal; as a result, there was little to eat, and no hotel rooms available whatever; it was impossible to purchase cigarettes or tobacco; prices were fantastically high. Mitropa informed us that all ships leaving Lisbon were sold out until February—and this was mid-October! Consular employees advised us that arrangements were being made by the Portuguese government to care for us in an open-air refugee camp during the several weeks or months that would elapse before we could sail; several of the Americans packed camping equipment to be prepared for this.

In the interim, there was the matter of the Spanish and Portuguese visas to be arranged, and this was by no means simple. The Spanish government had been completely intransigent in the matter; the regulations forbade male foreigners of military age to enter, or even pass through, Spain, and there was no intention of making an exception in our case. It was finally necessary for a Mitropa agent to go to Madrid, where he cajoled the necessary permission from a high official in the Franco government. (At that, our departure was delayed an extra day because of the Spanish government's refusal to issue a transit visa to a veteran of the Spanish-American War.)

We were, at any rate, assured that this was now arranged, but before I could obtain the two visas, it was essential to have my passport validated for travel in these countries by the U. S. consulate. Our passports had been transferred to Brussels, and thither I journeyed again, only to learn that the Brussels consulate had refused to validate the passports of American citizens residing in the Antwerp area, and that they had been returned to the Antwerp consulate. Back I went to Antwerp, arriving too late in the day to find the consulate open. Next morning, I put my thumbprint on the necessary forms, the consul put his in my passport, and gave me a letter to the Portuguese consul.

This consulate was just down the street. I filled out the forms, and was told to come back on the following day. I did so, received the visa without complications, and set out for the Spanish consulate, which, I had been assured at the American and Portuguese consulates, was "just across the street."

Three times, back and forth, I searched the length of several blocks, finding the Swedish consulate, various South and Central American consulates—but nothing even vaguely resembling a Spanish consulate. Back I went to the American consulate for the exact street address. Armed with this, I found the empty building where the Spanish consulate *had* been. A small card on the door indicated that it had been moved some two weeks before, but someone had thoughtfully torn off the lower half of the notice, giving the new address. I returned to the American consulate; after a good bit of scurrying about from one office to another, someone remembered that the Spanish consulate *had* moved, and found the new street address. By the time I found this building, in another part of town, the consulate was just closing its door for three days, because of some Spanish holiday or other. After three days, I came back, made out an imposing affidavit, left the requisite photographs, and on the following day received the necessary permission to cross Spain.

During all of this time, it was necessary to go to Brussels every two or three days to meet with Mr. Rummelspacher and receive the latest advice concerning the trip. This was inconvenient enough for me, from Antwerp, but for some of the Americans, traveling each time from a remote Belgian village, it was a real hardship. The date of the departure was first fixed for October 18, then the twenty-first, and finally the twenty-second.

Meanwhile, there were complicated financial arrangements to be made. I had a small sum in American Express checks, bought before the war; it was necessary to have official German permission to take this out of Belgium with me. We had been notified that baggage charges from Paris to Lisbon must be paid in France, in French currency; one must have official German permission to buy a certain sum in French francs (and one could only guess at the amount which might be required, since the rate was not known) and to take these francs out of Belgium. Lastly, I needed official German permission to buy a blocked check with my funds in Belgian francs and to take this check out of Belgium.

Fortunately, all of these permits were to be obtained from the same office, the financial branch of the Antwerp *kommandatur*. The consulate had prepared the necessary forms; I filled them out and the consulate placed the official seal on them. At the financial office I was received by a young captain, taciturn and efficient, who glanced at my documents and told me to return that afternoon. At the appointed time, I returned and was handed the permits. As was usually the case when dealing with the military authorities, this matter passed through with a minimum of complication, bother and red tape.

Unfortunately, while I was in Brussels the next morning, Mr. Rummelspacher announced that all of us must return on the following day at nine A.M. to go to the bank in a group with a consular employee to buy our blocked checks and French francs. These, he explained, would only be issued upon presentation of the pass for the departure of the entire group, and must therefore be done collectively. (This pass, incidentally, was signed by General von Falkenhausen, the former adviser to the Chinese government.)

I protested to Mr. Rummelspacher at this, and told him that the financial division in Antwerp had stated clearly that the transaction might be completed at any bank dealing in foreign exchange. He exploded with fury, and called on Heaven to explain why he must repeat so many times such elementary things to stupid tourists who did not even listen to what he said.

So, unwilling to take any risks at that late stage, I rose the next morning at five-thirty, and was in the Brussels consulate at nine. At nine-thirty, we were told that inquiry had shown that it was *not* necessary, after all, to buy our checks and francs in a group, and that we were therefore free to go to any bank in Brussels or Antwerp, individually, and obtain them. Mr. Rummelspacher showed some little embarrassment in my presence, and from then until the departure was exceedingly polite to me.

I went to the Brussels branch of the Guaranty Trust, because it was near by; the cashier curtly refused to sell me a blocked check; he did not have time for transactions of that sort, though I could not see that he was doing anything else. So I went first to a large Belgian bank, where, after two hours of standing in line, I obtained the French francs, then hurried to the National City Bank. Here, I found the staff completely unfamiliar with the necessary procedure, but quite disposed to be helpful, and with the assistance of the manager and most of the employees, the precious check was finally issued.

During all of this period, I was still doing my regular work in the laboratory, though this often meant spending most of the night there. There was unfinished work to be completed, preparations to be made for other projects to be continued in America, files to be put in order, inventories to be prepared, and endless items to be packed away in cases—not to mention packing my own baggage, most of which would have to remain behind.

There were, at that time, about three hundred Americans in Belgium. About half of this number had been able to meet the difficult conditions imposed by the Germans. As the German command was willing to furnish only one passenger coach and one small baggage car, only the first fifty-two persons to make reservations would leave on the twenty-second; luckily for me, my name was on that list.

The day fixed for the departure was a Tuesday; it would be necessary to be at the station in Brussels at ten A.M. Baggage must, however, be checked at that station on the previous day upon presentation of the ticket—and the tickets were to be issued at the consulate in Brussels at two o'clock sharp on Monday. I was becoming slightly bored with these interminable journeys between Antwerp and Brussels, and I determined to go to Brussels on Monday morning and remain there until my departure; this would also eliminate the risk of an uncertain train connection early Tuesday morning.

I spent most of Sunday trying to finish my packing.

Practically everything which I had accumulated during twelve years in Europe was in Antwerp, and it was no light task to decide what I was going to take with me, what I should risk leaving, and what I should discard. I was aided in this monotonous task by the elderly ex-cigarmaker whom I had met at the consulate in May; he hoped to leave with the proposed second or third group, if he could raise the money, and he had accompanied me on many of my errands during the difficult fortnight, in order to see for himself the various operations that were necessary.

We worked all of Sunday afternoon, had dinner at my *pension*, then went into town to see a few friends before my departure. We talked English in the streetcar on the way to town; the Flemish conductor came over, leaned down confidentially, and whispered that if we were English we shouldn't take the risk of speaking it where a German might overhear us. We explained that we were Americans, and he was reassured; he had, he assured us vehemently, "a belly full of these damned Germans!" They rode free of charge, crowding the cars and leaving honest civilians without sufficient transport facilities. He hoped to God England would "drive the dirty swine out of Belgium," but he feared it would take many years.

We entered the restaurant of my hotel still speaking English; a German officer, furious, got up, left his unfinished meal, and stormed out of the place. He must have heard the hearty laughter from Belgians and Germans alike that followed this outburst, for he did not reappear. One of those who was most amused, incidentally, was a plainclothes Gestapo agent, who knew that we were Americans.

It was not easy to say good-by to the friends with whom I had lived through so many difficult days—the staunch-hearted, elderly proprietress, whose daughter and grandchild were in Switzerland, which might be attacked any day; her daughter, Elvire, whose fiancé was somewhere at sea, in a ship which had been enrolled in the British merchant marine; Marie, the chambermaid, with one brother in a German prison camp, and another still missing. I was going home, to relative safety and comfort—but I was leaving them to face a future so vague that hope was almost forgotten. I proposed a round of drinks, but the old lady indignantly refused to allow me to pay for them. We talked of trivialities; there was little that was cheerful which could be said of the important things. They had made no secret, during the past fortnight, of their skepticism concerning my safe arrival in America; I knew that, living near the waterfront, they stood an excellent chance of being blown to bits in an R.A.F. raid before it was all over, and that with the best of luck they would probably be in for several very lean years—so we spoke of trivial things, far removed from our thoughts, and presently I rose to leave.

Farewells over, we departed with Charles, the proprietress's son, and his fiancée, to make a brief, last tour of a few Antwerp "night spots," such as they were. I was desperately tired out by the fortnight of strain and uncertainty, and I was determined to leave on a somewhat lighter note; an old phrase, remembered from somewhere, kept recurring in my mind: "Go out with a smile!" So I had kept a few hundred francs aside for this purpose, and we set out to see what Antwerp could still afford in nocturnal entertainment.

We went first to Chez Teresini, the most aristocratic of the drinking clubs. There was little to look at here save German officers, so after a couple of rounds we went to the Florida, where I had several acquaintances. We were in time for the floor show, and things were somewhat livelier, but at nine-thirty the music ceased, so I said good-by to my acquaintances among the entertainers, and we went to the Abbaye, which had been Antwerp's outstanding night club. As elsewhere, the place was crowded with German officers, sitting about with the girls of the establishment; the latter were not as beautiful as the *entraineuses* for which the Abbaye had been noted. A waiter explained to me that most of the former girls were now enjoying the "protection" of German officers; it was almost impossible to retain a good one, he said. There was an intermittent floor show, with dancing between the numbers, but few of the Germans availed themselves of it. Those who did, usually danced with wrinkled brow and solemn expression; one could feel them saying to themselves: "One, two— one, two—now turn—now straight ahead again." There was little noise and no gaiety; as usual, Germans amusing themselves made a grimly solemn business of it. From time to time a warning bell rang—the music stopped, and the orchestra leaped from the bandstand and hid in the checkroom. Then a German military police officer entered, saluted silently, examined the leave permits of soldiers, strode back to the door, pivoted smartly, clicked his heels so violently that he nearly fell on the waxed dance floor, raised his right arm stiffly, and with a sharp "Heil Hitler!" was gone. Almost before he was out the door, the musicians reappeared, took their places, and everything continued from where it had left off.

At eleven o'clock we terminated our evening, as Charles's fiancée had to pass a German street barrier in the outskirts before midnight. The ex-cigarmaker and I set out on foot for Oude-God through the darkened streets, and arrived there an hour and a half later to finish my packing. This seemed literally to have no end, and when we had filled the last case it was seven A.M. Once during the night, there was a violent air raid, which appeared to be in the direction of the near-by airport, but although the planes were directly overhead several times, we went on with the packing. When it was done, I went to have breakfast and my friend went to have a few hours' sleep before accompanying me to Brussels.

During the morning, I went around the factory taking leave of my colleagues and friends. Like everyone else, they expressed genuine pleasure at the fact that I was escaping from a German-dominated world. Never during the two years I had spent in Belgium had I been the recipient of such generosity and friendliness as were showered upon me during the fortnight after it became likely that I would be able to return to America. Close friends squandered ration stamps sufficient for a week on dinners which almost made one forget that hunger was just around the corner; men whom I had scarcely known invited me to their homes; invitations had been more numerous than I could accept; my landlady had insisted on giving me extra meals, to which I was not entitled; café proprietors had refused to accept ration stamps for my nightly cup of coffee, and had even given me extra sugar; several acquaintances presented me with food for the journey across France and Spain. Their tongues loosened by the fact that I was leaving, many of them expressed openly, for the first time, their hatred of the Germans and the hope that the enemy would one day be exterminated, "down to the last dog and cat in Germany." This included even some of those persons who had been, a few months before, strongly pro-German.

By noon, I was ready to leave for Brussels, but, unfortunately, it became clear that I should have to return to Antwerp to confer with one of the directors of the factory before leaving. The plant had given me a car in which to take my baggage to Brussels, thus solving a difficult problem, and it was arranged that I should return with the car, see the director, then take the last train back to Brussels early in the evening. We drove without incident to Brussels, where I received my ticket from the now amiable Mr. Rummelspacher, checked my baggage at the South Station, and set out to look for a hotel room for the night. This proved less simple than I had imagined; to rent a room in Brussels, it was necessary to go to a central German military office, which would assign me to whatever hotel it chose. We drove to this office, and I was given a permit to occupy a room in a hotel near the station, and ration stamps for twenty-four hours; as the Belgians often remarked, "the Germans thought of everything."

Back in Oude-God, I finished my business as rapidly as possible, then met my American friend, and went to my lodgings to get my hat, which I had forgotten. My landlady insisted that we have dinner before leaving, and the old Flemish peasant woman who did the cooking asked me, as she had almost every night since my arrival, how I had enjoyed the soup; after I had reassured her on that score, she explained mysteriously (as she had also done nearly every night) that the manner of its preparation was a secret known only to the women of her village; not even the proprietor knew how it was made.

Again there were leavetakings, and we raced to the station to catch the last Brussels train. Arrived in the capital, I took my friend to the office which issued hotel permits; fortunately, he was able to obtain one for the same hostelry. As it was not quite nine o'clock, and we had nothing more to do, I proposed that we visit one of the Brussels night clubs of which I had been a member in happier days. We found it with some little difficulty in the murky streets; like those in Antwerp, it was crowded with German officers, and the only places we could find free were at the bar. So we perched on the high stools and gave our orders. These were served, and as we sat, talking, the barman came over and said, very quietly, "Would you gentlemen mind drinking up, please?" For a moment, I suspected that for some reason not clear to me we were being turned out, and I protested. The barman smiled, and leaned over confidentially: "The boss heard you talking English, and from now on, your drinks are on the house; he says he hasn't heard English spoken since May."

From that moment on, the evening turned into a pro-Allied demonstration, and manager, waiters, artists and musicians crowded around us with expressions of sympathy for England, hope that America would aid the struggle, and that the *boches* would be smashed, with a fine disregard for the German officers sitting at tables all around us. Sentiment in Brussels was, it was very clear, much more sharply anti-German than in Antwerp. The time passed rapidly, and a little before eleven the barman warned us that we must not be on the streets after eleven P.M. This had not occurred to me (in Antwerp, one might

remain on the streets up to any hour), and we hastened
in search of a hotel we had never seen, in a city which
neither of us knew more than slightly—and in a blackout.
Several times we had to inquire the way of passing pedestrians, and each time the reply was, substantially, "Straight
on down this street—but don't let a policeman see you!"
At about eleven-thirty, we found the hotel; the front door
was locked and the place was in total darkness. We rang
the bell again and again, but nothing happened. We were
in something of a quandary: we had no right to be on a
street, and could not get into the hotel; we could not go
to another hotel, because our permits were for this one.
Finally, after twenty minutes, a sleepy proprietor, in
pajamas and dressing gown, came to the door, and looked
out at us without opening it. He shook his head, and
shouted through the door that we could not spend the
night there without a permit from the Germans. I assured
him that we had these, but it was not until I had shown
him the documents with the aid of my flashlight that he
grudgingly opened the door and showed us to rooms.

Next morning we were up early, and after breakfast I
made a few last-minute purchases with my remaining Belgian francs, which would no longer be of any use. At ten
we were at the station, and for the first time I really had
the sensation that I was actually going. The platform was
crowded with relatives of departing Americans—most of
those still in Belgium were people who had been there for
years, and in many cases had families there. I found an
empty place in a compartment, left my baggage, and
strolled outside until train-time. At ten-fifty-five, with a
great deal of waving and cheering, the train pulled out
and I settled down to the journey which would, with luck,

bring me to Lisbon on Friday.

I had at least a nodding acquaintance with most of my fifty-one fellow travelers; we had met so frequently at consulates and elsewhere the past fortnight that there were no strange faces. I felt fortunate, on the whole, in my choice of compartment; one of my companions was a former Russian, who had extensive mining properties in the Belgian Congo, and hoped to visit them before returning to America; another was an ex-naval commander of French origin, whose wife had a corset shop in New York; a third was an American boy who had been going to school in Belgium, and had now brought with him a complete tent and camping outfit so as to be prepared for the worst in Lisbon; a fourth was a middle-aged man of indefinite profession who had been in Dunkirk and Calais during the worst of the fighting, and was now in a badly shaken state; the fifth was a priest who had once lived for a few weeks at my hotel in Antwerp.

The morning passed quickly in comparing our respective experiences in getting away; all of them, I discovered, had in one way or another had a time just as complicated and difficult as my own, if not more so. For some obscure reason, luncheon was not included in our all-inclusive tour, but I had held a sufficient number of Belgian francs to cover that, and at noon the Russian and I went into the dining car. We were served an admirable meal—one such as we had not seen for months; having finally resolved to let us go, the Germans were, apparently, determined to make a good final impression.

All through the day, as the train made its slow course along the route through Belgium and across northern, occupied France, we saw constant reminders of what had happened along this route a few months before—Belgian anti-tank defenses in the fields, railway stations still a mass of wreckage, towns in which large areas were a heap of ruins, bridges still under repair, abandoned French tanks in a field, Frenchmen, still wearing their uniforms, walking behind a plow, and, interminably, German flying fields. It would scarcely be an exaggeration to say that during that day we were never out of sight of an air base. The Germans appeared to have their planes dispersed throughout the whole area in small groups of three to six planes; each machine had its V-shaped shelter into which it was wheeled, with careful camouflage. From time to time, there was a larger field, which no doubt served as the base for the planes at the small fields near it. Often, for long stretches of time, one field would not be out of sight before another was visible.

Nothing expressed the general state of dilapidation and ruin better than the telephone and telegraph wires along the right-of-way: at almost every pole, these hung in a tangle of cut strands, swaying with the breeze. Everything in France seemed to wear this air of ruin and neglect. People looked at one apathetically in the railway stations; men went about their work like sleep-walkers. Here and there were new red roofs, but most buildings bore no evidence of any attempt to repair the damage caused by the fighting.

We had an excellent evening meal in the Mitropa dining car, and arrived in Paris in the dark, at nine-thirty; our train was about an hour late. We had, incidentally, come by a different route from that indicated on our tickets; not improbably this was to prevent anyone in the party from meeting someone by previous arrangement en route.

We piled out of the train, each taking with him a single valise for the night, and leaving the rest to be transferred to the Austerlitz station, from which we should be leaving in the morning.

I had, over a period of a dozen years, arrived at the Gare du Nord many scores of times; from it, I had departed on the last civilian train to leave Paris, the night before the outbreak of war, and again in November, 1939. Then, it had been merely dismal; now, with the gray-uniformed invaders everywhere, dimly seen in the half-light, the tread of their hob-nailed boots resounding under the lofty roof, it was tragic. As we moved along the platform, a few German soldiers, with fixed bayonets, took up positions around us and accompanied us to the autobus waiting in the courtyard; whether they were there to protect us, or to watch us, was not quite clear.

The bus was the familiar Parisian conveyance I had known so well, but tonight it was the only bus running in all the city; such luxuries were not for conquered peoples. In the darkness we could see little; even the bus driver lost his way in trying to find the Square Louvois, where our hotel was located. The fronts of motion picture theaters were much more brightly illuminated than in Belgium; otherwise, the same blackout measures were in force as the Germans had applied elsewhere.

At the Hotel Louvois, Cross, of the American embassy staff (whose name was to become prominent months later when the German government asked for his recall), was awaiting us. He had heard that we were arriving, and had, as he said, come down "to see with his own eyes that a group of Americans had actually managed to leave Belgium." After our experiences in Belgium, it was pleasant to feel that one servant of the State Department, at least, took some degree of interest in our welfare.

We were also met in Paris by the tour conductor who was to accompany us all the way to Lisbon—Emil Möhring, formerly the Hamburg-Amerika agent in Paris, and now connected with Mitropa. He was a model of affability and good humor, but when I inquired about the possibility of going out for a bit, he replied somewhat impatiently that the police regulations in Paris forbade the circulation of civilians in the streets after ten P.M. I took the precaution of inquiring of the concierge, and learned that the curfew came into force at midnight, so after rooms had been assigned and everyone, including Mr. Möhring, was installed for the night, four of us went out to have a look around.

The appearance of things was not encouraging. We all had pocket flashlights, so it was not too difficult to find our way about in the "City of Light," but there did not appear to be much to justify the effort. We walked as far as the grand boulevards, and could only see darkness and desolation on all sides; no vehicles and no pedestrians marred the tranquillity of the somber streets, so we returned to the vicinity of our hotel.

We went into a neighborhood café at random. A few men were playing *belote* without enthusiasm; the proprietress, behind the bar, surveyed us without interest. We seated ourselves and ordered cognac. Madame shook her head; this was not a day for alcohol. We might have wine if we wished; it was too late in the day to be permitted to serve coffee. So we sampled the wine, which was vile stuff, and decided to try elsewhere. In the next café, the wine was equally bad, but I managed to buy a few packages of cigarettes for the journey. In a third café, larger than the other two, there were half a dozen clients but no animation; they talked in low tones and never smiled; the service was apathetic. The wine was as bad as it had been elsewhere, but two members of the party managed to buy bottles of reasonably good vintage wines to take with them. The atmosphere was depressing, and we did not linger longer than necessary.

On Wednesday morning, our train was due to leave at eight-thirty. This meant rising at seven, which was really five A.M., Greenwich time, and when we left the hotel it was still dark. We had arrived in obscurity—we were leaving the same way; on the whole, I was as well pleased that it was so; I had seen as much as I wished, though I regretted not having had the opportunity to see a few acquaintances who might possibly be in Paris.

The run from Paris to Bordeaux has never been especially attractive, and this time it was less so. We were never able to forget the war; the tiniest French village through which we passed had its contingent of German soldiers and railway men; the entire right-of-way was guarded by sentries at frequent intervals. As we left Paris behind, there was less and less evidence of destruction, however, and the external appearance of the towns became more normal, if not more animated. There were not nearly as many flying fields, as was to be expected. At Bordeaux, considerable concentrations of anti-aircraft guns protected the bridges and the port.

We were supposed to cross into Spain that evening, and to arrive in San Sebastian about midnight, but when our train reached Hendaye, on the French side of the border, it became evident that something had gone wrong with our itinerary. Our train remained motionless for an hour, while Möhring held excited conferences with angry French railway employees, dashing off at intervals to telephone the German headquarters in Paris. We could not find out a great deal about what was happening, but we did learn that the Spanish border had just been closed; for how long, no one could say. For a time, it appeared that we were to spend the night in a hotel in Hendaye, but the German officials seemed curiously reluctant to have us do so. I learned, presently, that all British subjects in the vicinity, who were not already in a concentration camp, had been arrested that day. It was obvious that something important was in the wind, and eventually a German soldier admitted that high personalities of the German and Spanish governments were meeting in Hendaye that night.

Eventually, orders came from the German command to take us to Biarritz for the night, and the French railway employees who had insisted that there were no locomotives available, found one in a few minutes. We arrived in Biarritz in the dark—we were growing accustomed to that— and stumbled through the streets to the local *kommandatur*, to be assigned to hotel rooms. The young officers on duty received us courteously, and after a short delay, rooms were found in two hotels. Everyone was tired, and after having sandwiches in the lounge of our hotel, we turned in for a sound night's rest.

Next morning, we had a rather inadequate breakfast at our hotel, consisting of rolls without butter and black coffee without sugar—and this in Biarritz! I had, luckily, provided for such contingencies, and brought with me a small bag of sugar, as had several of the others. After breakfast, we were told that we should not leave for an hour and a half, so with Pierre, the young Belgian-American in my compartment, I went for a long walk along the waterfront. The morning was warm and sunny, but except for a number of German soldiers, there was no one on the beach. The casino was open for a few nights a week; shop windows still displayed atrocious pseudo-Basque handicraft and souvenirs, and except for an occasional German plane flying over, there was little indication that we were in a war area.

Later, walking through the center of town on our way back to the railway station, we saw evidences of the horde of refugees which had come thus far and no farther during the great exodus. On every hand were tattered posters, placed there by the former French authorities, advising refugees where to go for assistance, and regulations concerning the refugee problem. There were, too, many posters placed there by the Germans, and chiefly that one which showed a mother, with a baby in her arms, weeping, while her husband, crippled, surveyed the ruins of their home; in the background, the shadowy figure of a British officer, a sneer on his face, laughed mockingly; across the top was a single phrase: "It is the British who have done that!"

At the station, some little complication was occasioned by the fact that we did not yet have permission to return to Hendaye but were obliged, for some reason, to leave Biarritz. Again there were excited conferences, and again Möhring dashed off to telephone somewhere or other, and eventually our two coaches were taken to the little village of La Negresse, where they remained on a siding for several hours, directly opposite several tank cars filled with gasoline and guarded by impassive sentries.

When it became evident that we should be there for some time, Pierre, the Russian and I decided to do a bit of exploring, since we, like everyone else, were becoming exceedingly hungry. Several members of our party had been as far as the little station, and reported that there was nothing to be had there, though the soldiers had given them a loaf of gray army bread. We walked to the station, where we encountered a German nurse. She explained to me how to find a small café, where we might obtain something to eat. We located the establishment after some little search. A few Germans were sitting on the terrace. We passed inside, hopefully, but the proprietress was not encouraging. The Germans had closed down the meat market a few days before, and there was little to eat in La Negresse. We ordered a glass of wine, and presently madame suggested, diffidently, that she could let us have a tin of sardines and a bit of bread, if that would interest us. It not only interested us, but before we finished we had consumed several tins of the excellent sardines and crisp-crusted bread, washed down with the really admirable wine, a local product. When we returned to the train, we took with us a further supply, for there was little assurance as to when we might reach San Sebastian, our next stop.

Eventually, the train which had left Paris twenty-four hours after ours arrived, and our coaches were joined to it. This time, at Hendaye, there was a long list of formalities to be gone through with the German authorities—declaring all of our money, in any currency, giving up our permits to take out money, passport examination—and, of course, the German officials insisted on a thorough search of all baggage. Möhring protested violently at this, and an argument went on in his compartment for nearly half an hour. In the end, the officers agreed to select one valise at random in each compartment, and, if these disclosed nothing dangerous, to let it go at that. This was rapidly completed, and the question of the registered trunks sealed in the baggage car occasioned another lengthy argument. Finally, with not too good grace, the officials consented to a similar procedure: they would select three trunks at random, and, if the results were not unfavorable, the examination would be terminated.

Our stay in Hendaye, though prolonged, was not dull, for we were all extremely curious to know what had happened there during the night as the cause of our delay. It was not difficult to guess, for the platform was still decorated with enormous Nazi and Spanish flags, branches of evergreen were fastened to the uprights along the platform, a bandstand had been erected at one side, great numbers of German soldiers were still about the station, and others were rolling up long, rubber-covered microphone cables. There had been, obviously, an important Hispano-German meeting, but had it been a conference between von Ribbentrop and Suñer, as some insisted, or, as I strongly suspected, an encounter between the German Führer and the Spanish Caudillo? Before our train pulled out, I learned that it had been the latter. The news was not reassuring. We knew that at least six hundred thousand German soldiers were massed near the Spanish frontier in France, and we had visions of Portugal being invaded before we could leave for America—perhaps before we could reach Lisbon!

All things must end, and the time finally arrived when the German officials could find no further reason for detaining us. Our train slowly pulled out of the station and across the international bridge to Irun; I leaned far out of the window, watching the German sentry at the French end of the bridge—he was, I hoped, the last gray-uniformed figure I should see for some time to come; I had acquired, I realized, a very definite aversion to that particular color, which was likely to be of long duration.

We were quickly in Irun, and our train halted again as Spanish officials, more picturesquely dressed, came to inspect us. Möhring greeted them with a hearty Nazi salute, and disappeared into the station with them for another of his interminable conferences. We were accustomed to these delays, however, and no longer complained, so long as we occasionally moved a bit further in the direction of freedom. When Möhring reappeared, we were asked to file into the station. There was no customs examination, but each person was required to first pass a window to declare all currency being transported, then into an office for a passport and visa check-up, and as there were still fifty-two of us, we began to wonder when we would reach San Sebastian; we had been promised lunch first at noon, then at two-thirty, and we now wondered whether we would arrive there in time for dinner.

Eventually our train departed, without any visible signs of haste, in the direction of San Sebastian, where we arrived after dark. Buses took us to the palatial Maria Christina Hotel; Möhring explained to us that since we had missed our lunch, he had arranged to serve us an especially generous dinner. It was perhaps fortunate that he had done so, for after eating our lunch-and-dinner-in-one, we left the Maria Christina only slightly less famished than we had arrived. Pierre and I consoled ourselves on the way back to the train with the thought that we still had a quantity of delectable sardines, bread and wine from La Negresse. Our jubilation was short-lived. All baggage had been transferred to a Spanish coach, dirtier and more unkempt than any railway equipment I have ever seen. When we took our places in this miserable coach, where we were to sit up all night and all the next day, we discovered two delightful facts: the hand baggage had been so completely scrambled in the transfer that no one could find anything, and the Spanish soldiers posted to guard our property had stolen every scrap of food and every drop of wine or water in the car. Möhring found this very amusing, and remarked that one could scarcely expect anything else from Spanish soldiers.

Everyone was tired and in a bad temper by this time, and no one's feelings were improved when it was discovered that there was not a drop of water in the washrooms at the two ends of the coach. Those who wanted to go to sleep immediately, turned out the lights; those who wanted to read, turned them on again; some persons tried to stretch out over several seats, in order to get a little rest; when the occupants of these seats returned, there were bitter words exchanged; for hours, in the darkness, dim figures were prowling up and down the corridor with flashlights, looking at each baggage rack in turn in an effort to find some bit of their luggage; those who slept snored, and those who stayed awake talked and disturbed those asleep. Somehow, almost incredibly, we got through the night without any physical violence. Next morning, everyone was extremely dirty and tired; many had been so badly bitten by vermin that they resembled patients with advanced cases of measles. We were not enjoying Spain.

As the morning wore on, our unhurried train made occasional stops, and at one of these, Möhring announced that he had arranged for us to have coffee in the station restaurant. There was a scramble to reach the oasis, and in a few moments the station restaurant was a bedlam of confusion. Matters were so badly arranged that less than half the party had been served when we had to return to the train; Mr. Möhring had had *his,* however, so no doubt everything was all right. His popularity, which had been high at the moment of leaving Paris, was steadily waning, and as the end of our journey came within view, his manners were less and less those of a travel agent and more and more those of a Prussian drill sergeant. However, even with that qualification, we were lucky to be traveling in his company: from Belgium to the Portuguese border, German auspices were, after all, the most helpful that we could have.

The impression of Spain, as seen from the car window during the forenoon, continued to be depressing. We had just come from countries ravaged by war, but in comparison with Spain, the memory of them now seemed opulent. Except for complacent, well-fed officials, the men we saw were more pitiable than anything we had seen in the war zone: hollow-cheeked and pale, with burning, sullen eyes and listless manner. The women, and especially the younger ones, appeared far more cheerful, and certainly in better physical shape, than the men; the same could not be said of the children, however; as for the animals we saw, they were little more than skin draped over skeletons. One of our group threw a scrap of bread to a famished-looking dog; before the animal could reach it, a man had dashed up, kicked him out of the way, brushed off the piece of bread, and shoved it in his pocket; in another case, a passenger offered some food to a small boy, and a Spanish official prevented his accepting it; no doubt he was determined to show us that there was no shortage of food in Franco's domain.

Arrived at the border, our persons were searched for the first time by Spanish officials chiefly interested in illegal export of currency. Some hours passed here, and we grew very tired of the shabby little station and pompous officials —especially as we knew that a dining car was to be attached to our train on the Portuguese side of the frontier. At last, well into the afternoon, our train steamed out of Spain and crossed to Vilar Formoso—"Beautiful City." Formalities here were quickly gone through; passport control was to be carried out in the train. The very air we breathed seemed subtly different. The dining car was spotlessly clean. The passport control officer was positively amiable. The few soldiers whom we saw appeared neither pompous nor brutal. No one wore a worried, harassed expression. People talked in loud voices—and even laughed! Victor Hugo had once infuriated the Spanish, I recalled, by saying that "Europe ends at the Pyrenees"; now it might be said, I felt, that "Europe ends at the borders of Portugal; outside of them lies only the Nazi empire of darkness." The rotund dining car steward knew, I think, that we were refugees, and that it was some time since we had seen a decent meal—there could be no other explanation for the number of courses and of second helpings set before us; he beamed as he watched us methodically devour everything set before us. So great was the

wonder of it that I cannot now recall a single course that
was served—but I remember that the bread was white,
and the butter was not margarine, that a second cup of
coffee was available for the asking and that there was
sugar on the table—in short, I knew that I had never tasted
such a heavenly meal, and might never taste one with such
relish again.

After that, we were prepared, and even determined,
to like Portugal, and we found no difficulty in doing so.
The rugged mountain scenery was distinctive and breath-
takingly beautiful; the villages and farms we saw seemed
spotless, after what we had recently passed through; the
people looked happy and amiable.

Toward evening, as we neared Lisbon, Pierre and I
discussed the hotel problem. So far we had failed to find
the penury of food that we had been warned to expect in
Portugal, but there was still no guarantee that we would
have a place to sleep that night. Pierre, to be sure, had his
tent—but the police might not view favorably our efforts
to erect it in one of the public parks. On the mimeographed
forms given us at the consulate in Brussels, it had been
clearly stated by Mitropa: "Our services terminate with
the arrival in Lisbon." This had even been underscored,
and Möhring had repeatedly emphasized that we should
have to shift for ourselves in the Portuguese capital,
though Mitropa would assist if it proved possible. Cross,
of the Paris embassy, had assured me that we would have
no trouble in finding rooms in Estoril, the seaside resort
just outside Lisbon, but we wanted to be in the center,
if possible. We decided to ask the advice of the young
passport officer, and found him in the dining car. He confirmed the fact that Lisbon was crowded, owing partly to

refugees and partly to an exposition then in progress, marking the eighth centennial of Portugal. He assured us, however, that it was nonetheless possible to find rooms, and gave us two addresses of hotels which he knew personally; a room and meals would probably cost us, he thought, about thirty escudos (or one dollar and twenty cents) a day.

Upon arrival in Lisbon, Möhring was met by a local representative. After a brief talk with him, Möhring made a little speech on the platform, referring contemptuously to the American consular service and its inability and unwillingness to do anything for us, and finished by announcing that *he* had arranged rooms for us all at Sintra, some twenty-five miles from Lisbon; we were now to take buses to Sintra, and would be brought back to Lisbon at ten in the morning to sign up for our steamship tickets. This meant that there would be no opportunity to see the consulate, talk with steamship agents, or find out anything whatever about the general situation before we had bound ourselves hand and foot with the German agency. It sounded very much like a "squeeze play" to me, and I would have none of it. Furthermore, I resented Möhring's remarks about the American consular service; I largely agreed with what he had said, but I did not feel that it came with especially good grace from an agent of an official Nazi travel bureau.

Pierre agreed with me in this, so while the others piled into the two big buses, we had a porter put our baggage in a taxi. Möhring saw this, and vehemently ordered the porter to put our baggage on top of a bus. He started to do so—I ordered it back in the taxi—Möhring ordered it put on the bus—and seeing that this might continue indefinitely, we decided to wait our turn. So we took places in the bus and rode the twenty-five miles through the mountains to Sintra; it was, I believe, a beautiful journey, but we did not greatly appreciate its loveliness. Arrived at the Central Hotel, the others followed Möhring inside, and I, summoning my few phrases of Portuguese, asked the chauffeur when he was returning to Lisbon; as he was leaving in about ten minutes, I inquired if we might return to town with him. He said that we might, and added that there would be no charge. By that time, someone had informed our tour conductor that we were returning to Lisbon. He came out, white-faced and almost speechless.

"I understand," he said, angrily, "that you two wish to return to Lisbon tonight. Is that correct?"

"No," I replied, very quietly, "you have been misinformed. We *are* going back to Lisbon tonight."

He paid no further attention to us, but turned to the driver, addressing him in Portuguese and obviously assuming that we would not understand:

"Don't take them to a hotetl! Take them to the garage, and let them shift for themselves!"

Then, turning to us again, he bowed and said, in honeyed tones: "Good-by! I'm *sure* you'll find hotel rooms!"

The ride back was a delight. We had no notion whether we should find a place to sleep that night—but for the first time we felt that we were no longer spied upon, controlled and ordered about; we were free! The driver proved most friendly, and quite obviously did not like Germans; we later found that a great many Portuguese shared that feeling. He took us to the garage, about two miles outside Lisbon, then found a taxicab for us, and came with us in search of a hotel—for all of which he refused to accept the slightest gratuity; we were beginning positively to love the Portuguese.

The first hotel of which we had the address was full up; the taxi driver took us to a second which he knew, which also had no rooms. We began to be a bit apprehensive, but at the second hotel on our list, a sleepy night porter came to the door, and, in response to our anxious inquiry, assured us that he could give us two rooms. We placed our baggage upstairs, then, intoxicated with our sudden feeling of freedom, decided to go out for a cup of coffee, though it was already two A.M.

We did not know which way to go, and when we heard a woman coming out of the hotel leading a dog speak to the man with her in a voice unmistakably American, I took the liberty of introducing myself and asking her advice in the matter. Within five minutes we had discovered a half dozen mutual acquaintances in New York, London and on the Riviera, and the four of us retired to the nearest café, where we found a Scotch and soda to be an acceptable substitute for the coffee we had had in mind. The man proved to be connected with the Spanish diplomatic service in some capacity, and while I differed with him in politics more than he perhaps realized, he was agreeable and well informed about many things which interested me.

He asserted—and I subsequently found good reason to believe that he knew what he was talking about—that Hitler had demanded permission to occupy a strip twelve miles wide around the entire Spanish coast (and, of course, Portugal) at his meeting with Franco. He also claimed that Franco had refused, and had said that German soldiers could, no doubt, enter Spain by force—but that they would enter in no other way.

Franco feared, my informant explained, that the entry of German troops into Spain would bring his régime tumbling down and return Spain to a state of civil war, so bitterly were the Germans hated. Eighty per cent of the population of Spain was literally starving to death, he went on, somberly, because Hitler insisted on his pound of flesh —Spanish food now, in return for German planes then. Franco had begged him to grant Spain a moratorium for one year, two years—so that the Spanish workers might have enough to eat to be able to produce something again; Hitler had contemptuously refused. There was not a drop of olive oil to be had in all Spain, yet he, my informant, had recently seen, in New York, Spanish olive oil packed in Germany and exported from there to America by a devious route. We had, ourselves, seen great shipments of Spanish dried fruits at Hendaye being sent to the German troops in France.

The next morning, with a magnificent, warm sun shining, Pierre and I set out to explore the town. A broad and spotless avenue led toward the center of the city; the sidewalks were inlaid with mosaic tiles, and tall palm trees accorded well with the Moorish nature of the architecture. The men were handsome, and the women amazing; apparently, despite the very mixed origins of the people, centuries of comparative isolation had developed a "pure" racial type.

We called at the consulate, where we registered, and obtained the addresses of the shipping agencies; went to a bank and changed some money; then went to the office where Möhring was making his headquarters to pay him the one dollar charge each for the bus to Sintra the night before. There was no real reason why we should pay it, but it was worth it, just to tell Möhring how easily we had found hotel rooms, in the heart of Lisbon, for materially less than the others were paying out of town; childish, of course, but gratifying!

We knew that a Greek boat, the "Nea Hellas," was leaving shortly, with rates materially lower than the American boats for which Mitropa wanted to book us, so we determined to wait a bit. Six members of our party left on the following day's boat, on mattresses in the music room; we had intended to see them off but were unable, because of a previous appointment with the representative of an American motion picture company, at Estoril.

The week that followed was one of the happiest of my life. The weather was splendid, our hotel was comfortable, and the meals were not only tasty but so generous that no normal human being could have eaten everything served up—but we, who had just arrived from the occupied areas, went stolidly through every item on the menu, and put on pounds daily. Three days went by before we could see the manager, to learn what all of this was going to cost us. Despite this, and despite the fact that he knew we would have difficulty in finding anything else, the rate he quoted was exactly what the passport official has promised us—a dollar and twenty cents a day. Every contact we made with the Portuguese increased our respect for their civilized character. Their amiability and helpfulness knew no bounds. A shopkeeper who did not have what you wanted asked you to wait, while he rushed about all the shops in the neighborhood, locating it for you. The information booths in the street were more than helpful, as were the police. If, through lack of acquaintance with the money,

you paid too much for something, the clerk or waiter
rushed after you to refund the difference. Prices were
ridiculously low, despite the number of refugees in the
country. The American lady whom we had met on the
first evening had assured us that Lisbon was very lovely,
but that there simply was no night life in the place; I
could write another entire book about how wrong I found
her to be—but I don't know that it would be advisable!

The days sped by, each pleasanter than the one before.
We visited the exposition, expecting little; perhaps for that
very reason, we were astounded; for sheer good taste, I
could think of nothing since the Paris exposition of deco-
rative arts in 1925 to equal it. Imagine, if you can, an
exposition spread out over a vast area along the waterfront, with tasteful buildings separated by great open
spaces and beds of incredible flowers, and, behind the principal buildings, reproductions of old Portuguese streets,
Mexican and South American villages. Around the grounds
were hidden loudspeakers, and during the entire afternoon
we were there, these relayed nothing but the music of Bach,
Handel, Chopin and Mendelssohn; that item was typical
of the mellow, civilized manner in which the whole was
conducted. Our visit ended with a complete inspection of
a ship lying near the entrance; this gaily painted and
gilded craft was an exact reproduction of a Portuguese
vessel of the time of Columbus and the great explorers.
Even the members of the crew were in authentic costume;
later, we were given to understand, she was going to be
sailed to America as a publicity scheme.

Had there not been the ever-present fear of a German
invasion of Portugal, we should have been in no haste to
leave. I still did not have enough cash on hand to cover

the boat ticket, and information concerning the chances of clearing the blocked check through New York was not encouraging. Then Pierre received a considerable sum of money, and offered to lend me the amount necessary for my passage until we reached New York, so we decided to investigate the possibility of making reservations.

At the American Export offices we were told flatly that we could only book through Möhring; although we were American citizens, we could only have places in an American boat by booking through a German tourist agency! I learned, later, that several members of our party had gotten around this by passing generous gratuities to Portuguese members of the office staff, but that is another story.

We went first to the offices handling the bookings for the "Nea Hellas," about which we had excellent information. We were pleasantly received, and within a quarter of an hour had booked and paid for excellent berths in the Greek vessel. Jubilant, we returned to our hotel for lunch. As we were attacking the first course, the manager walked into the dining room. "Have you heard the news?" he inquired. "Greece was invaded this morning." And that was that! We returned to the shipping office in the afternoon; there was some little awkwardness over the matter of returning our passage money, since they proposed to substitute a Yugoslav boat somewhat later in the month. We declined this, and were offered our money back, minus a twenty-five per cent charge for the reservation we were canceling. Several Americans were in the same situation, and the American consul went in person to the shipping office, where, after a certain amount of warm discussion, it was agreed that we should receive our passage money back without any deduction whatever.

I came in contact, several times during the week, with the efforts of the American consulate to handle the situation created by the flood of refugees, and it seemed to me that, within the somewhat inelastic limits set by the State Department, the consulate was doing a pretty fine job of it. Cases came to my attention in which members of the consular staff had dug into their own pockets to pay the passage of some particularly destitute American, whom the American government could not afford to help. Work had been found for a great many more on shipboard, and loans had been made in as many deserving cases as the limited funds available had permitted. There was hardship among Americans in Lisbon, and sometimes bitter hardship—but no one, so far, had been completely stranded. There was nothing in the situation to make me feel proud of my government, but there was little to be ashamed of in the splendid effort being made by the consular staff.

On the way back to the hotel, a surprising thing happened. Passing the Avenida Hotel, I was loudly and enthusiastically hailed by a smiling and delighted Möhring. "Come to the American Export office at three o'clock tomorrow," he shouted. "I have places for you in the boat on Saturday." Pierre and I looked at each other in astonishment. Next day, which was Thursday, we met him as arranged, still feeling skeptical. To the man ahead of us he said: "You can have an excellent berth in a cabin for three hundred, or a mattress in the music room for two hundred and sixty-two." The passenger, who was our friend, the ex-navy commander, took the mattress. Then, to us, Möhring said, amiably: "For you, I have splendid berths in a well-placed cabin." I replied that I did not care to pay three hundred, and would take a mattress. "No, no," protested Möhring, "I have you down for berths, at two hundred and sixty-two dollars." He made out the order, and the Portuguese employee refused to issue us the tickets, on the grounds that we were getting three-hundred-dollar accommodations for less money; finally, the manager had to be called in to make him see reason. We received our tickets, and left; our departure for America was only forty-eight hours away!

Just why the enigmatic Mr. Möhring should have so suddenly taken a fancy to us, after the previous marked coolness on his part, must remain a mystery. Perhaps—and only perhaps—it had some connection with the fact that Pierre had casually mentioned to Möhring's assistant, earlier in the week, that I was an ex-newspaperman, and would be writing a book about my experiences when I returned to America. Could it be that he had repeated that innocent remark to his chief?

My worries, at any rate, were over. Two days later, I embarked on the "Exeter," for a calm and uneventful return to New York. In the boat were one hundred and eighty refugees, from every corner of Europe, many of whom had been waiting in Lisbon for months. During the entire ten days, my time was spent in discussing the one topic that interested any of us at that moment.

Americans newly arrived from London told me of the courage and determination of the British people; those from Holland and Denmark brought stories similar to my own experiences in Belgium; those from occupied and unoccupied France confirmed my belief that the situation throughout Europe differed only in minor details in particular areas; those from Germany confirmed the impressions of the German morale which I had gained from the occupation troops.

If I were to tell in full the stories which I heard, in half a dozen languages, during that ten-day period, another volume would be required, and I do not feel that they would add a great deal to what has already been said; in many cases, details from them have been incorporated in earlier chapters.

I have tried to report, fairly and accurately, what the occupation meant to me as an individual—not because one individual experience is of importance in a world in upheaval, but in the hope that the description of one typical experience may give some notion, at least, of what is happening to millions. In writing it, I have tried to keep faith with my friends—in Belgium, in England, in Germany— by writing nothing for which I would have to feel ashamed, should they see it. If I have succeeded in this, then I have kept faith with the reader.

XIII

Where Will It End?

NEARLY EVERYONE WITH WHOM I HAVE TALKED ABOUT
the present war, since my return to America, has been seeking the answers to a great many questions: When will
the war end? Can the Allies win? Can England hold out?
What will Russia do? How can Germany be prevented
from starting another war in twenty-five years? What will
be left of Europe after the war? Should America enter
the conflict?

Since these questions cannot fairly be discussed in terms
of the Belgian situation alone, it seems to me advisable
to make clear at this point that my residence in Europe
was not confined to the country where I was made a virtual prisoner by the outbreak of war. In 1925, I visited all
of the major European countries. In 1927, I moved to
Paris, and worked there, in Nice and in French northern
Africa. In 1929, I spent more than half a year in Italy,
then went to London; I worked there until 1932, with frequent trips to France and Germany. In 1932, I went to
the Soviet Union, where I remained until 1937, and was
one of the very few non-Russian and non-Communist engineers to hold a responsible executive position, in a scientific research institute. During these years, I made three
trips to France, Germany and England. In 1937, I returned to England to become research director of a British corporation, but spent at least half of each month in

Paris. The successive crises and mobilizations as Hitler entered one country after another made it increasingly difficult to carry on research work in London, and in the spring of 1939 I arranged the transfer of our laboratories to Antwerp. I continued to work in my place in Paris part of each month, and frequently visited England and Germany. I was in Paris when the general mobilization was ordered, left for Belgium at once, crossed the border just after Great Britain declared war on Germany and arrived in Antwerp to learn that France had just followed suit. I returned to Paris once, in November, 1939; other than that, I remained in Belgium until my recent departure for Lisbon and New York.

I mention these otherwise extraneous facts because it seems to me essential that the reader bear in mind, in considering the observations which I shall report, that I saw at first hand not only the war itself, but most of the major developments which led up to it. In most of the countries mentioned, my work brought me into direct contact with political and military figures of importance on frequent occasions, and I was often in an advantageous position to observe what was going on behind the scenes. Once war had been declared, I was virtually isolated in Belgium, and my direct observation was restricted to events in that country. Despite this limitation, Antwerp remained an important seaport, and I had frequent contacts with visitors from every corner of Europe.

This was interrupted in May, 1940, by the invasion, but my journey across France and Spain, my stay in Lisborn and my crossing to New York in a boat carrying one hundred and eighty passengers, chiefly refugees from all parts of Europe, enabled me to fill in a great many of

the gaps. A young couple from Riga told of the entry of
Soviet troops into the Latvian capital, and of conditions in
Sweden, where they had fled immediately after. An American military observer shed new light on the smashing of
the Mannerheim line. American diplomatic and consular
employees, returning to the United States, told intimate
details of current daily life in Berlin, in Amsterdam and
elsewhere. A South American diplomat, and former foreign minister of his country, told of an encounter in Bar-
celona with Pierlot and Spaak, heads of the Belgian government, before they were rescued and taken to London in
a British submarine. Dozens of refugees described to me
the harrowing days of their long treks from Holland or
Belgium to the channel ports or the south of France. A
woman refugee, escaped from Poland, gave me fresh information about the situation in that unhappy country. A
Dane who had just left Copenhagen brought news of recent conditions there; a Wall Street broker had just come
from Germany and Switzerland. A French officer, who
had escaped from southern France by way of Morocco,
and an American businessman, told of conditions in unoccupied France and of the Vichy government, which they
described as "no government at all, but a dozen different
cliques, each, for its own greedy ends, trying to influence
the aged *Maréchal*, the idol of France but no longer in full
possession of his faculties." There were scores of others—
a cabinet minister in the Dollfuss government, a French
aviator who had been attached to the R.A.F. in Flanders
and France, refugees who had escaped from prison camps
and had crossed illegally half of the closed frontiers of
Europe, the Berlin correspondent of an American radio
chain, an American who had driven an ambulance in Po-

land and in France—these, and many more. Their stories, as such, do not belong in this volume, but they helped me to understand more clearly many of the things I had seen, and to report them with greater impartiality.

All of the questions which people are asking about the war simmer down to two major topics:

1. What will be the further development of the war, and when and how will it end?

2. What will be the situation in Europe after the war?

I should have to be both an astrologer and a military expert to give unequivocal answers to those questions with any degree of self-assurance—and thus far, the most consistent aspect of the whole war has been the uniform regularity with which both prophets and military experts have been wrong about practically everything. Most of them have been wrong, I believe, because they have thought of the war solely in terms of strategic military or geographic positions, raw materials and guns, forgetting that the fighting must, in the last analysis, be done by human beings. The degree of sacrifice which men will make is conditioned very largely by their degree of belief in the cause for which they are fighting—by their faith in the social and economic system which they are defending. Few of the prophets and experts have considered these social factors at all; other analysts have recognized their existence, but have been so afraid of the underlying currents implicit in the situation that they have allowed wishful thinking to cloud their judgment. The causes of this war have their roots in social discontent, and I believe that the fruits of the war will be social change, whatever the outcome.

What follows below is not an attempt at prediction; it is, rather, an effort to present the trends inherent in the situation, as they appeared to an American living in Europe during the greater part of the long armistice between the two wars and the first fourteen months of the present conflict. Some of the points upon which I shall touch have been mentioned in other chapters, but it seems to me important to bring them together in an integrated pattern.

When and how will the war end?

The very general belief in Europe, when I left there, was that the war would terminate not earlier than the spring of 1942, and not later than the spring of 1944. It will end, many well-informed persons believe, with a German collapse, but not with a decisive British military victory. (I am speaking here, of course, of opinion on the Continent; I have been out of direct touch with British opinion since May, 1940.) Points at which the internal upheaval in Germany may well start are such cities as Hamburg and Vienna, and the German fleet, Germans conversant with the situation told me.

This opinion is naturally subject to Great Britain's ability to hold out, and upon every aid from America short of fighting men. (For that matter, many Europeans believe that Germany will overreach herself, sooner or later, and force America into the war.) Concerning Britain's ability to continue the struggle, there are two vital factors: morale and materials. The second question, that of material resources, is obviously more serious; the destruction of production facilities by mass air raids, and of supplies and ships by submarine warfare, makes American material aid the decisive factor in the situation. There is a very general opinion in Europe that both Spain and Ireland are letting Germany use submarine bases along their coasts. Regarding the former, I have talked with many eyewitnesses among shipping men who claimed to have seen German U-boats in Spanish harbors from the beginning of the war; for the second, I have only the gossip of German soldiers and sailors, which may be groundless. Regardless of this, Germany's possession of submarine bases near the English Channel, along the French coast, makes the situation for England much more grave than in the First World War, and the U-boat of today is a far deadlier weapon than that used by the Germans twenty-five years ago. The methods of detecting submarines, and destroying them after they have been located, have lost much of their efficacy, and there is little indication as yet that new and superior defensive weapons have been found. Few persons in Europe believe that a war can be won with air raids, however vast they may be—but it is recognized that there is a very real danger that the submarine menace might leave England without the means of carrying on the struggle.

Europeans do not generally believe that England can mobilize sufficient striking power to drive Hitler out of the Continent which he has occupied—but they believe that this is not necessary; they are convinced that if England can checkmate Hitler and prevent further successes on his part, Germany will eventually collapse. The German people are back of Hitler because, thus far, he has managed to keep them convinced that war pays, and pays handsomely. When he can no longer protect them from retaliatory blows, and there is no more booty to be divided up among his soldiers, his support will dwindle.

My own observation has convinced me that the German army is much stronger on the offensive than it is likely to be on the defensive. The German is the finest soldier in the world—when he is winning; no people shows less courage and less sportsmanship when losing. In that sense, British mastery of the skies at some future time would have a tremendous importance; it would place the entirety of the German forces on the Continent on the defensive, in at least one sense, and the effect on their morale would be out of all proportion to the actual damage which air raids might cause.

Nearly all Europeans with whom I have come into contact have attached a great deal of importance to the role which they expect Russia ultimately to play in the present conflict. Nothing in the whole situation has seemed more remarkable to me than the drastic alteration in the views expressed on this subject since the war entered on its acute phase. During the few years previous to this, successive Russian trials and purges largely alienated the sympathy of the great mass of European liberals for the Soviet Union; the Finnish campaign convinced them that the Russian colossus had no important military strength; the Nazi-Soviet pact helped to make Soviet Russia unpopular, even in working-class circles.

The invasion and a few months of German occupation sufficed to bring about a change in the general attitude not limited by geographical borders or class boundaries. The feeling of the average European today about Russia might fairly be summed up as follows:

"Russia is not a friend of Germany, nor is she deceived into believing that Nazi Germany is her friend. She has given Germany some aid and will give her more—but never as much as Germany expects and never in greater amount than the strict minimum necessary to keep the pact in force and protect Russia from German attack for

the present. Russia did not make a pact with the Allies
for much the same reason that the Low Countries refused
to do so—lack of sufficient faith in the willingness and
ability of France and England to defend democracy. Had
Russia made a pact with the Allies, she would inevitably
have been drawn into the war at once. By making a pact
with her most dangerous enemy, she has kept the war away
from her own doorstep—and the first duty of any government is to take every possible step which may keep its
people out of war. The two great, traditional enemies of
Russia are Germany and Great Britain, and at present
these two are weakening each other, while Russia goes on
arming and building up further strength. When the proper
moment comes, Russia will enter the war—and that will
probably be at the moment when she believes Nazi Germany is ready to collapse or revolt. If, by that time, conditions in Great Britain have altered sufficiently so that
Russia no longer fears British aggression, she may actively
ally herself with the democratic powers, influenced in this
direction by her enmity against Japan, the traditional enemy of America."

So much for the general opinion in the occupied countries in regard to the Soviet Union. I do not fully share
the optimism felt there concerning an ultimate Russian
attack on Germany, but it is significant that such an opinion should be widely held.

When I visited Germany, after my return from the
Soviet Union, I was surprised to find a considerable proportion of Soviet sympathizers among Germans in various
walks of life with whom I talk. More astonishing still,
those Germans who disliked Russia were definitely and unmistakably afraid of it. For years Hitler had screamed

at them the story of the "Russian menace," and the result had been twofold: he had made the Germans afraid of a Soviet attack, but he had also convinced many of them that if Russia were as grave a danger as the Leader insisted, then things in Russia could not possibly be going so badly as the German propaganda stories pretended.

Among the German soldiers in Belgium, I found a similar mixture of sympathy and mistrust. Many made little secret of their admiration for the Soviet Union, and their hope that Germany would ultimately have a similar government. The majority, however, openly asserted that war between Germany and the Soviet Union was inevitable, one day or another, and admitted the consternation they had felt when they had first learned of the Nazi-Soviet pact. Many of them boasted that one German soldier was worth fifty Red Army men, but when they discussed the possibility seriously, they did not hesitate to admit that such a campaign would be a hard and costly one.

If the German soldier is scornful of the fighting ability of the Russian, it would be difficult to find words to convey the depth of his scorn for the Italian army. A group of soldiers staying at my hotel brought me the news of Italy's entry into the war slightly before the radio announced it. They were jubilant at this development, but when I suggested that they had better send an army to Italy quickly, before that country collapsed, their smiles changed to roars of appreciative laughter. At no time, then or later, did they trouble to disguise their total lack of respect for the Italian military machine.

I have discussed extensively, in an earlier chapter, a matter also likely to have an important bearing on future developments in the war, i.e., the decline in the morale of the German troops stationed in the subjugated countries. This, as I have pointed out, seems to be serious, and under certain circumstances might eventually create a discontent sufficient to cause many of the soldiers to join with the suppressed populations in an attempt at revolt. Short of such a situation, as I have also pointed out, I do not believe that there is any serious hope of revolt in the occupied countries on the part of the civilian population; only with the help of a considerable proportion of the German soldiery could such an uprising have the slightest chance of success, for reasons which I have stated earlier.

An interesting feature of the present war, which seems to have been little remarked, has been the relatively small role played by espionage, in comparison with the First World War. The French *Deuxième Bureau* and the British intelligence service were rated as good as any in the world, but the speed of the German advance through the Low Countries and across France left them helpless and disorganized. This is not surprising, if it be considered that the position of the front at any given moment was so uncertain that every German military vehicle had to carry a square of yellow bunting flat across the top to warn German fliers that it was not to be bombed. Had the Allied espionage been able to communicate this fact rapidly to the French and British, whole Allied convoys of vehicles could have moved with complete freedom from interference from the air. Shortly before I left Belgium, I saw direct evidence that the British military intelligence was adapting itself to the new kind of warfare, and learning to fight fire with fire. It would not be fair to describe this in detail at the present time, merely for the sake of a good story. I am revealing no secrets, however, if I state that I saw convincing proof that the British secret service was capable of outwitting the Nazi counter-espionage forces. If this can be maintained, it will have an important bearing on future aerial bombardments and other attacks designed to harry the Germans.

I have spoken at length, in the opening chapters of this book, about the importance of faith and morale in total warfare, and stated there my convicion that the rapid collapse of Belgium was due not only to an overwhelming German military superiority, but also to the fact that the Belgian people as a whole no longer believed in "democratic capitalism," and were not prepared to sacrifice their lives to defend it as freely and recklessly as they had done in 1914. Similarly, many Dutch citizens became Nazi sympathizers because they no longer believed in their own political and economic institutions. The great mass of the Polish people had little faith in either their economic system or their political leaders, for the one had brought them only misery and unbelievable poverty, and the other had at the head Colonel Beck, who they knew had once been expelled from France as a German spy, and who had for years tried to "run with the hares and the hounds" in his alternating loyalties to France and Germany.

Not one, but dozens of German officers and soldiers have told me that the grimmest resistance met by the German army in the present war, and the greatest proportion of casualties, occurred in Norway. Now Norway was certainly the most poorly armed of any of the countries overrun by Hitler—but the Norwegian people had something to fight for. The three Scandinavian countries were the pioneers in social legislation of the entire world, and they had, by peaceful evolution, carried social reform farther toward practical realization than perhaps any other nation. There was little corruption in public life, and, with the possible exception of Sweden, little concentration of wealth in a few hands. Denmark, it is true, did not seriously oppose the invasion, but her geographical position and size, and total disarmament a few years earlier, made armed resistance almost out of the question.

It is true that in Holland, Belgium and France, German propaganda had done much to foster dissatisfaction and tear down confidence in the régime, but this is a superficial statement of the matter. Propaganda does not find a serious foothold among a contented people, or a people which has faith. It is only when one political system has failed that people turn to another. To say that Nazis in Holland, or Communists in France, brought about the collapse of the Allied cause in the summer of 1940 is not to state a reason; the important thing is to ask: *"Why* did people in Holland become Nazis, and citizens of France Communists? *Why* were citizens of these various countries dissatisfied with capitalism, and *why* had they lost faith in democracy?" Merely feeling indignation that such things have occurred provide neither an answer nor a remedy. The simple truth, as it appeared almost universally to the people I talked to in Europe, is that both the capitalists and the democratic political leaders of Europe fell down pretty badly on their jobs during the long armistice. The capitalists were unable to give the people of Europe even a relative security; European economic life, between 1918 and 1939, was merely a sequence of depressions, crises, inflations and collapses. Political leaders failed as badly; public life was rotten with corruption, and the peoples of Europe lost faith with each passing day. It is not my purpose here to condone or condemn the capitalists and politicians who made this situation; this book is not a political or economic treatise. I believe, however, that it is extremely vital to recognize the lesson inherent in the situation, because it has a direct bearing upon American defense.

What will Europe be when the war is over?

This question, of course, lies in the field of pure prophecy, but I am not going to try to tell what *I* think Europe will be after the war; rather, I should like to describe what Europeans in every walk of life have told me of what *they* believed and hoped the future Europe would be. I am naturally most familiar with Belgium opinion, but I have talked with many others as well without noting any serious differences. The average European, who has been through this war and remembers something, at least, of the other, believes the following:

1. That capitalism is dead, not dying, and that any discussion of "the future of capitalism" would be purely academic.

2. That economic security, with equality of opportunity and privilege, is going to be more important in the Europe of tomorrow than political freedom. If it is possible to have both, so much the better, but if one must be sacrificed, then let it be liberty.

3. That the day of nationalism in Europe is ended; that a system of confederation must be found, within the framework of which small nations may guard their cultural autonomy but relinquish the direction of foreign policy and defense to a more powerful central body; that, in a word, a United States of Europe must, in some form or other, come into being.

4. That there will only be two major world powers at the close of the present struggle: America and the U.S.S.R.; that these two nations represent the only hope of the oppressed peoples of Europe; that it is desirable that they should dictate the peace, and set up a Europe in which private greed will be secondary to considerations of stability and justice.

5. That the political and economic systems which have brought Europe to "this" twice in twenty-five years must be considered a failure, and must give way to something offering at least the hope of improvement.

These points, which I do not propose either to defend or attack here, represent in brief the opinions expressed to me by men and women in every walk of life. The most astonishing thing, to me, was the surprising unanimity of opinion in this respect, whether I talked to a banker or an unemployed laborer.

A former university professor, now a consulting engineer, said to me, a few days before my departure: "I have just been obliged to surrender to the Germans all of my stocks and bonds. I still have a little money; I am spending that on building an addition to my house. If it isn't bombed, I will at least have that when the war is over. Otherwise, the savings of a lifetime are wiped out, and the same thing is happening all over Belgium, all over Europe. After this is over, we can only have socialism or communism of some sort; nothing else will be possible."

A wealthy industrialist, politically conservative and a devout Catholic, said to me on the day before my departure: "All this must change, after the war. We can't have capitalism bring us to this again—and anyway, there is no basis left on which to rebuild capitalism. There are no wealthy people left in Europe, or soon there will be none. Bit by bit, every scrap of wealth in Europe is being destroyed, and there is only one class left—the poor. Germany, even if she is smashed, can never pay for what she has annihilated. After the war, no one—literally no one— will have anything to lose; therefore, no one will oppose any economic, social or political experiment which offers even a faint hope of a better future for our children. Whether it be called Communism, or something else, does not matter." And this from a man who, only a year before, had tacitly avoided references in our talks with me to the fact that I had once worked in Russia, since he invariably became infuriated.

A Belgian small businessman, conservative in his views, said: "Russia will help us, when the time comes. She is playing a game with Germany, pretending to be her friend, but the day will come when Russia will co-operate with a more truly democratic England in liberating us from the Germans." That view, incidentally, was a common one.

A diamond cutter, unemployed for years: "After this, there will be a Soviet Union of European states, or something perhaps similar to the American union of states. Nobody would oppose that idea any longer. Belgium has fought for her independence for centuries—but from now on, we want somebody bigger than we are to assure our safety."

A Brussels banker: "The Allies will smash Germany, with American aid—then they will all adopt Germany's present economic system. The day of uncontrolled capitalism is over, forever. Belgium's entire gold reserve consists of four bars of the metal in a vault in Brussels; all the rest is in America, and Belgium's external debt is greater than the total value of this. The same is going to be true everywhere except in America—so how are you going to use the gold standard again?"

A Catholic priest: "I am beginning to feel that perhaps the Church should not have supported Franco so strongly. Perhaps there are worse things than Communism; nothing could be more wicked than the state to which the old system has brought Europe."

I might add indefinitely to this list of quotations, but these are typical of the whole. There is less unanimity on the question of what Germany will be after the war, and what should be done to her if the Allies win. There are those—and their number is not few—who bitterly demand the virtual destruction of Germany, breaking her up into small states and leaving a powerful army of occupation for twenty-five years. Others—and I believe these are in the majority—feel that it is time to recognize that Germany is one of the major nations of the European continent; that notwithstanding this, she should be taught, once and for all, that "crime does not pay." After which a redistribution of world sources of raw materials and world markets should be made to give Germany a share commensurate with her indubitable ability to work and to produce; that, in a word, the rest of the world needs what a Germany redirected into constructive channels could contribute to civilization.

One point should be mentioned in passing. Hitler has "sold" socialism to the German people to a deeper extent than most observers have realized. Whether he has given them socialism or not is another matter, but as time has gone by, he has introduced an increasing number of re-

forms which have made a great many Germans believe that
they enjoy a large measure of socialism—and that belief
is perhaps more important than the objective truth of the
matter. Hitler has, with passing years, put increasing restrictions on capital in Germany—more so than is generally realized abroad. Whatever his motives, he has created
an economic situation and a public opinion which would
make difficult, if not impossible, the restoration of capitalism along the old lines in Germany. He has paved the
way for some sort of socialist, collective economic system
in Germany by a long series of socialistic (or pseudo-
socialistic) measures—he has paved the way for a new economic system in the rest of Europe, first, by the destruction
of a vast amount of property, then by the requisition and
confiscation of what wealth remained. The old status quo
can no more be restored in the economic field than it is
likely to be geographically.

Most of the confused thinking about this war springs
from the fact that the issues of the war are in themselves
confused. Three struggles are going on, not one: a con-
tinuation of the old struggle between the German and British imperialisms, a struggle between capitalism and economic change, and a struggle between the free, democratic
way of government and the totalitarian way. Unfortunately, the division between the two major opponents is
not a simple, geographic one. Hitler is fighting for German imperialism, for economic change and for the totalitarian way of government. Great Britain, in the beginning,
was fighting for British imperialism, and for the freer
form of government, against economic change. Thus, the
issues between the two were not clear-cut. As it became

evident in England that the men of Munich could not successfully conduct the war, and that without the support of labor the war could not be fought at all, changes began to appear in the structure of the government which carried it toward the progressive camp. Today, there seems to be an increasing recognition in England of the fact that the old order is dead, and that it would be better to give it a decent burial before the putrefying corpse spreads corruption and decay throughout the world. It seems to be recognized in England that the old imperialisms can, in any case, no longer be restored, and that social change (as one of the earlier and wiser Russian czars once said) had better come voluntarily from the top than by explosion from the bottom. Thus, the issue has become increasingly one between two ways of life—that of compulsion, and that of free choice—and that phase of the struggle today dominates the world situation.

In the midst of this confusion of issues and the nightmare of war, the eyes of the conquered peoples turn most of all to the United States of America and to the U.S.S.R., the one as the pattern of the European confederation of states and political system which they are at last convinced would mean peace in Europe, and the other as the model of the economic change which they believe must follow this war. Curiously enough, however discouraged they may be about the immediate future, the peoples of Europe are not pessimistic about the ultimate outcome. They believe that they are witnessing the passing of an old order, and see no reason to doubt that it is possible to build a new and better system which will give some promise of economic security and the hope of fewer wars in Europe. To that end, they will sacrifice a great deal of national pride, and, if need be, a great measure of political freedom. Most of all, they would like to see a new Europe in which the economic system offered little place for private greed, and the political system recognized the dignity of man and his right to be governed as he wishes. Whether such a union of economic and political reforms is possible in Europe only the future can tell, but there are many who believe it, and far more who hope.

It seems to me that few Americans realize just how encouraging a degree of social and economic progress has been made in America during the past decade by the decent, civilized, ballot-box method. Those who have been in America continuously during that period do not fully realize the difference between the American scene in, say, 1931 and 1941. I have been away from America for thirteen years. I have spent much of that time in totalitarian countries, where the process of change has been at work the hard way, with bloodshed and sadism and oppression. Back in America, I find a degree of change which I would not have deemed possible at the time I went away, brought about with no street fighting, no torture and no bombings or political assassinations.

To Europeans, now engaged in a bloody struggle to decide those same issues, this is little short of a miracle. To Europeans, America typifies much of what little hope is left in a blacked-out world. What America has done, Europe must learn to do, and the peoples of the oppressed countries of Europe turn with the confidence born of despair to the one proof left in the world that perhaps the decent way of life pays best, after all. To them, the President of the United States is not merely a man of flesh and blood; he is the symbol incarnate of the expectation of a better tomorrow. To those who are still fighting, his presence at the head of the American state brings the hope of ultimate victory; to those who have already been subjugated, his words bring the hope of liberation.

THE END